ENGLISH LANGUAGE SERIES

TITLE NO 12
Designs in Prose

ENGLISH LANGUAGE SERIES

General Editor: Randolph Quirk

Designs in Prose

A study of compositional problems and methods

WALTER NASH

University of Nottingham

LONGMAN
LONDON AND NEW YORK

LONGMAN GROUP LIMITED *LONDON*

Associated companies, branches and representatives
throughout the world
Published in the United States of America by Longman Inc., New York

© Longman Group Limited 1980

First published 1980

ISBN 0 582 29100 3 cased
ISBN 0 582 29101 1 paper

British Library Cataloguing in Publication Data
Nash, Walter
    Designs in Prose (English language series; 12)
    1. English language – Rhetoric
    I. Title II. Series
    8081.042   PE1408   79–41021

    ISBN 0-582-29100-3
    ISBN 0-582-29101-1 Pbk

Printed and bound in Great Britain by
William Clowes (Beccles) Limited, Beccles and London

Foreword

Most books in this series – indeed most books on English language – aim at describing phenomena: explaining, for example, how grammatical relations work, or analysing textual material into its components so as to demonstrate their structure and the rules involved. Even a book with so frankly a prescriptive title as J L Austin's *How to do things with words* was solidly in the genre of describing. It tells us – however revolutionarily – how things *are done* with words. The goal of such studies is to help us understand something of the complexity of processes deeply within us – and they serve a subsidiary purpose, dear to the heart of scientific inquiry, in helping the reader formulate comparable analytic studies of his own.

But to the extent that their authors hope to enable readers to use language more effectively (and many would energetically disclaim any such intention), the lesson is imparted indirectly and inexplicitly. Having understood this or that analysis (of the English sentence, for example), your actual synthesis of the next sentence you form may well reflect this understanding. Even books on rhetoric and composition have been written with such an oblique orientation.

There is nothing indirect or inexplicit about Dr Nash's approach in the present work. Indeed the communicative momentum is the exact reverse of what we have been discussing. If the reader finds (as I am convinced he will) that he is better able to analyse some one else's prose and to understand the complex network that holds it together, it will be because he himself has been squarely faced with the manifold practical tasks involved in shaping a piece of language for himself and putting it on to paper.

Nor will anyone read far in this volume before realising that Dr Nash is no armchair critic, telling others how writing is created without experience of venturing on to Parnassus himself. Though quite unjustifiably shy about his own achievements, Dr Nash is fortunate in possessing a highly creative imagination, both playful and profound, as those know well who are privileged to enjoy the poems, stories, and witty parodies he never bothers to publish. In a prefatory page to an earlier book, *Our Experience of Language*, he significantly quotes W H Auden: 'Words are for those with promises to keep'.

In so insightfully directing readers how best to deploy their words and fulfil their promise, *Designs in Prose* is a welcome addition to the present series. As English has increasingly come into world-wide use, there has arisen a correspondingly increasing need for more information on the language and the ways in which it is used. The English Language Series seeks to meet this need and to play a part in further stimulating the study and teaching of English by providing up-to-date and scholarly treatments of topics most relevant to present-day English – including its history and traditions, its sound patterns, its grammar, its lexicology, its rich variety and complexity in speech and writing, and its standards in Britain, the USA, and the other principal areas where the language is used.

University College London   RANDOLPH QUIRK
February 1980

Preface

When I began this book I had no idea of writing anything resembling a manual of composition. My original intention was to study some aspects of cohesion in written English – some 'designs in prose' – selecting for objective analysis passages of exposition, description, and narrative. Quite soon, however, I became occupied with the technical and psychological problems of the writer, and without pretensions to anything more than routine competence found myself trying to make an insider's assessment of compositional skills. This revised aim is ambitiously formulated in a phrase occurring at the end of my first chapter: *to make the motes of grammar dance in imagination's festive light.*

The material used for analysis throughout the book, from the briefest examples of phrasing to passages of essay length, is almost entirely of my own devising. (There are, I think, three extracts not composed by me.) The decision to create my own resources has rescued me from presumptuous meddling with other people's work, and has allowed me on occasion to demonstrate mistakes in composition without feeling embarrassed on behalf of the composer. In any case, I have never understood why teachers of English should not be expected (like teachers of music or drawing) to show themselves capable of practising what they preach, in sketches exemplifying basic procedures in writing. There appears to be a myth of objectivity, involving the belief that for purposes of analysis the analyst's own works are somehow not valid, not 'real'. I have felt the power of this superstition in my own occasional doubts, but hope that the book as a whole will justify my resistance to it.

The exercises with which the book concludes are designed in the first instance to invite the reader's practical assessment of points discussed in the preceding chapters. To that end, I have tried to indicate as fully as possible the points of reference between the exercises and the main text, and I have also tried to give something like tutorial guidance in the instructions that introduce each project. Exercises, however, are notoriously difficult to devise; what works very well for one apprentice or one instructor may fail miserably with another teacher and a different group. If the material I have supplied is unsuitable, I trust that readers will feel free to criticize and amend it; otherwise I would hope that text and exercises together might provide an interesting programme of investigation, whether for the private reader or the student following courses at university or college of education level.

I must express my warmest thanks to friends and colleagues for their support and help during the preparation of this book. My deepest debt is to Randolph Quirk, whose editorial tact has saved me from many blunders. I am grateful for his kindness and encouragement, and for the sustaining friendship of Chris Butler, Ron Carter, Peggy Cooke, Martin Gray, Norma Hazzledine and Helen Hunter. I hope that the work will prove worthy of the interest they have shown in it.

University of Nottingham   WN

Contents

I suffer as always from the fear of putting down the first line. It is amazing the terrors, the magics, the prayers, the straitening shyness that assails one. It is as though the words were not only indelible but that they spread out like dye in water and color everything around them. A strange and mystic business, writing. Almost no progress has taken place since it was invented.

JOHN STEINBECK, *Journal of a Novel*

Chapter 1

Layout and rhetorical pattern

In his play *Le Bourgeois Gentilhomme*, Molière pokes fun at one M. Jourdain, a good-natured, pudding-headed man of business who is deeply gratified to learn that he enjoys a totally unsuspected accomplishment; all his life, he is told, he has been speaking prose. The scene always raises a laugh, and yet there is something to be said in defence of its comic victim. Irresistible though the joke may be in its context, it is misdirected as a general proposition because it requires a definition of prose that few of us would accept. We do not associate prose with the daily run of talk, any more than the innocent M. Jourdain did. We identify it, rather, with the act of writing, and therefore with careful premeditation, with deliberate processes of selection and correction, with the patient search for a coherent, convincingly demonstrated pattern of discourse. Talk, with its approximate if sometimes brilliant matchings of language and situation, is involved in our experience, shapes it, comments on it; prose, however urgent in effect, is necessarily marked by the detachment that comes between experience and the record duly committed to the page.

The very mechanics of putting something into written shape are of no little importance. We have developed conventions of layout which often have communicative significance as the contours, so to speak, of prose design – outlines modified from within by the pressure of material that has to be arrayed, or 'programmed', in a way that corresponds effectively to the writer's intentions. Such programming calls for many decisions: about the order in which items of information are presented, about the demonstration of relationships between one item and another, about the permissibility of digressions from the main expository path, about the need for repetition and recapitulation. It is from this basic marshalling process that the drive and conviction of good writing proceed, and its importance is obviously such that we may be tempted to dismiss the graphic presentation, the layout, as a mere editorial imposition not integrally related to the message the writer has to convey.

Yet even if this were wholly the case the fact would remain that layout is at least very useful as an orientational device, serving reader and writer alike. It helps to clarify the writer's intentions, and so presents to the reader a kind of route map by means of which he makes his way through the text. To the writer himself it offers a means of coping with the bulk of the work by piecing it out in sections of manageable proportion. To have an unbroken text in prospect is to have a perplexing burden on the mind. The load lightens, and the possibilities of design become apparent, as soon as we begin to work out some principle of segmentation. For these reasons alone we might suppose that it would reward us to begin our enquiries by examining some versions of layout in some recurrent types of text.

1.1 Versions of layout: (a) lines for copy

Texts of all kinds invade our lives: the novel, the scholarly treatise, the reference book, the minutes of last Friday's meeting, the leader in today's newspaper, the insurance policy, the instructions for the operation of the washing machine. Seemingly the forms that printed material can take are endless, yet from all this variety, if we examine the matter, there emerge a few simple conventions of layout or segmentation. These are indeed so commonplace that our indoctrinated minds rarely question them; we assume that the outward shape of the text is appropriate to – is, indeed, *part and parcel of* – its content. A linguist might express this by saying that the *graphology* of the text, its complex of distinctive features in layout, script, or print, is an aspect of its *register*, meaning the communicative purpose for which it is designed and the language considered appropriate to that purpose.

Custom, no doubt, makes us more or less oblivious of the linguistic features that characterize a familiar register, and often our attention is retrieved only when we are made to notice some incongruity between language and ostensible purpose. There is, for example, a deliberate mismatching or cross-breeding of layout and content in the following:

[1] Pamper yourself with the Archduke Trio
Go on – put it on

(Beethoven won't mind)
Paradise is for tomorrow – here's a little bliss to be going on
with

Revel in that heavenly length
(You've never known such generous movements)
Bask in every blessed, buoyant, brilliant bar
And it's forever, the miracle
You need never slip another disc
Unless, of course, you'd care to try the Trout Quintet
And why not do that too?
(Schubert won't mind)

Everybody will recognize the graphological convention that this text imitates; it obviously exploits the line-by-line segmentation that is characteristic of the language of advertisement. Just as obviously, it is not a genuine piece of copywriting. We are hardly likely to find on a record sleeve a text recommending a piece of chamber music as though it were some kind of fashionable indulgence.

This might also seem a very strange way of saying that the 'Archduke' Trio and the 'Trout' Quintet are never-failing sources of pleasure and consolation; yet the method is not without its point. It exemplifies a stratagem sometimes known as 'register borrowing', one of the aims of which is to create, with interesting and perhaps revelatory consequences, a new tension between form and content, giving commonplace thoughts an original turn and conventional language an unexpected vivacity. When language is used with creative intent, if only (as here) for the mildest of jokes, a major effect must be to open our eyes to the value of familiar conventions. Certainly, one consequence of our 'Archduke' Trio exercise ought to be that the reader's attention is focused upon the convention of line-by-line layout, with its provocative spacings and indentations.

The layout is vital to this text. It accords with a jocular intimacy of idiom, a colloquialism that would sit awkwardly in almost any other presentation; it reinforces, through the isolative focus on one line at a time, the blatant punning and word-play upon which the 'advertisement' turns; but most of all it creates an acceptance for its own joke, for the line-breaks and spaces give point to semantic shufflings that might seem flatly absurd if the sentences making up the text were laid out in continuous sequence. This raises an interesting and possibly disturbing point. Can I compel the interest and even the assent of the reader merely by virtue of the shape my text makes on the page?

If the point were put to a classical rhetorician (conveniently translated into our own times) he would perhaps be ready to concede that such use of layout as a persuasive apparatus is only a modern extension of an old tradition. He might point out that the disjunctions, the insets, the parentheses, etc, are no more than notations of the gestures and vocal inflections which rhetoric has always allowed as part of the armoury of effective pleading. In the layout of advertising copy there is often a strong visual interest, but together with this there may be an even stronger appeal in the reader's sense of vocal performance. The carefully plotted sentences make up a script presenting equivalents to certain *paralinguistic* elements in speech *eg* gesture, intonation, stress, the loudness or softness of the voice, vocal timbre. In the 'Archduke' Trio example, the bracketed sentences obviously suggest some kind of *sotto voce* rendering, or even the intrusion of another voice; while the fact that some lines are set in from the margin could be seen as an indication of how a delivery of the passage might be timed.

Thus the copywriter's layout takes the eye with a pleasing shape (which of course must often be accommodated to the outline of a photograph or an illustration) but may also tease the phonetic sense, the inward ear, with the possibility of a vocal performance. There is evidently some correlation between graphic presentation and what might be called the *scoring* of a text. If the writer wishes to convey to the reader a certain sense of phrasing and intonation, it appears that one way in which he may do so quite powerfully is by cutting his text into rather short segments and laying them out on the page in such a way that visual spacing corresponds to oral timing.

The uses of this rawly effective procedure are obviously limited. Apart from the fact that it consumes a great deal of space, there is no doubt that more than a little of it would prove tedious and self-defeating; very probably the reader would soon cease to attach any significance to the irregular visual pattern of the text. Furthermore, this kind of layout sets disproportionate store by visual and vocal appeal, reducing the content of the text to a mere apparatus for the verbal conjurer. If all texts were written in this way, we should certainly pay too high a price for the facility of giving graphic equivalence to some vocal effects. But this is a convention of restricted scope. In other forms of writing, in the extended prose of essays, expositions, editorials, and the like, we may remain on nodding terms with the shaping presence of speech, but generally the vocal echo occurs as an incidental grace of rhetoric and not as its primary object. There are, moreover, some types of composition in which it is virtually suppressed.

1.2 Versions of layout: (b) sections for documents

In texts such as the following, 'scoring' is largely ignored:

[2]2 EXAMINATIONS

2.1 There shall be one Final Honours examination for each subject in the academic year.

2.2 Before entering upon his Junior Honours year, a candidate must have passed the degree examinations in the first two years of the normal curriculum for the Honours group.

2.3 A candidate aspiring to Honours in a subject or subjects for which an Intermediate Honours examination is prescribed must, before presenting himself for Final Honours examination, have passed the Intermediate Honours examination in each subject or subjects.

2.4 A candidate who satisfies the examiners in the Final Honours examination shall be awarded Honours in one of the three grades to be denominated respectively First Class, Second Class, (Upper and Lower Divisions) and Third Class. The names of candidates shall be arranged for publication in alphabetical order according to grades or sub-divisions of grades.

(Edinburgh University Calendar, Regulations for the degree of Bachelor of Education, p. 531.)

There are few paralinguistic echoes in this extract; its author has obviously not been concerned with the problem of relaying expressive gestures and inflections. What it offers is a quite rigorous method of controlling the flow of information from writer to reader. Information is presented in a series of labelled boxes; the labels in this instance are numerals, but in other varieties of the same layout they might consist of short titles, key words, or even repetitions of some typographical device, such as the asterisk. The labelled sections are essentially self-contained, in that each has a content which is not drawn out of its predecessor and does not overflow into a following unit; on the other hand, the boxes may well be set out in an optimum order, so that the reader must acquaint himself with one section before he can properly understand the next. Each section, in short, establishes a point in a programme – which suggests that the effect of this section-by-section layout might be summed up in the term *programming*.

This is a useful convention, freely employed in the presentation of all kinds of official and informative material; we meet it in public notices, in brochures and pamphlets, in codes of procedure, statutes, ordinances, regulations, in many kinds of document and in a good many textbooks. One of its characteristics is that with each section the writer can begin afresh and need hardly trouble himself with the problem of forging elaborate discursive links between one segment and the next. Another is that the jargon of a technical register governs the presentation, making it unnecessary for the writer to concern himself with the establishment of a personal style. These are advantages as long as all that is required is the effective and unambiguous transfer of information, but the scope of the method is limited. We can hardly imagine a short story, a literary essay, or even an advertisement being written in this way. The demand for strict programming tyrannizes over the material, making insignificant allowance for the translation of vocal effect and excluding the devices of continuity and cohesion that can create a well-articulated prose structure. This is certainly a good way of packaging information; but most of us would feel that it is hardly a suitable format in which to conduct *discourse*.

1.3 Versions of layout: (c) paragraphs for discourse

But what do we mean by discourse? In the present context the word refers to written composition in continous development. Discourse has a purpose that reaches beyond the allocutory gestures of copywriting, and a structure that requires progressions and transitions ignored by the compilers of statutes, minutes, and manuals of instruction. In discourse the organizing principles here identified as 'scoring' and 'programming' are subordinated to the more complex operations suggested by the word *expounding*. There is a programme of assertions, examples, qualifications, but these are not presented as a series of distinctly labelled positions. Instead, they are related to each other in a progressively unfolding pattern, the turns and connections of which are demonstrated in various ways: sometimes by means of syntactic devices, sometimes through the kinship of elements in vocabulary, sometimes by the management of punctuation and typography.

This is the appearance and structure of the sort of writing we mean when we talk about discursive or expository prose:

[3] The 'idea of a university' is often taken for granted, as something so obvious that discussion is hardly necessary. Yet it would appear that there are various and sometimes conflicting assumptions about the purpose for which a university exists. For some a university is primarily a centre of research and scholarly enquiry; for others it is above all a place of education, where the young are taught to think and make judgments; while there are those who regard it as the first duty of a university to serve the community by producing people trained to fill responsible positions in industry and public service.

There is no reason why these aims, each in itself quite valid, cannot be reconciled, even though we might disagree about priorities. Indeed, each of these purposes may be said to be involved with the others. A university *does* exist to promote research, but the purpose is not wholly self-sustaining; it cannot continue without the communication of a heritage from generation to generation, and this continuity of experience is in its turn dependent on general acceptance of the university as a positive force in society.

These two paragraphs set out an argument and match its progress to a structural principle: the first proposes a problem while the second offers some kind of solution. Within each paragraph there is a clear programme of contributory points, but these are incorporated into the text at different levels, some occupying whole sentences while others are embodied in constituent clauses or even in phrases. There are one or two minor effects of scoring in the text. For example, in the first sentence of the second paragraph the phrase *each in itself quite valid*, interpolated between commas, may actually be thought to evoke the intonation a speaker might use when slipping this qualifying point into the argument. What we should notice as a general principle, however, is that both the programmatic structure and the scoring here have a subordinate place in a greater design.

Now obviously this expository design is something made and unmade at the writer's will. There is no pressing reason why the material used in our example should have been programmed in two paragraphs, even though the accomplished fact might seem to assert its own rightness. The programme might have extended into a third paragraph, or have been so adroitly managed as to occupy only one. Paragraphs, it could be said, are for the choosing; they are not governed by immutable rules. The fact that writers use them and even find them indispensable adjuncts to thoughtful composition confers upon them no status as 'linguistic' units.

Paragraphing is a simple stratagem guided by compound motivations. The paragraph may be shaped in the actual process of writing, as the author begins to discern and respond to patterns in his work; it may result from his sense of the text as a visual and vocal burden needing to be lightened by periodic interruptions; and it may be imposed retrospectively during the correction and editing of the text. By each and all of these criteria it is a subjective thing, not lending itself to formal definition, amenable to the writer's first ideas and second thoughts. This does not detract one whit from its usefulness and significance in prose structure. It simply invalidates the notion of the paragraph as an entity conforming to some kind of rule. It would be altogether misleading to regard it as though it were a unit in grammar, the next station beyond the sentence. Its domain of significance is not grammar, but rather the sister art of rhetoric.

Since 'rhetoric' has for some time been a suspect (not to say pejorative) term, let us be quite clear what we mean by it in this context. We do not mean empty verbal gesture – mere grandiloquence – and we do not use the term in restricted reference to the figures and tropes of poetic language. The word is here used in an old-fashioned and honourable sense, as a general designation for the techniques of composition. In this sense a writer can no more dispense with rhetoric than a musician can abandon his score or a painter can forget about his palette. When we condemn a piece of writing as mere rhetoric, we are as a rule pointing to a disproportion between an ostentatious technique and a trivial theme. Thus it has come to be felt that rhetoric is the last bad resort of those who have nothing to say. Good rhetoric, the skilful practice of an appropriate technique, either goes unnoticed or is commended by some more favourable name.

In the rhetoric of prose the paragraph functions as a viewfinder, freely used to define the groupings and transitions of a compositional design. With its help the writer may frame a dominant motif spanning a number of subordinate details, or may perhaps outline a sequence of related propositions. There is a free and unending play of possibilities, and in any text the design will flow and overflow among paragraphs which the writer constructs in an attempt to circumscribe the sinuous procedures of composition.

1.4 Varieties of rhetorical design: (a) the Step

Casual consultation of the nearest bookshelf may be enough to show how intricate compositional procedures can be. Even in the simplest prose there can be a freedom and ostensible randomness of development that challenges description, and sometimes the design-at-large is slow to emerge from a medley of constituents. But just as graphic design has its basic shapes which are fundamental to the most elaborate compositions, so the rhetoric of expository prose is reducible to a number of primary stratagems, or, as we shall now call them, 'designs'. Some elementary patterns can be illustrated with the help of material composed for the purpose.

A very simple and familiar species of text exemplifies one of the most common of structural devices:

> [4] First, check that the gear lever is in neutral. Then insert the key in the lock, and turn till the engine fires. Be sure that you have a clear view in your rear mirror. Depress the clutch and engage first gear. Release the handbrake. Before moving off, check your mirror again, and glance over your right shoulder to make sure that no other vehicle is approaching from your rear. Signal your intention to move out into the traffic. Then slowly let in the clutch while accelerating gently.

This hardly merits the name of expository prose, belonging as it does to a technical register; it is questionable whether a set of instructions can really be called an exposition. One symptom of the uncertain status of the text is that it might well have been laid out as a column of separate and perhaps numbered sentences – a format in which it would be no less effective than in the continuous sequence seen here. Indeed, the passage is little more than a sample of programming.

Its ordered development, however, conveniently illustrates an important principle. Each sentence is a Step in a procedure, and each

intelligibility –
sticking
together

Step is a discrete unit. No great attempt is made to construct relationships between sentences; the coherence of the passage depends on the reader's perception of an underlying context of situation. We are to assume, in other words, that the sentences refer separately and collectively to one event. Given this presupposition, the text offers us a graduated account of the process of getting a motor vehicle to move. The reason for calling its governing design the Step hardly needs to be laboured.

We can point in this example to some linguistic features which are in fact symptoms of the instructional register but which also help to outline the step device. One evident characteristic of the passage is the dominance of the imperative verb forms (often supplemented by an object or an adverbial) which are the focus of each sentence in the series. Another feature, and one that ostensibly marks the step process, is the use of ordinal expressions like *first, then, before,* to introduce subsequent phases of the instructional account. Such expressions function as positional markers, but they are by no means necessary to the effectiveness of the rhetorical scheme. They could in fact be deleted here without loss; the Steps which the reader is invited to follow are really constituted by the series of imperative constructions.

This pattern will obviously be found in instructional texts (recipes, 'directions for use', and so forth) but it is not restricted to these. The syntactic recursion which is one of its most striking features – and which in fact imposes a textual unity on a series of contextually associated items – may be observed in other kinds of writing. A dramatist's stage directions, for example, might very well conform to a step pattern:

[5] Round a centrally-placed coffee-table there are three armchairs. To the left of the fireplace is an alcove with built-in bookshelves, to the right a table carrying a television set. Against the wall facing the fireplace stands an upright piano.

In this example the progression from Step to Step has been emphasized by the deliberate location of a recurrent syntactic element (the place adverbial) at the head of each sentence, like a number or some other positional label. When the effect is so obviously sought it is bound to figure a little crudely. With subtler location a less obtrusive framework might be created and it is possible that many descriptions of place or landscape are presented in Steps only half noticed by the reader.

Even in narrative the device is not uncommon. It occurs quite frequently as a method of setting the action, and is sometimes a vehicle for dramatic or humorous effects:

[6] The garden party was a huge success. The sun blazed on a green and cheerful campus. Champagne came and went. Strawberries disappeared down a hundred throats. Gowns fluttered. Girls giggled. A porter fell into the chocolate mousse. Gaiety reigned supreme. But then as though to prove the cruel transience of mortal joys, something altogether unforeseen and unreasonable occurred. An enormous green alligator of hideously malign aspect came waddling over the Vice-Chancellor's lawn.

The sequence of Steps in this burlesque example is made fairly obvious by the recurrence of identical or near-identical sentence-structures. Sentence after sentence is subject-headed, the subjects consisting of simple noun phrases (*The garden party, The sun, A porter*) some of which are unmarked by any determiner in the form of an article, a demonstrative, etc, (*eg: Champagne, Strawberries, Gowns, Girls, Gaiety*). The verbs are preponderantly intransitive and in some instances carry no adjunct or complement (*Gowns fluttered, Girls giggled*); adverbials, where they occur, indicate place or direction (*on a green and cheerful campus, down a hundred throats, into the chocolate mousse*). This syntactic regularity sets up a pattern which the reader can predict and begin to enjoy – the more so, perhaps, because the orderly linguistic procedure is imposed on a wayward and unpredictable content. The penultimate sentence introduces a fairly complex variation from the established pattern, creating a moment of suspense until, in the final sentence, the syntactic norm is emphatically reasserted – now, however, with a much more elaborate noun phrase as subject of the sentence. Evidently the whole paragraph has been homing onto this phrase, *an enormous green alligator of hideously malign aspect*. It is highlighted, brought into stylistic prominence.

This example has of course been deliberately constructed to illustrate one of the uses of a rhetorical device, and is to that extent an artificial contrivance. However, it would not be difficult to find in novels or short stories passages following similar procedures. Perhaps the only difference in principle between them and this jocose invention would be that in serious narrative such a text is usually shaped by some implicit logic of descriptive procedure; there is in fact a programme, not set out with numbers or key words but nonetheless carefully followed. Our invented passage (and this is of course a clue to its attempted humour) appears to respect this programmatic convention, but in fact takes mischievous liberties with it.

1.5 Varieties of rhetorical design: (b) the Stack

The principle governing our second pattern is one of definition and extension; a topic is announced at the beginning of the text or segment of text, and becomes the nodal point of divergence and convergence, the home key, as it were, for the ensuing discourse. Here is an example:

> [7] There is something wrong with the morality of a saying like 'Honesty is the best policy'. The wrongness lies in equating virtue with profit. Any tolerably observant person must see that the equation is false. There are countless occurrences in life when doing what we believe to be right does not bring us material rewards. Indeed we may sometimes suffer for it. To offer sound policy as an excitement to good morals is therefore in itself dishonest. Honesty, if it requires a motive, must be valued for reasons other than politic.

This is a common form of exposition. There are many such passages in which a thematic or 'topic' sentence is followed by a Stack of amplifying comments which may possibly be rounded off by some kind of summary formulation. Thus in the present instance the topic sentence is *There must be something wrong with the morality of a saying like 'Honesty is the best policy'*, and the summary is *Honesty . . . must be valued for reasons other than politic*. Often, one suspects, the topic sentence and the summary are termini which the writer has established in his own mind before he begins to work out his argument. The working is demonstrated in the intervening sentences which form the Stack. Each of these sentences, it may be noted, extends the ground laid by its predecessor; but what is even more important is that each sentence is an offshoot of the original proposition. This process of reversion, through developing stages, to a governing topic, is the distinctive mark of the device.

It is in the formation of the stacked commentary, in the means used to order and interrelate the constituent items, that the interest of the pattern lies. Here, for example, the argument is made to cohere lexically – that is to say, echoes and correspondences in the vocabulary are made to do the work of holding the text together. Thus the phrase *something wrong* in the topic sentence is echoed by *wrongness* in the sentence that follows; the word *equating* in the second sentence is further echoed by *equation* in the third; and the words *policy*, *incitement*, and *good morals* in the penultimate sentence have semantic equivalents in the *politic*, *motive*, and *honesty* of the summary.

This is one way of negotiating the ground between proposition and conclusion. There are of course other paths. An alternative version of the same argument might read as follows:

[8] There is something wrong about the morality of a saying like 'Honesty is the best policy'. For one thing, the readiness to weigh virtue in the scale of calculable profit is in itself deplorable. For another, there are clearly a great many occasions when being honest not only fails to bring material reward but may even invite suffering. Furthermore, if we encourage young people to believe that they will always be materially or socially better off for being honest, they will discover by experience the falsity of this claim and will be inclined to regard us as fools or hypocrites. All in all, it seems clear that honesty, if it requires a motive, must be valued for reasons other than politic.

Here, continuity of exposition depends on a series of phrases which, like so many enumerating fingers, tick off successive points: *For one thing, For another, Furthermore, All in all*. This is possibly a somewhat cruder way of assembling the argument, but it is a method that is very likely to suggest itself to a writer faced with this kind of expository task; it is in effect a primary stratagem.

The Stack appears, with various modifications of shape, in writings often quite remote from the register in which it is most familiar. It is clearly a stereotype for the presentation of argument, and as such is most likely to be found in essays on moral, philosophical, or social concerns. Yet it also turns up in fiction, in passages of narrative or description. Such occurrences might be described as sophisticated examples of register borrowing; on the other hand, it is possible that this is an archetypal pattern to which we make frequent reference, whatever the compositional task in hand might be. Like the Step, it offers the possibility of dealing *predictively* with a piece of text. It is a small map, of limited range and scale, but one that shows the writer a destination and suggests to him a route.

1.6 Varieties of rhetorical design: (c) the Chain

Such 'predictive' stereotypes relieve the writer of one of the major burdens of expository composition: the bewilderment, sometimes bordering on paralysis, of being lost among so many avenues of choice and of not knowing how to set about finding an issue. Yet it would clearly be too much to expect that an extended piece of writing might be carried out by the mere reduplication of such compositional formulae. Often the writer's procedures are less *predictive* than *exploratory*; he works through the expository maze, seeing no more than a sentence ahead, placing his trust in the clues afforded by syntactic or lexical connections.

This process of maze-threading is illustrated by our next example:

[9] Our Labrador bitch, Candy, was the greediest animal I have ever known, myself not excluded. She combined the vice of greed with the virtue of patience, and would sit for hours with her nose pointing unswervingly at the larder door. Behind the door, as well she knew, there stood a large paper bag full of biscuits allegedly shaped like bones and called (not surprisingly) Bonios. Bonios were to her what chocolates are to portly matrons. They were not, however, her exclusive diet. If they had been, we should merely have been faced with the simple task of visiting the local petshop quite frequently to fetch home a sack of biscuits. As it was, we had the double chore of visiting the petshop *and* Messrs Sainsbury's, whose shelves were stacked with tins of evil-smelling meat beloved of all Labradors. Those shelves were emptied once a week on behalf of our dog Candy.

The pattern of construction underlying this passage is chain-like: it presents a series of items each of which is related to its predecessor by means of explicit verbal links. There are connectives running from one sentence to the next in a scheme of linkage which may be tabulated as follows:

sentences 1–2:	*Candy* (+ *greediest*)	*She* (+ *greed*)
sentences 2–3:	*the larder door*	*behind the door*
sentences 3–4:	*Bonios*	*Bonios*
sentences 4–5:	*Bonios*	*They*
sentences 5–6:	*They were not*	*If they had been*
sentences 6–7:	(*If they had been* +)	(*As it was* +)
	the simple task	*the double chore*
sentences 7–8:	*shelves*	*those shelves*
	(+ *all Labradors*)	(+ *our dog Candy*)

It will appear that the links between sentences may be forged through the repetition of a word (*eg: greed, door, Bonios, shelves*), by making a parallel or echoic construction (*eg: the simple task . . . the double chore*), by spanning sentences with a syntactic bracket (*eg: If they had been . . . As it was*), by the use of pronouns or demonstratives, or by a combination of these methods. Often, as in 1–2, 6–7, 7–8, there may be a doubling of the linkage between sentences. Such solidity of structure might be a characteristic of highly wrought, densely figured 'literary' prose. In cases like the present, however, it is more likely to be a symptom of the writer's need for security of procedure. His explorations depend on the strength of the discursive Chain paid out behind him.

1.7 Varieties of rhetorical design: (d) the Balance

In another type of exploratory procedure, the track runs crooked, beating between thesis and antithesis:

> [10] To be able to drive is undoubtedly a useful accomplishment, and the ownership of a car is for many people a fact of life that reaches beyond convenience into sheer necessity. On the other hand, all possessions are a burden, and a car may rank among the heaviest. It is expensive to maintain, it makes the owner a prey to vandals, thieves and pedestrian acquaintances, and it exposes him to the risk of accident. Against these considerations he has to weigh the privilege of travelling in door-to-door comfort, the freedom of deciding when he will travel, the value of time saved, and (if he cares for such things) the pride and joy of property.

Here we see a shift between proposition and counter-proposition, with the apparent intention of giving real weight to a discursive counterpoise and of inviting the synthesis of conflicting claims in argument. There is no sign of an inclination to prejudge the issue. *On the other hand* and *Against these considerations* are signals of a genuine intent to explore alternative paths; the same concessive spirit is reflected by the parenthesis in the final sentence.

Our example illustrates the use of the Balance as an exploratory procedure. It should be added that it is possible to use the same device in a way that is more predictive than exploratory. In the following instance the exploratory gestures barely conceal the tendentiousness of the argument:

> [11] During the first three or four months of the year, it is true, Cumbria is particularly prone to bad weather, and some of the remoter parts of the district may even be quite difficult to reach. On the other hand, a visit in mid-March may be well worth while, if only for the freedom from overcrowding and the absence of the tourist traffic that builds up later in the season. Our climate nowadays is in any case so unpredictable that March may well turn out to be a good month. But even if it rains, Cumbrian hospitality is warm, and the visitor who makes a wise choice from the ever-growing list of hotels and guest-houses need not regret his decision to take an early holiday.

Here the writing imitates the classical orator's trick of propounding antitheses with all the appearance of wanting to give fair representation to rival cases or conflicting considerations. The issue, however, is settled in advance, and the counterpoises merely buttress a foregone conclusion; we know from the outset that this paragraph is designed to recommend Cumbria at all costs. In this invented passage, as in many actual specimens of literary salesmanship, the Balance is used ambivalently; the reader may enjoy the comfortable illusion that he is exploring the topic along with the writer, but for the latter the route and the destination are already predicted. His 'map' leads him via the corners and crossroads of phrases such as *it is true, on the other hand, in any case,* and *but even if,* yet these ostensibly divergent signposts all point in the same ultimate direction.

1.8 The compounding of devices

The rhetorical devices described here are perhaps stereotypes expressing the writer's psychological responses to the manifold challenges of composition. They are certainly not formulae applicable to distinct tasks, even though we may sometimes be able to identify a common connection between a register and a rhetorical plan (*eg* the customary use of step patterns in instructional registers). No writer works from the assumption that there is a form ready-made and waiting for his particular content. To expect anything of the kind would be to ignore the infinitely variable problems of writing, which cannot be solved so mechanically. To some extent the writer works instinctively, appraising and moulding his material as he goes along; to some extent he edits and revises his text after the initial effort of composition, in an attempt to impose upon it a form answering to his intuitions about the orderly progression of his theme.

Since the pattern of virtually any piece of discursive writing is the result of the combined working of instinctive and editorial forces, it is almost inevitably complex. A reader looking for the structures that inform a given passage will rarely find that one dominant device excludes all others; instead, he will become aware of one procedure invading another, one device abandoned in favour of another, one pattern begun, interrupted, and perhaps resumed. The rhetorical impulses blend and change, kaleidoscopically, as the writer discovers his subject and progressively shifts his ground.

As an example of the compounding of devices, here is a passage from a newspaper article:

[12] It was clear from the beginning that the London Broadcasting Company would have the most difficult task of all the commercial radio stations to be set up in Britain. All-news radio stations have proved successful in the United States, but this is a new experience for Britain. Whether there is an effective economic demand for the kind of service that LBC is contracted to provide has yet to be proved. This is not because British listeners are less interested in news than Americans. It is rather that, despite the appearance of ploughing virgin territory, LBC has in fact had to compete with established broadcasting interests. In the provision of news it has had to compete with the BBC's Radio 4 which generally does a pretty good job and has the corporation's large resources and long years of tradition behind it. In the provision of general features on London life LBC has had to compete with the BBC's Radio London, though that competition is less daunting.

This is discernibly based on the procedure we have called the Stack, but the general pattern is blurred by the intrusion into the argument of an antithetical shift of position. There are in effect two Stacks, the first of which runs from the beginning of the paragraph down to the words *has yet to be proved*. The two ensuing sentences (*This is not because . . . It is rather that . . .*) form a minor balance, the second sentence of which incorporates the topic of the following Stack (*. . . LBC has in fact had to compete with established broadcasting interests*). This analysis is demonstrated in the scheme set out on *p* 19, where the layout isolates the balance element in the pattern and clearly presents the topic-shift, or rotation of perspective, which the writer is obliged to make in pursuit of his exposition.

1.9 Textual cohesion

The same layout also presents certain expressions in italics. If these are studied, it will quickly be evident that they are the rivets and hinges of the textual apparatus. The sentences of the first Stack are held together by recurrent words and phrases – *LBC, radio station, Britain, have proved*; the sentences constituting a Balance cohere by virtue of a syntactic bracket – *This is not because . . . It is rather that*; while in the second Stack the cohesive principle is once again expressed through repeated words or phrases – *had to compete with, in the provision of*.

The cohesion of a text is a matter of the first importance – the ground, it might be said, of secure writing and comfortable reading. The writer is concerned with it from the moment he sets pen to paper. The internal cohesion of sentences has to be resolved so that the reader will readily perceive their structure and the relationship of their syntactic constituents. Connections between sentences often have to be demonstrated, for we need to bear in mind that to write two sentences in succession is to create a semantic hiatus, a gap with implications of what may be more than one meaning. For the reader's sake this gap must be filled and the desired meaning made evident. In the same way it is necessary that the text as a whole should be furnished with indications of structure that enable the reader to keep in view the connection and relationship of passages that may be spatially remote. From first to last, therefore, from the structure of a sentence to the connection between sentences to the integrity of an

1ST STACK

Topic: It was clear from the
beginning that the *London
Broadcasting Company* would
have the most difficult task
of all the commercial *radio
stations* to be set up in *Britain.*

1 All-news *radio stations have
proved* successful in the
United States, but this is a
new experience for *Britain.*

2 Whether there is an
effective economic demand
for the kind of service that
LBC is contracted to
provide *has yet to be proved.*

BALANCE SWINGING TO 2ND STACK

Poise: *This is not because* British   *Counter:* It is *rather that,* despite the
listeners are less interested   appearance of ploughing
in news than Americans.   virgin territory,

2ND STACK

Topic: LBC has in fact *had to
compete with* established
broadcasting interests.

1 *In the provision of news, it has
had to compete with* the
BBC's Radio 4, which
generally does a pretty
good job and has the
corporation's resources and
long years of tradition
behind it.

2 *In the provision of general
features on London life LBC
has had to compete with*
the BBC's Radio London,
though that competition is
less daunting.

entire text, the writer is unceasingly concerned with the problem of giving cohesive shape to his work. Various types of cohesion are incidentally exemplified by the passages used for illustration in this chapter. The 'advertisement' for the 'Archduke' Trio, in example [1], raises the spectre of a vocal performance, and thereby suggests the type of cohesion we would call *phonological*; the auditory matchings and echoes are implicit in the layout of the text. The passage from a set of university regulations, [2], exemplifies *graphological* cohesion; the numbering and the section-by-section layout impose a unity where other indices may be lacking. In further examples the cohesive method is *syntactic*, as in passages [10] and [11], illustrating the balance device, or both syntactic and *lexical*, as in the illustration of the chain device in [9].

In our continued explorations a primary concern will be the relationship between cohesion (particularly syntactic and lexical cohesion) and the creation of effective rhetorical designs in expository or simple descriptive prose. This concern is in the main practical and functional. Its end is not to expand the theory of stylistics or to open up new perspectives in literary criticism. It is rather to strengthen our common intuitions about elementary structures in discourse and to make a workshop of sorts for the academic journeyman in language – the mostly-reader who is obliged to be partly-writer. This is ostensibly a humble and a limited aim, yet it is one that may after all extend our views of composition so far as to reveal a little of what it means to use words creatively, to make the motes of grammar dance in imagination's festive light.

Chapter 2

The gaps between sentences

Between sentences there are indeed gaps: not the intervals obviously required by typography, but blanks of articulation, spaces which interpretation must leap. Consider, for instance, the following:

[1] Nottingham is a city which has undergone a great deal of 'development'. It retains some of the charm that once earned for it the title of Queen of the Midlands.

Here is a minor puzzle. How are we to relate these two sentences? Perhaps there is a clue in the inverted commas round 'development', which look like an invitation to read the word pejoratively. If that were the case, the relationship between the two assertions might be expressed in this fashion:

[2] Nottingham is a city which has undergone a great deal of 'development'. Nevertheless, it retains some of the charm that once earned for it the title of Queen of the Midlands.

However, this reading is not necessarily implicit in the two sentences as originally set out. Notwithstanding those tell-tale inverted commas, it could be argued that the relationship between the two statements is to be understood thus:

[3] Nottingham is a city which has undergone a great deal of 'development'. Consequently it retains some of the charm that once earned for it the title of Queen of the Midlands.

In this version, *consequently* imposes a different meaning on the inverted commas. They now merely quote a term currently in fashion, perhaps registering a feeling that the word is a piece of jargon, but without implying an attitude of disapproval towards what it denotes. In fact we are now explicitly informed that 'development' has had beneficial results for Nottingham. It appears that the two sentences of [1] are separated by a 'gap' which may be bridged in different ways. One kind of bridge is made by connective expressions such as *nevertheless, however, in spite of that, all the same,* etc, while another kind is constructed by *consequently, in consequence, as a result (of this/that), because of (this/that), thanks to (this/that),* and so forth. Despite the apparent simplicity of the example some overt mark of transition, some directive clue, is evidently necessary; and there are countless instances in the making of prose where the clarity of the text would be affected by the absence of such connectives.

An extension of the example will show how it is possible to create from a perfectly reasonable and well-ordered programme a text so lacking in cohesion that it crumbles into apparent absurdity:

[4] Nottingham is a city which has undergone a great deal of 'development'. It retains some of the charm that once earned for it the title of Queen of the Midlands. It is a provincial city with many of the drawbacks implied in that epithet. There are distinct advantages in living there. It is possible to live quite near the city centre. For most people transport is a minor problem. At certain times of day the bus services are overcrowded. It is difficult to find parking space in the inner city area. It is still fairly easy to get about.

At first reading, this is a ramble through a series of non sequiturs. On further consideration it presents itself as a 'raw' text, a set of propositions which make collective sense only if one can supply the links and articulations that demonstrate an expository process. Those links are realized in the following version:

[5] Nottingham is a city which has undergone a great deal of 'development'. *For all that,* it still retains some of the charm that once earned for it the title of Queen of the Midlands. It is *admittedly* a provincial city, with many of the drawbacks implied in that epithet. There are distinct advantages in living there, *all the same. For one thing,* it is possible to live quite near the city centre. *This means that* for most people transport is *only* a minor problem. At certain times of day, *of course,* the buses are overcrowded. It is *also* difficult to find parking space in the inner city area. *Nevertheless,* it is still fairly easy to get about.

The ramble has now become a route march, the stages of which are marked out by the italicized expressions. These words and phrases structure the text, making it possible for us to pick up a thread of intelligible discourse. There may still be defects of presentation, points of style and emphasis that the writer might wish to adjust. For instance, the penultimate sentence might be conflated with its predecessor, and the attitudinal focus of the text could be sharpened by substituting *suffered* for *undergone* in the first line. But amendments of this kind belong to a phase of stylistic polishing that comes fairly late in the process of composition. There is no point in undertaking them before the basic structure of the text has been firmly realized.

2.1 Expository structure: (a) enumerative terms

We have at hand a syntactic repertoire which enables us to create varied and flexible structures in prose exposition. One of the simplest of stratagems is to construct a pattern of argument round a set of enumerations, thus:

[6] Smoking is undoubtedly a pleasure to many people, but it can hardly be thought a good habit to acquire. In the first place, its correlation with bronchitis, heart disease and cancer of the lung is too well established to be doubted. In the second place, tobacco and cigarettes are no longer modestly priced and the smoker has to pay dearly for his enjoyment. Furthermore, what is a pleasure to him is often an ordeal to others, whose reactions may give him the unpleasant sensation of being a social outcast. It might seem, in short, that the next best thing to giving up smoking is never to have acquired the habit.

It is easy to see how this text hangs on a series of positional pegs: *in the first place, in the second place, furthermore, in short*. Basically these terms may be regarded as the equivalents of numerals or letter-indices, but they are more subtly involved in the gradation and attitudinal colouring of the text. The term *furthermore* presents a finer differentiation than would be conveyed by a *3* or a *(c)* or even by the word *thirdly*; it suggests that the third point is an addition to two others which are sufficiently powerful in themselves, and also that it broadens and even shifts the ground of the argument. In similar fashion, the phrase *in short* has more comprehensive implications than a *4* or a *(d)*, because it tells the reader that this is the last item in a series and one that summarizes the purport of all preceding items.

In some cases, therefore, these enumerative terms are not only structure *markers* – equivalents of *a, b, c, d*, etc – but also structure *shapers*, devices having a certain stylistic value. It is for the writer to determine whether his organizational terms should merely peg out the text like so many numerals, or whether they might enter more significantly into its structure. He has a fairly large range of expressions from which to choose. Here are some:

(i)	*Ordinal numerals and adverbs*		*first(ly), second(ly) third(ly)*, etc
(ii)	*Ordinal or 'proponent' phrases*	a. 'initial'	*in the first place, to begin with, to start with, first and foremost, for one thing, apart from anything else*, etc
		b. 'medial'	*in the second place, then, next, after that, to continue, furthermore, what is more, moreover, in addition, for one thing*, etc
		c. 'final'	*finally, lastly, all in all, last but not least, in short, to sum up, by way of conclusion, in conclusion, one final point*, etc

Set down in random sequence and out of context, these words and phrases of course present a stylistic rag-bag. The list tells us nothing about the compatibility of items (does *firstly* always presuppose *secondly*?) and it can give no indication of their syntactic versatility, *ie* the possibility of locating them in positions other than at the beginning of the sentence. An even more significant defect is the lack of any guidance on questions of register. Different levels of formality are represented here, and in certain contexts some of these items would make unlikely company. It might appear, for instance, that one of the connectives in the following example is stylistically out of place:

[7] No one with a sound mind and a reasonable chance of backing

a Derby winner would think of sitting down to write a textbook. Apart from anything else, it strikes at the heart of domestic life by keeping a man away from his television set. Then there is the slow loss of sanity to be considered, the remorseless grinding away of a serviceable wit that has sturdily resisted the very worst that income-tax inspectors and Faculty Board meetings can inflict. What is more, the financial rewards are a little less than handsome, thanks to the price of books and the determined unenlightenment of the British public. By way of conclusion, I would say that the text-book writer is not so much a harmless drudge (Dr Johnson's description of the lexicographer) as a toiling nincompoop.

The phrase that must surely strike a discordant note is *by way of conclusion*. In the language of formal address it has its place, and it would probably sort well enough with *first and foremost, furthermore,* and *moreover*; it figures very awkwardly, however, in the company of *apart from anything else, then,* and *what is more*. It would have been much more appropriate to the style of [7] had the last sentence begun *All in all* or *By and large*.

2.2 The function of enumeratives

Evidently there are constraints of usage on these apparently simple terms, and it appears that some of the constraints are personal; here as elsewhere each of us has his own preferences, his own notions of stylistic propriety and compatibility. Such reservations, however, do not affect the generally accepted conventions of using enumerative terms to shape a text. They can be adapted to a remarkably broad range of structural purposes. Here are some examples (for the sake of clarity the enumerative words and phrases are italicized):

[8]i *Marking a position in a series:*
First the canvas is stretched on a properly-constructed frame. *Next* it is given a coat of glue-size. *After that* it is primed with two or more coats of white paint. *Then and only then* is it ready for use.

ii *Indicating ascending order:*
The first important point is to ensure your own safety. *Even more important* is the necessity of protecting your passengers. *Most important of all* is your duty to other road users.

iii *Indicating descending order:*
What are the priorities of a university teacher's work? *First and foremost*, I would maintain, we have a duty to teach our pupils. *Next*, in support of that duty, we are required to study. *Only in the third and final place* is there an obligation upon us to become administrators.

iv *Setting out a complex of loosely interdependent points in argument:*
Money is conventionally denounced as the root of all evil, but it might just as well be blessed as the source of much that is good. *For one thing*, the security and well-being of an individual and his family is a matter of no small consequence. *Moreover*, there is no real evidence that poverty makes people generous and compassionate or that affluence has the opposite effect. *In general* the kindest and most tolerant communities are those in which the benefits of money are widely distributed.

The examples may point to an affinity between the enumerative sequences and certain of the rhetorical designs examined in Chapter 1 – notably the patterns called the Step and the Stack. The Steps of an instructional series are often marked out by enumerative signals, though as example [5] in Ch.1 suggests, their purely position-marking function can often be dispensed with. It is in building the Stack of routine arguments – the stuff of day-to-day debate – that the enumeratives come into their own. Many of the examples in this and the preceding chapter correspond to the formula *topic sentence – items with 'initial' marking – items with 'medial' marking – item with 'final' marking.*

This is a commonplace and perhaps in some instances a facile method of exposition. Often there may be better ways of knitting an argument. Compare, for example, the formulaically assembled passage [8], beginning *There is something wrong with the morality of a saying like 'Honesty is the best policy'*, with a version of the same theme, [7], in which the cohesion of the argument does not depend on enumeratives. The comparison possibly shows up the enumerative strategy as a rather pedestrian if easy device. It is nevertheless a useful resort and one that can be used in conjunction with others that increase its range and flexibility.

2.3 Expository structure: (b) extensional terms

Through the use of enumerative terms we can create a framework for exposition which is simple and reasonably effective, but limited in scope. We must have recourse to further sets of terms which will enable us, at need, to expand this structural formula, to enlarge or modify terms in argument, to introduce an element of personal comment. Such terms invite the name *extensional*. A few of them appear in the following passage, governing its cohesion in ostensibly casual style:

[9] Stereotypes of national character are generally falsehoods raised upon some buried and broken stratum of fact. The Scots, to take a typical case, are commonly traduced (and even take pleasure in denouncing themselves) as the flinty guardians of ancient pence. In other words, they are reckoned to be mean. They are further alleged to be dour, unsmiling and taciturn, particularly in the presence of the glib Englishman. Actually, as any visiting Sassenach knows, they are the most generous people on earth, compulsive spenders, affable companions, generous to a fault; the southerner sits tongue-tied in their company, brooding over his innocent wallet and his miserly outlay of words. They are not mean and never have been. They may insist gleefully on their parsimony, but the simple and beautiful truth is that they are lairds of largesse. As far as the stereotype is concerned, they have known penury, and with it the desperate need for prudence. A Scot seeking his living in eighteenth century London, for example, would as a rule be bound to consider his purse and would have little to lay out on extravagances. Consequently he would run the risk of incurring a totally unjustified reputation for meanness; the stereotype can be traced to its origins in the entirely honourable caution of proud men.

Scanning this passage for the expressions that fill the gaps between sentences, we find *to take a typical case, in other words, further, actually, as far as X is concerned, for example,* and *consequently.* Two of these (*to take a typical case, for example*) mark illustrations; one (*further*) introduces an additional or parallel example; one suggests the reformulation of an elaborate and perhaps extravagantly obscure description (*in other words*): two (*actually, as far as X is concerned*) imply an enlarged or corrected point of view; and one (*consequently*) points towards the result of the argument or the inference we can draw from the facts supplied. Collectively, these terms suggest one governing power, namely that of personality. Through them the writer begins to intervene in the life of his text, selecting, evaluating, taking a stance, even creating a bias.

2.4 The extensional repertoire

The following list, though far from complete, may serve to exemplify the repertoire of extensional terms:

1 ADDITION AND SPECIFICATION

These terms introduce additional points or indicate the particular scope of a given instance.

Examples: *in addition, equally, similarly, in the same way, by the same token, also, further, not only . . . but also, as well, even, besides, too; in particular, particularly, chiefly, especially, mostly.*

2 EXEMPLIFICATION (OR APPOSITION)

The role of these terms is to mark an illustration or introduce an explanatory comment.

Examples: *for example, for instance, a case in point, to take (quote, cite) a typical case (instance, example), that is, that is to say, by way of illustration (elucidation, explanation).*

3 RESULT AND INFERENCE

The terms indicate some goal or consequence in the process of exposition.

Examples: *consequently, in consequence, as a result, as a result of which, in view of which, in which case, in that case, so, thus, therefore, for, then.*

4 REFORMULATION

The terms announce that some foregoing expression is to be rephrased, or mark an idiosyncratic formulation.

Examples: *in other words, or rather, to put it another way, differently put, alternatively; as it were, so to speak, if you will.*

5 DISJUNCTION, ENLARGEMENT, TRANSITION

The terms indicate a revised point of view. The writer ostensibly detaches himself from his theme and takes an objective stance; or enlarges his argument so that misapprehensions are corrected; or moves forward to a new phase in the exposition. Among the examples listed below, the 'disjuncts' (here, the items preceding the semi-colon) suggest an appeal to the imagined reader-over-one's shoulder.

Examples: *in fact, indeed, evidently, clearly, of course, admittedly, actually; now, turning to, as for, as far as X is concerned.*

2.5 The role of extensional terms in discourse

The five subdivisions of 2.4 cover a very wide variety of syntactic operators. If we now ask ourselves just what it is that these ostensibly diverse types have in common, it must surely be evident that they not only *extend* discourse in the sense of enabling the writer to create a protracted verbal structure, but also *expand* it by implying the attitudinal presences of a writer and a reader among the variables that govern the making of a text. As long as writing merely involves the enumeration of data or the creation of simple step patterns of instruction and description, the personalities of author and reader are kept at a distance. But no sooner do we allow anything in the shape of reasoning or demonstration to enter discourse than we imply a kind of social relationship between author and reader, and a play of personality round that relationship. The extensional terms therefore imply a phase in the growth of prose discourse as presented in these pages; we move from simple statements of 'position' to connected sequences of 'composition', and so eventually to 'exposition', in which a connected text is manifestly designed and controlled by the personality of the writer.

When the enumerative and extensional techniques are combined, the result may be a quite elaborate development of the stack design, a possibility which is illustrated in the following example:

[10] Despite the objections of the pundits, it is arguable that one good television adaptation of a classic novel may do more for literature than all the lectures and learned analyses of critics and scholars. In the first place, a TV production is based on the assumption that the work exists to be *enjoyed*, irrespective of whether the viewer is acquainted with the author's general ideas, with the peculiarities of his style, or with his status in the history of literature. *War and Peace*, for example, has been confidently offered, as an absorbing spectacle, to a public not in the least concerned with Tolstoy's philosophy of history.

Indeed, the majority of viewers of the recent production probably had the sketchiest notions of the historical events and political trends of the time in which the novel is set. Consequently, the work had to meet one paramount requirement: that it should contain within itself the power to please, to excite, to engage and move the sympathies of millions to whom its cultural origins might be of no significance.

Secondly, the writer and producer of a TV adaptation must strive to bring out what is essential to the work, and to discard matter that from an artistic point of view is incidental or merely discursive – however great its ostensible importance in the text. In addition, they must consider the best way of realizing these essential features in the new medium. Their activity is therefore responsible and creative. They function as the author's critical sponsors, or rather as midwives of his artistic intention in a new world of narrative. They cannot, of course, depart radically from the plot and structure of the story they are adapting, but their sense of what makes good television might identify something in the story that a reader could easily overlook. As a result, a TV adaptation may successfully re-establish an unfashionable work, or make an original statement about a well-tried favourite.

The 'Stack' is here so large that it extends over two long paragraphs – and indeed might be further extended. Two enumerative terms, ie: in the first place (following the opening 'topic' sentence) and secondly (at the beginning of the second paragraph) control the general design. The other sentence-connecting devices (for example, indeed, consequently, in addition, therefore, of course, as a result) belong to the extensional range and illustrate the dual effect of protracting discourse and of reflecting the presence of a governing personality.

2.6 Expository structure: (c) endophoric terms

With the protraction of discourse into extended patterns comes the need to demonstrate the strength of an exposition by showing clearly the bonding of a sequence of sentences. In the following illustration each sentence contains some small expression that functions like a rivet or shackle, making a tie with the sentences that precede or follow:

[11] Recently there has been some unrest among students, chiefly about the size of their annual grants. This is understandable, since the cost of living has long been far too heavy for the student purse. But that is no justification for obstructive actions which bear chiefly on University servants and others who have no responsibility for the demonstrators' plight. Such conduct cannot help the students. It can only serve to raise against them the resentment of those whose sympathy they can ill afford to lose.

The foregoing argument, or something like it, would be accepted by most people, even by the students themselves. But it leaves unanswered the question of remedies. The following measures at least might be considered: (a) the establishment of an annual reviewing board, on which student delegates would sit, (b) the institution of a fund to meet special cases, and (c) the working out of a procedure to deal with grievances. Here are three possible developments, some further suggestions for which are set out below.

In this example the connective items are mostly retrospective – signposts, as it were, pointing to some expression in the preceding sentence: *this* (– 'there has been some unrest'), *(but) that* (– 'the cost of living has been far too heavy etc'), *such (conduct)* (– 'obstructive actions'), *it* (– 'conduct' – 'obstructive actions'), *the foregoing argument* (– the whole of the first paragraph), *here* (– the 'measures' just described).

These backward-pointing items are called *anaphoric*. Our text also includes one or two expressions that are prospective, or *cataphoric* in function, *eg: the following, below*. The two types of connection are comprised under the heading *endophoric*. Such functions, let it be noted, are essentially *textual*. Enumerative terms have some extra-textual scope; they make provision in the text for the ordering of the 'theme' or 'message'. Extensional terms, as we have seen, expand and explain the text; they help to create a 'context' by relating the text to the writer's controlling responses. Endophoric terms differ from these in that they give second place to extra-textual reference. Their function is clearly intra-textual; they relate *text to text*, supplying words that refer in the first instance to other words and only secondarily to persons, objects, or ideas.

2.7 The endophoric repertoire

This description might suggest that endophoric cohesion is the most abstract of the processes so far reviewed; that in fact it may be like the symbolic language of mathematics or logic, inasmuch as one expression can represent or imply another. Yet the exponents of this ostensibly abstruse process are reassuringly commonplace. Here are some examples of endophoric words and phrases:

1 ANAPHORA

These terms have the effect of pointing back to a preceding reference. They resemble 'pro-forms' (see below) in that they stand in for a word, phrase, or even longer stretch of text, but they are further marked by their *deictic* (*ie* 'pointing') function and their consequent occurrence in positions where spoken stress is implied.

Examples: *this, that, these, those, the foregoing, the above, here, such.*

2 CATAPHORA

The terms point forward (or, as the Greek suggests, 'downward') to a subsequent reference.

Examples: *below, the following, as follows, this, these, here, thus, like this, in this (the following) way.*

3 PRO-FORMS

These are grammatical stand-ins for preceding items or stretches of text. They are like anaphora in their retrospective function, but lack the deictic force and in the case of personal pronouns do not imply a spoken stress.

Examples: *he, she, it, him, her, they, them, his, hers, its, theirs; one, all, some, any, many, each, none, the same.*

2.8 The role of endophoric terms in discourse

With the addition of a further range of terms to the connective repertoire we increase the possibility of ensuring strength and clarity of exposition. We gain, furthermore, a certain security in composition, since these endophoric items can serve the writer as clues by means of which he marks his own path through the textual labyrinth. This aspect of writing has been touched on in 1.6; it is illustrated in the type of rhetorical structure for which the name

Chain was suggested. Here indeed is a basic method of close-knitting a text, though it is one that may sometimes have to be evaluated against other possibilities. Compare, for instance, the following passages:

[12]i Hamlet is said to represent the indecisions that plague us all. He reflects, with tragic intensity, the lesser despair of common mortals. This is surely an explanation of the play's appeal. It survives the politics of its own time and speaks directly to our century of the common man.

ii Hamlet is said to represent the indecisions that plague us all. The melancholy prince reflects, with tragic intensity, the lesser despair of common mortals. That our ordinary anguish, our routine paralysis of the will, should thus acquire a poetic magnitude is surely an explanation of the play's appeal. Shakespeare's brooding masterpiece survives the politics of its own time and speaks directly to our century of the common man.

These may lack something as samples of prose ([12ii] is a little inflated) but they serve well enough to make a point. If what is required is a muted, matt-surfaced, quietly unfolding exposition, then all the writer need do is to supply a few simple syntactic links of the kind we see in [12i], where *he, this, it* quite adequately control the cohesion of the text. If on the other hand the writing is to be more demonstrative, its emphases more heavily underscored, its tone pitched higher, then possibly, as in [12ii], a scheme of lexical cohesion will be used. The simple endophoric items of [12i] are replaced in [12ii] by elaborate periphrases: *the melancholy prince* (='Hamlet'), *our ordinary anguish, our routine paralysis of the will* (='lesser despair of common mortals'), *Shakespeare's brooding masterpiece* (='it', 'the play'). These weigh cumbrously upon the style, but they overlay the basic statement with an attitudinal comment: *melancholy, anguish, paralysis, brooding* invite the reader – or perhaps exhort him – to share a state of mind. Another compensatory aspect of this talkative strategy is that it may give explicit strength to points that syntactic cohesion merely elides; for instance, in the second sentence of [12ii] there is a clear counterpoise between *the prince* and *common mortals*, a contrast not so strikingly apparent at the corresponding juncture in [12i].

The choice here illustrated is between textual economy and affective power: between concise statement and elaborate, rhetorically charged assertion. In the one case simple endophoric terms serve well enough, but if we choose the other goal we must have access to devices which are to be examined at length in another chapter.

2.9 Expository structure: (d) interruptive terms

By means of enumerative, extensional, and endophoric terms a piece of writing can be carefully protracted and shaped into a continuously developing pattern, the elements of which are clearly ordered and related. For any writer the ability to devise such continuity of exposition must clearly be a matter of primary competence. But he must also be able to interrupt the pattern, break continuity, perhaps even introduce a series of counter-assertions; something of the kind is demonstrated in 1.7, in connection with the device called the Balance. Another set of terms is now required. We shall call them *interruptive*:

[13] In the past, it is true, Latin and Greek have been staple subjects in the school curriculum. But times change, and we can no longer take for granted the sovereignty of the 'classical' education. The Classics have admittedly provided a formative discipline for many minds. It can hardly be said, however, that we lack other disciplines, equally rigorous. The case system of Latin may indeed test the wits. By comparison the grammar of many modern languages is simple enough. On the other hand, Russian presents problems of form and inflection every bit as exacting as those posed by the construction of passages in Latin and Greek. But we must surely stop thinking in terms of the rivalry of disciplines in competition for the mind of the learner, as if academic subjects were so many street-traders with wares and services to peddle. Instead, we should try to reinstate Latin and Greek as what they have always been – indispensable adjuncts to the study of a foundation era of European civilisation.

Here we find a number of expressions which promote the cohesion of the text while constantly questioning, modifying, rebutting, and generally making distinctions between the assertions that constitute its theme, *ie: it is true, but, admittedly, however, indeed, by comparison, on the other hand, instead.* Of these, *by comparison, on the other hand,* and *instead* have something like the anaphoric function (*by comparison* relates to 'the case system of Latin', *on the other hand* to 'the grammar . . . is simple enough', and *instead* to 'thinking in terms of the rivalry of disciplines'); while items such as *it is true, admittedly, however, indeed,* are viewpoint adjuncts sharing some ground with the disjuncts listed in 2.4(v).

2.10 The repertoire of interruptive terms

The range of terms is substantial, and may be referred to the following categories:

1 CONTRADICTIVES
These terms introduce a statement which directly opposes or excludes a foregoing proposition.
Examples: *but, on the contrary, on the other hand, against that, instead.*

2 CONTRASTIVES
Here the terms countervail a foregoing assertion, without, however, excluding it.
Examples: *nevertheless, notwithstanding, however, yet, still, all the same, for all that; by (in) contrast, looking at it another way.*

3 CONCESSIVES
These are terms used to acknowledge or forestall criticism, possible objections, the awareness that something has been omitted or only partially stated, etc.
Examples: *admittedly, assuredly, certainly, naturally, of course, true, it is true, to be sure.*

2.11 Expository structure: (e) time definers

The simple devices so far discussed provide a structure for the majority of texts; to enumerate points, to extend argument, to make close-knit textual patterns and counter-patterns, is the ordinary business of expository prose, as exemplified by the composition presented and analysed in 2.15 below. Before turning to that summarizing example, however, we must draw attention to further connective strategies, prominent in certain types of writing. For example, in histories and biographies the dimension of time is so obviously important that the frequent temporal references become a

major element in textual organization. Here is a piece of autobiographical text in which *time definers* are essential agents of
continuity and cohesion:

[14] Until 1952 I had been quite content to eke out an existence in
London, though even in those uninflated days an assistant
lecturer's salary (paid quarterly in arrears) required very
careful budgeting. At the time I had a room in a cheap
boarding house in Brunswick Square, in an elegant if decaying
terrace that was subsequently demolished to make room for a
red slab of modern brutality. That was the base from which I
made my raids on London: not the London of the theatres and
stores, but a London of byways, barrows, pubs, chop-houses. I
enjoyed it enormously and after two years had begun to think
of myself as a Londoner. Meanwhile, however, my scholarly
career – if such it could be called – had stagnated, for two
associated reasons. The interest I had hitherto felt in the
paratactic and hypotactic patterns of seventeenth-century
prose had noticeably waned. At the same time I had developed
a compensating enthusiasm for a very personable young
woman who fed me solicitously, supervised my wardrobe and
kept an eye on my health. Many an assistant lecturer has fallen
gratefully by courtship's wayside, and I was happy to continue
the tradition. When I left London, shortly afterwards, there
were pleasant domestic prospects to console me for whatever
sadness I might have felt on parting from my little room in
Bloomsbury. Only in later years did I sometimes feel, in self-
dramatising moods, that maybe the room had contained the
last and best of my youth.

Many of the structural pegs in this text are expressions of time:
*until 1952, (even) in those (uninflated) days, at the time, subsequently, after two
years, meanwhile, hitherto, at the same time, shortly afterwards, in later years.*
They are not all of a piece, it will be noted. Some are time-indicative,
locating a point in time or defining a period as a point; *eg: in those days,
at the time.* Others are time-relative, taking bearings (as it were)
between points in time; *eg: hitherto, meanwhile, shortly afterwards.*

Time relaters might be subclassified as expressions of *precedence* (*eg:
hitherto, until*) or *co-occurrence* (*eg: meanwhile, at the same time*), or
subsequence (*eg: afterwards, in later years*). Another kind of time-definition
is expressed in our text by the word *quarterly*, which neither locates a

point, like *at the time*, nor defines a relationship, like *shortly afterwards*. Its function is to record distribution or frequency. Words and phrases like *quarterly, frequently, every so often, on alternate Fridays*, are frequentatives; akin to them (but not exemplified in [14]) are expressions of duration such as *briefly* or *for many years*. In composition, then, time is defined punctually, relatively, distributively, often in subtle shifts of perspective requiring the support of the verb in its changes of tense or aspect. (Note, for example, the interaction of time definers and tense throughout [14].)

2.12 The repertoire of time definers

The following examples are representative of time definers in their text-sustaining role:

1 TIME INDICATORS
Examples: *then, just then, at that time, in those days, last Friday, last year, next Easter, in 1978, at the beginning of June, on the stroke of ten, at four o'clock sharp, five months ago, when these events began*.

2 TIME RELATERS
Examples: (a) *Precedence*: *until (then), by (then), before (then), hitherto, up to that time, in the preceding months (weeks, days, etc), in the weeks (months, days, etc) leading up to, prior to*. Beginning a narrative sequence: *at first, to begin with, at the outset, in the beginning*.

(b) *Cooccurrence*: *at the same time, in the meantime, meanwhile, simultaneously, at that (very) moment, (even) while (this was going on), as (these events were unfolding), all the while, all along*.

(c) *Subsequence*: *subsequently, afterwards, then, next, thereafter, presently, by and by, after a while, later (on), in later days, at a later period, in days (time) to come; in due course, eventually, finally, at last, at length, at the finish, in the long run, in the end*.

3 TIME DISTRIBUTORS
Examples: (a) *Frequency*: *frequently, hourly, daily, weekly, monthly*, etc; *occasionally, now and then, every so often, again and again, from time to time, as the years (time) go(es) by; day after day, year after year*, etc (see also *duration*)

(b) *Duration*: *briefly, for some moments, for many years, during those hours; second by second, minute by minute, hour by (after) hours*, etc, *for days (hours, etc) on end, for hours (etc) at a stretch*.

2.13 Expository structure: (f) place definers

In descriptions of landscape, furnishings, the setting of a stage, etc, another kind of dimensional reference gives cohesion to the text. Observe the importance of *place definers* in the following passage:

[15] My room does double duty as a writer's workplace and a painter's studio, and in this joint capacity presents an unseemly clutter. Under the window stands my desk, two or three feet behind the desk I have set my easel, and round these fixed points the room is all too unfixedly organised. The wall to the right of the window was to have been reserved for books, that to the left for painting materials, but I have not been very successful in keeping my own ordinances. To one side of me as I sit at my desk there is indeed a large hanging bookshelf, below which, however, leaning against the wall, there are two small folding easels, a drawing board, a portfolio and several sheets of mounting card. Access to my books, moreover, is hindered by a display of little sketches and paintings propped up against the spines of the ranked volumes, watercolour roses cheek by jowl with *Beowulf*, an abstract squiggle hard by *History of Western Philosophy*, a dark townscape alongside Edward Lear's jolly dust-jacket. On the opposite side of the room, flanking the chimney-breast, are two alcoves. In one of them is a cupboard containing files, folders, paint-boxes, palettes and what-not, piled higgledy-piggledy one on top of the other. In the neighbouring alcove is a small oil sketch, beneath which stands a chest of drawers bearing a litter of books, jars of brushes, photographs, paperweights and miscellaneous ornaments. The adjoining wall boasts a serving hatch, which looks out of place in a study and is a relic of a former occupancy when this was a dining room. Beyond the hatch is the kitchen; all round it – all over the wall, in fact, ranging upwards and outwards from the one space where a picture cannot be hung – are framed paintings and prints; in front of it is a half-moon table with the telephone, the directories, and the usual cargo of jottings, doodles, and bric-à-brac. In short, the room is a pleasant little chaos; I vow reform, but know myself to be an inveterate sloven.

Here only the first sentence and the last make no reference to position or spatial relationship; the linkages in the intervening text require a continual process of place definition, by prepositions, by adverbs and adverbial phrases, by adjectives (*neighbouring, adjoining*) and even by verbs (*eg: flanking* in *flanking the chimney breast*). In general these place definers either express the relationship of separately positioned objects (*eg: below*), or locate a positional juncture (*eg: on*), or indicate a direction (*eg: outwards*). Our exemplary passage gives particular prominence to expressions of spatial relationship: *under, behind, beneath, below, in front of, (all) round, to the right of, to the left of, to one side of, on the opposite side of.* The nature of the compositional task here – the description of an interior from a central point of observation – might very well account for this prominence.

Other categories are not so well represented. There are expressions of positional juncture in *on top of* and *in*, and of direction in *all over, outwards, upwards.* Some terms, however, function in a way that suggests further sub-types. The sentence beginning *Access to my books*, for example, introduces expressions indicative of *proximity* (*against, cheek by jowl with, hard by, alongside*) and somewhat later in the passage there is one word (*ie: beyond*) that suggests the converse relationship of *distance*. These categorical distinctions have a compositional interest in their relationship to the design of a text. Note, for example, how in [15] there is an 'outer' scheme of spatial expressions, a scheme which contains – or is interrupted by – an 'inner' scheme of terms indicating proximity and contact. Thus in the general account the bookshelf is described as standing *to one side of me*, while in the particular description of that feature the small drawings and paintings are said to be propped *up against* the spines of the ranked volumes.

2.14 The repertoire of place definers

The examples in the following categories do not cover every conceivable expression of space or place, but typify such words and phrases as might be important in the structuring of a text. Some items occur in more than one function:

1 JUNCTURE (see also *proximity*)
Examples: *at, in, on, on top of, here, there, where* (*eg* 'where the bookcase is fixed to the wall the plaster is stained'), *against, touching.*

2 SPATIAL RELATIONSHIP (see also *distance* and *direction*)
Examples: *above, below, beneath, behind, facing, flanking, inside, within, on one side, to one side (of), to the right (of), to the left (of), on the opposite side (of), in front (of), before, (all) round.*

3 DIRECTION
Examples: *across, along, aside, up, down, to, to and fro, forward(s) backward(s), upwards(s), downward(s), inward(s), obliquely, sideways, longways, at an angle, (all) over, to the right, to the left, (to the) north, south, east, west.*

4 PROXIMITY
Examples: *adjoining, adjacent (to), (up) against, alongside, near, nearby, next to, (hard) by, close to, face to face, back to back, cheek by jowl, touching, neighbouring, (close) at hand, in the foreground.*

5 DISTANCE
Examples: *beyond, in the distance, in the background, past, far away (off), on the far side, at the farther end, yonder, there, outside, to the north, south, east, west.*

2.15 General design and syntactic cohesion: an extended text

In this chapter we have presented a simplified and selective view of syntactic cohesion that leaves many things out of account or postpones them for later discussion. Nevertheless these preliminary explorations should be of some use in identifying the rudiments of textual design. To put the matter to the test, let us attempt something a little more ambitious than our standard exemplary paragraph. It might be proposed, for example, to write a short essay in praise of opera, with the following text as the result (paragraphs are numbered marginally for ease of subsequent reference):

[16] There are people who love a good play and willingly attend symphony concerts, but who cannot bear the opera at any price. Though I think they are wrong, I would not condemn them out of hand. I am myself a rank philistine as far as some operas are concerned. Only the most compelling inducements – the rack, a life annuity, a sudden descent of in-laws – would

persuade me to attend a performance of *Parsifal*, for example. On the other hand, I pity that man whose pulses do not drum with cheerful anticipation when Mozart's brisk overture draws to a close, and the curtain rises to reveal the immortal Figaro measuring his bedroom while the ever-blessed Susanna tries on her new bonnet. Some operas abide our question; others it is our human duty to adore.

2 Allowing, then, for individual preference and prejudice, the fact remains that opera offers a peculiar and perhaps unique pleasure. It reflects enchantingly what many feel to be a condition of real life, the existence of poetry in the heart of the preposterous. It is, so to speak, a compendium of fairy-tale and philosophy, an amalgam of sublime silliness and profound symbolism, a mixture of dramatic business and pictorial tableau. This commingling of qualities leads some to dismiss it with irritation as a hopelessly contaminated art form. For others, however, its very magic springs from the fact that it is indeed a family alliance of all the arts, with the possible exception of the dance; and even that has a place in some operas.

3 The scenery of an opera, to begin with, differs in function and appeal from that of a play. In a play the setting is exactly what that word implies – a more or less realistic background against which the action is presented. In an opera it is something more. It adds pictorial qualities of colour, shape and perspective to the musical dimensions of tone and harmony and the histrionic properties of costume, grouping and movement; in the great set pieces which are the delight of all operatic composers it is an essential element in the tableau of sight and sound.

4 Then there is the music itself. This is, at one level of perception, a vehicle for the expression of character and action; how marvellously, for example, an opera like Britten's *Peter Grimes* reflects in music the physical and mental natures, the very muscle and thought, of its personages. At another level, the composition for voices of differing range and quality presents itself as a pure art, like chamber music; we forget the action and listen only to the music of trio or quartet, reposing and soaring in an ecstasy of art that transcends all the pother of the fable. At such moments the conviction steals upon the

opera-goer that there are after all worlds beyond this world and that our vulgar sufferings may be the staves and crotchets of a timeless music.

5 But what above all gives opera its hold upon its devotees is the convergence of setting, action and music in intense moments of poetic revelation. Such moments live on in the mind and acquire a talismanic or symbolic quality, expressing values that rule beyond the opera-house. Towards the close of *The Marriage of Figaro*, for example, there is a moment when the womanizing Count Almaviva, ridiculously trapped in yet another escapade, at last recognizes his folly and turns to his greatly wronged Countess to ask her pardon; whereupon she proclaims his forgiveness in music that descends like a grace, a benediction, an absolution for all our grubby wrongs. At the heart of that supremely merry opera there is this moment of stillness, of benign gravity, when we are reminded – if reminder were necessary – that without love and forgiveness all action falls apart in a rattle of meaningless gestures and callous jokes.

6 None of this, perhaps, will overcome the prejudice of those who are determined not to be pleased by operatic performances. What deters them above all else is the barrier of operatic conventions. They cannot bear to hear characters exchanging the time of day in recitative, or converting an oath into an aria; and when a man is run through with a sword and luxuriates in five melodious minutes of dying, or a buxom soprano gives all her lungs to the demise of a consumptive heroine, their credulity is stretched beyond endurance. Besides, they say, the plots are unbelievably silly. Who could attempt a serious account of the action of *The Magic Flute*, for example, without feeling just a little embarrassed?

7 Such objections, it is true, have probably occurred to all of us at one time or another. There is indeed an artificial strain in the conventions of recitative and aria. On the other hand, the conventions of the Greek drama, in which a chorus comments on the action, or the Elizabethan stage, in which heroes reveal their minds in extended blank verse, are every whit as artificial. And while the plots of some operas are admittedly fantastic, there are plays by Shakespeare in which the action is no less grotesque. *The Tempest*, to take an obvious case, asks us

to believe in an exiled Duke who by a long course of study has acquired supernatural powers and who has, among other things, rescued a fairy from a centuries-long imprisonment in an oak tree. Compared with this, *The Flying Dutchman* is a reasonable tale.

8 Besides, the fact is surely that for the devotee the absurd conventions add to, rather than detract from, the pleasures of the opera. He sees them as delightful in themselves, is amused at their extravagance, is appreciative when they are skilfully exploited. When all is said and done, every art is a play of conventions, benignly-contrived illusions which are recognized and accepted as such. It is hard to believe that there is some extravagance in the conventions of the opera which makes them harder to accept than, say, the conventions of mediaeval Romance or the film 'Western'; but if there is, then those of us who like operas can only congratulate ourselves on having learned to ignore reason for the sake of revelation.

There are perhaps features of this essay that are not accessible to the terms of reference we have so far established, but some important points of compositional technique can nonetheless be identified. In the first place, there is a clearly defined paragraph scheme. This in fact emerged as the work progressed, and reflects the writer's feeling about the logic of his procedures. (There is no contradiction in terms here; prose has its 'logic', but the writer is always guided by the 'feel' of his work.) The first two sentences or so of each paragraph are leaders in the unfolding theme, announcing sub-topics which are then extended in whatever rhetorical design has seemed appropriate to the author; the stack pattern, for example, occurs more than once.

Then there is the fact that a part of this paragraph scheme is set up on a basis of enumerative terms which not only introduce their respective points in exposition but also make connections between paragraphs. Thus paras. 2 and 3 are linked by *to begin with*, paras. 3 and 4 by *then*, and paras. 4 and 5 by *(but what) above all*. Other paragraphs are linked extensionally or endophorically; the transition from paras. 1 to 2 is indicated by a resultative *then*, from paras. 5 to 6 by the anaphoric phrase *none of this* plus the concessive *perhaps*, from paras. 6 to 7 by the anaphoric *such objections* followed by the concessive *it is true*, and from paras. 7 to 8 by the extensional *besides*.

The tactics of cohesion within each of the paragraphs invite study. It is striking that extensional terms of the kind that imply a point of view, an authorial stance, occur predominantly in the first and last paragraphs: *as far as some operas are concerned, for example, besides, when all is said and done.* This distribution may be symptomatic of an approach to composition. The writer makes his entry and takes his leave in a style that suggests a sort of literary socializing; between the greeting and the leavetaking comes the matter of getting down to argumentative business.

Another distributional feature is the concentration of interruptives in para. 7, where some attempt is made to deal with the kind of objections that are raised by critics of the opera. Here the cohesive tactics are evolved in response to the pressure of the argument, as indeed they also are in para. 4, where the text is poised on two enumerative stress-points, *ie: at one level of perception* and *at another level.*

These are some salient features of the text, aspects of structure that now fall within our descriptive view. They were not consciously devised in the course of writing so that they might subsequently be discovered in a pedagogic routine, though perhaps it will seem that whoever mixed the pudding ought to know where to find the sixpences. Compositional choices are never quite so deliberately made. They are, rather, always under subconscious review. When we have arrived at them we can attempt to rationalize them and perhaps raise new schemes of patterning upon them, but no writer ever set out with the notion of trimming his words to a hard-and-fast formula. The discernible laws of his craft are confirmed in the workings of his instinct.

Chapter 3

The lexicology of composition

The forging of syntactic links from sentence to sentence is a primary compositional process, but not the sole means of ensuring cohesion and rhetorical power. Key words, seminal phrases, turns of metaphor, figures of speech, the various features a linguistic analyst would refer to as the *lexicon*, also have a part to play in the shaping of a text. Indeed, their role is so clearly important that it is constantly stressed in our casual talk about the problems of composition. We complain, for example, about the difficulty of 'finding the right word' far more often than we deplore the equally crucial task of discovering the right sentence-structure. This is perhaps because syntactic choices are relatively limited, while the lexicon seems to lie wide open to us, offering tantalizingly rich and complex possibilities. We rub and scrub at the text, cancelling this idiom, that synonym, fretfully convinced that there is always something a little more precise lying just out of mind's reach, blessing and cursing English for its enormous and unrelenting fecundity.

Actually, the sense of boundless choice is an illusion. Factors too numerous and complex for brief discussion set limitations on the writer's lexicon. Theme and register must play a major part in that they dictate the items and general range of vocabulary required by the author in conveying the purely informative part of his message. But few messages consist simply and solely of information. There is usually an attitudinal element, an implication of judgements and stances, commonly involving the writer's relationship with his reader. Questions of stylistic variation also arise, and with them the not unimportant fact that syntax often has a determinant power over lexical choice. To give a very simple example of this last point: the construction *I think* has a general correspondence with *It seems to me* and hence with *It is apparent* and other quasi-synonymous expressions.

It may even be paraphrased by means of a viewpoint adjunct such as *evidently*. From one phrasal alternative to the next there is the gradual slide of meaning that characterizes all synonymy, but the significant point is that in the course of these shifts lexical variation is bound up with grammatical variation.

It is the struggle to reconcile all these constraints that so often makes the right word elusive. This is the central problem in the lexicology of composition and one that can hardly be avoided, though there is no formula for its solution and there would be no point in labouring to devise one. Instead, let us consider some types of lexical choice made on two planes, the *textual* and the *textural*. By the *textual plane* we shall understand that level of composition at which the writer is concerned with the cohesion and continuity of his text, while the phrase *textural plane*, or the adjective *textural*, will refer to the colouring and fleshing of the text with imagery, metaphor, dominant motifs, figures of speech, powerfully evocative language, and all the resources of address and persuasion. These 'planes' are essentially interlocked, as subsequent illustration may show, but the distinction is convenient for expository purposes.

3.1 Text and texture: (a) reiteration

One effective device of lexical cohesion is simply to reiterate a word until it becomes a pervasive motif, insistently claiming and directing the reader's attention. Here is an impromptu on a random theme:

> [1] Before me I see those two familiar workmen and labouring strangers, my hands; Tom and Dick, pottering round the typewriter keyboard, working at their own sweet pace, stumbling and fumbling, at times seeming quite oblivious of their governor, the brain. Suddenly I am struck by the fanciful thought that these hands of mine, these functionaries, would live their own careless lives if they were not unremittingly forced to attend upon me and my needs. Fetchers and carriers for an importunate body, sanitation engineers, constructors, practitioners of the arts, emissaries in the transactions of love – for years they have been as busy as hands can be, keeping the record of my existence.
>   A man's hands know him and show him for what he is. Like his face they may reveal his nature, his avocations, his

passions. My hands, now, are soft in the palm (a sign of easy living) and yet the nails are often bruised or broken, and along the knuckles at the first finger-joint are callouses I have had for years, where the porous grain of the skin has been rubbed into smooth, leathery little pads. It would take no great detective to read into my hands a liking for pursuits more strenuous than typing. Tom and Dick are indeed acquainted with tools and tackle, with spanners and hammers and tillers and warps, and their instinct for these things is encoded in their appearance and posture. It is extraordinary, now that I begin to pay attention to them, how clearly they announce their history. And there is something even more extraordinary. Watching them go about their business, I have the uncanny feeling that I have seen these hands before, working for someone else. A gesture betrays them; in it I recognize my father's hands. This is indeed a strange and unsettling experience. I have inherited no more than a general family share of his face, but his hands are mine. These hands are shaped as his were shaped, and move as his hands moved.

This example illustrates immediately the interlocking of the textual and the textural planes. The cohesive function of the single word *hands*, occurring eleven times, is quite obvious; the whole text is constructed round it. Equally obvious is the power of this reiteration to stain the text with ever-deepening colours of emotion. It is apparent that the writer of this passage has responded to the stimulus of the repetition as he might respond to the allure of a hypnotist's bauble; the text begins in something like a spirit of levity or amusement (*Tom and Dick* is a symptomatic phrase) but ends in an almost chastened mood of solemn fixation. In short, the word *hands* gradually accumulates *textural* value as a powerfully emotive item, in the course of discharging its *textual* function of keeping the reader attuned to the cohesion of the passage.

The word recurs in phrasal contexts which make their own contribution to the strength of textual cohesion and emphasis: *hands, my hands, these hands, a man's hands, my father's hands, his hands*. The artfulness of the device, in other words, does not lie solely in the repetition of the noun; it also involves a grammatical orientation relating that noun to the text's unfolding pattern of meaning. Initially, the hands described in the text are merely parts of the body; by the end of the passage they have become emblems of human life and symbols of a personal relationship. These shifts of perspective are marked by the apparently casual switching from *my* to *these* to *a man's* to *my father's*. In this ringing of the phrasal changes there is a dynamic intention to keep the text on the move, in play, with its meaning always one bounce beyond the reader's conclusive grasp. If *hands* had the same contextual associations throughout, the mere repetition of the word might be stylistically crippling; textually adequate, possibly, but texturally dead. There is a kindred intention in the figurative variations which at the beginning of the text accompany and indeed outplay the repetitions: *these two familiar workmen and labouring strangers, Tom and Dick, these functionaries, fetchers and carriers, sanitation engineers, constructors, practitioners of the arts, emissaries in the transactions of love*. Such phrases are not only useful as metaphors or periphrases which vary and illuminate the *hands* theme; they also set up, collectively, a secondary pattern of variation and repetition, a kind of lexical subplot. Thus *these two familiar workmen* reappear in a textural variant as *Tom and Dick*; but somewhat later in the passage that same variant functions textually, as a synonym establishing lexical cohesion with *my hands* in the preceding sentence (*It would take no great detective to read in my hands a liking for pursuits more strenuous than typing. Tom and Dick are indeed acquainted with tools and tackle*, etc . . .). Another textural variant of *these two familiar workmen* is *these functionaries*, and that phrase in its turn becomes a superordinate expression presiding over a series of subordinate phrases indicating various personified functions of the hands (*eg: sanitation engineers, constructors, practitioners of the arts*). At first sight these figures and variations no doubt appear to be nothing more than fanciful ornaments, but in fact they enter significantly into the structuring of the text – so that, for example, when the author writes *go about their business* (towards the end of the passage) he can feel secure in the knowledge that he has established a lexical history that will justify that expression.

3.2 Text and texture: (b) variation

The hazard of reiteration is of course its potential clumsiness; the majestic tread of formal prose can so easily become a club-footed one-step. We should distinguish, perhaps, between planned reiteration and the lexical stammer of ungainly repetition. Words sometimes follow each other in close paradigmatic association (*eg:*

repeat might have *repetition* as its near neighbour), and there may often be a case for allowing the recurrence of a word in successive clauses or sentences, but style is ludicrously crippled when one lexical form is repeated within close syntactic limits, *eg* within the structure of a clause. It would clearly be unacceptable to write *Some good arguments were produced in the course of the argument*, or *The contest was hotly contested.* In such instances we have obvious recourse to the synonymic equivalents which allow such formulations as *Some good arguments were produced in the course of the debate*, or *The match was hotly contested*, or *The contest was hotly fought.* Synonymy rescues us from our stylistic difficulties, but often does so at the price of a slight distortion of meaning, a warping of the strictly accurate grain. It may be, for example, that *debate*, as a synonym for *argument*, implies rather more than the writer would wish to claim.

This looseness of semantic fit makes for weakness in passages where lexical equivalents are extensively used. A comparison of the techniques of reiteration and variation in two not-quite-satisfactory examples may help to make the point:

[2]i How commonplace, yet how intensely poignant, at times of crisis, our thoughts may be! I remember my own thoughts as I lay waiting for a serious operation. Thoughts of my home and family were succeeded by thoughts of a summer when I had been happy doing nothing in particular, and those thoughts yielded in turn to thoughts of very homely and enormously appetizing food. My body may have been preparing for heaven, but my thoughts remained stubbornly earthbound.

ii How commonplace, yet how intensely poignant, at times of crisis, our thoughts may be! I remember my own cogitations as I lay waiting for a serious operation. Memories of my home and family were succeeded by recollections of a summer when I had been happy doing nothing in particular, and those reflections yielded in turn to animadversions on very homely and enormously appetizing food. My body may have been preparing for heaven, but my deliberations remained stubbornly earthbound.

Each of these passages has its manifest faults. The intention in [2i] is perhaps to be gravely emotive, to make *thoughts* a word that tolls evocatively through the passage; but the reiterations follow too closely, and what was intended to be a solemn resonance is reduced to a busy clanking. Yet the textural instinct is right, while [2ii], on the other hand, is texturally bizarre, a composition resounding with heavily accented false notes. (It is all too obvious, in fact, that the writer in [2ii] is straining to avoid repetitions.) The Latinate words – *cogitations, deliberations, animadversions* – disturb the simple and confidential manner which is the attitudinal ground of the passage, and which is better represented in [2i]. Any affective power which [2i] might have is dissipated in [2ii]. What is worse, the synonymic variants in [2ii] refract meaning in a way that is simply not legitimate if the sense of [2i] is to be preserved. For example, *deliberations* suggests an intellectual method quite alien to the *thoughts* of a man lying on the operating table. Furthermore, the various words substituted for *thoughts* lack synonymic concord among themselves; *memories* and *recollections* are roughly synonymous, but hardly belong to the same set as *cogitations* and *animadversions*. In fact it would be appropriate in this case to avoid the word 'synonym' and to describe *thoughts, cogitations, memories, recollections, animadversions* and *deliberations* as lexical 'equivalents' having a textual, *ie* a cohesive, function.

These equivalents, as we have seen, fit rather loosely. Something of the rattle could have been taken out of [2ii] if the mind of its author had been less rigidly set on making a pattern of equivalent nouns, corresponding to the number of occurrences of the word *thoughts* in [2i]. It is possible to make the variation flexible, to distribute the weight of equivalence across the grammatical categories, to construct a phrase where a word is wanting. Another version of [2i] and [2ii] might read like this:

> [3] How commonplace, yet how intensely poignant, at times of crisis, our thoughts may be! I remember the images that drifted through my head as I lay waiting for a serious operation. My home and family came to mind, and a summer when I had been happy doing nothing in particular, and then I found myself thinking about very homely and enormously appetizing food. My body may have been preparing for heaven, but my brain lingered among earthly things.

Textually this is a sound construction, but in texture it is far removed from the original draft in [2i]; the would-be-evocative manner has been completely discarded. The obvious equivalences of [2ii] have also disappeared, to be replaced by a more flexible pattern of variations. One aspect of this flexibility is that the writer has looked for syntactic solutions to lexical problems, so that where in [2ii], for example, we find *Memories of my home and family were succeeded by recollections of a summer . . .* etc, in [3] we read *My home and family came to mind, and a summer . . .* etc. The work done in the one case by two nouns (*memories, recollections*) is performed in the second instance by one governing verb phrase (*came to mind*).

The interplay of lexicon and syntax is seen in other instances where the mobility of [3] may be compared with the fixities of [2i] and [2ii]. The passage begins with *thoughts,* for which the noun-equivalent *images* is promptly devised. To show, however, that these are cerebral images, the writer now introduces a verb phrase *drifted through my head.* An equivalent verb phrase, *came to mind,* follows in the next sentence, and the dictionary connection with *thoughts* is reasserted in *I found myself thinking.* In this version idiomatic verb phrases have assumed the burden carried by nouns in [2i] and [2ii]; the effect is perhaps one of greater suppleness of movement. In the last sentence, however, noun-equivalence is restored, and here the word *brain* provides the pointed antithesis to *body* that is blurred in [2i] and broken in [2ii]. It is possible now because of the stylistic accommodations the writer has been prepared to make. He is not committed, as in [2i], to the reiteration of a word, or obliged, as in [2ii], to find an equivalent that will suggest a mental process. The freedom of the preceding variations (*images, head, mind, thinking*) leaves room for this final choice of *brain,* as a word that subsumes all the rest while filling precisely its own antithetical slot.

In certain cases, eg when the composition is obviously governed by a spirit of irony, self-deprecating mockery, or burlesque humour, the approximations of synonymy or lexical equivalence can be exploited for stylistic purposes. The resulting texture is often deliberately florid:

[4] 'It suits our outlook,' the well-groomed housewife and mother of two would proclaim, in a certain TV commercial. 'It' was a hair shampoo. I am always ready to take these declarations seriously, and why not? Possibly her shampoo *did* suit the lady's outlook. Probably her toothpaste accorded well with her views, and her favourite brand of margarine squared agreeably with her philosophy. No doubt her conscience, scrupulously examined, could be reconciled to her taste in bacon-flavoured stomach-powders or cholesterol-free chicken noodles. Reason and composure are barely disturbed by such

claims, for indeed it takes all sorts to make a world. My mind only threatens to boggle a little when the preferences of winsome shampoo-loving matrons are protracted into imperatives on my own conduct: when it is implied that unless I hurry along to the chemist's, scurry down to the grocer's, hasten to the market and hie me to the stores in search of the appropriate dandruff-defeating, plaque-scouring, artery-coddling nostrum there will shortly be something rotten in the state of my Weltanschauung. It is at this point that I feel obliged to withhold my consent from the propositions urged upon me. 'You keep your outlook and I'll keep mine,' I wheeze, baring my stained teeth and brushing the fallen hair from my rounded shoulders.

This has the air of a free-wheeling exercise in sardonic burlesque, involving blatant, though clearly intentional, contrasts of texture. The manner veers from the wryly academic to the ruthlessly colloquial; Shakespearean allusion mingles with echoes of copy-writer cliché, tarnished pieces of literary currency (*boggle*, *hie me*) jingle against flashy new coinages (*dandruff-defeating*, *plaque-scouring*, *artery-coddling*), the dry tones of the disputant (*I feel obliged to withhold my consent from the propositions urged upon me*) fade into the casual assertions of the armchair lounger (*You keep your outlook and I'll keep mine*).

Stylistically, then, this may look like a free and wilful blending of registers, a defiant hotch-potch. In fact it is quite closely designed on the principle of lexical equivalence which governs both its textual cohesion and its textural diversity. Its would-be-playful energy stems from the one word *outlook*, which occurs in the first sentence and the last, completing a textual circuit. In the body of the text there is a series of equivalents, *ie: views, philosophy, conscience, Weltanschauung*, which play very loosely with whatever notion is implied in *outlook*. In this case, however, the distortions or distensions of meaning are deliberate; they are part of the writer's programme of ironic attack on a foolish and empty usage, and with each occurrence the suggested equivalent is more absurdly ambitious till we arrive at the ludicrous extreme of *Weltanschauung*. A similar campaign of attrition is conducted against the word *suit*; the text proceeds in mock solemnity from *suit* to *accord well* to *square agreeably* to *be reconciled* and in the process manages to convey ironically the absurd suggestion that there is some moral or religious element in commercial choices.

The shaping of the text generally facilitates the occurrence of correspondent points in lexicon and syntax. For example, a series of sentence-introducing adjuncts – *possibly, frankly, no doubt* – takes the reader from sentence to sentence in a train of increasingly flamboyant parallels. Lexical counterpoises are seen in the matching of *reason* with *mind*, *disturbed* with *boggle*, and in the sequence *hurry along, scurry down, hasten,* and *hie me*. In the last example, the matching items are carried along by a rhythmic impulse; rhythm is the strength of a further series – *dandruff-defeating, plaque-scouring, artery-coddling* – this time of morphological parallels, *ie* of analogously formed expressions. These compounds, moreover, are textually related to expressions previously used (*dandruff-defeating=shampoo; plaque-scouring= toothpaste; artery-coddling=cholesterol-free*) and thus play a part in the cohesion as well as in the decoration of the text. It is evident from such instances that the principle of equivalence invades the text and in some way underlies every turn of style.

3.3 Text and texture: (c) periphrasis

As textual strategies, reiteration and variation are major alternatives, appropriate to different purposes, suggesting different postures on the part of the writer, projecting different kinds of relationship with the reader. The lexical items that serve as equivalents are generally synonyms or hyponyms, but there are other ways of ringing the lexical changes, one of which is to exploit the possibilities of periphrasis. The device is so familiar in a certain style of journalism – 'columnese' – that the temptation to parody is difficult to avoid:

[5] Policemen are sorely beset in their traditional battle with the common criminal; now they have another opponent and an increasingly dangerous one, the urban terrorist. The ordinary ratepayer, alas, expects far too much of the everyday guardian of the law, looking for security not only from the practising hoodlum and housebreaker but also from the theorist of violence who lives by the outrageous code of the bomb. The officer on the beat, with all his competence and courage, is simply not equipped to meet this threat. Apart from anything else, the force is undermanned. Every year sees fewer men in blue, because the public will not urge the justice of paying them a wage that might compensate for some of their dangers

and hardships. As far as terrorism is concerned, there might be a case for establishing a special force to deal with the politicized enemies of society. To the right-minded tele-viewer that might sound uncomfortably like a version of the Gestapo, and indeed the necessary democratic checks and balances would have to be most scrupulously devised. One fact is clear, however; if we really want our protectors of public safety, in whatever form they come, we are going to have to pay for them.

What appears as noble ornament in the style of the *Odyssey* or *Beowulf*, where the frequent periphrases gradually illuminate a character or a theme, occurs in journalese as an ingenious recipe enabling the columnist to avoid repetitions and at the same time to give his writing an evaluative slant. This tendency is imitated in [5], where the *policeman* appears as *the everyday guardian of the law* and *the protector of public safety* as well as *the officer on the beat* and *the man in blue.* The other actors and objects on this polemic stage likewise have their periphrastic guises: *the common criminal* is also *the practising hoodlum and housebreaker, the urban terrorist* is *the theorist of violence* and *the politicized enemy of society,* terrorism is *the outrageous code of the bomb,* and *the ordinary ratepayer* is somewhat loosely equated with *the right-minded televiewer.* From such variations we derive not so much a programme of information as a display of the attitudes the writer is inviting his reader to share. This sly process of persuasion by renaming is one of the important functions of periphrasis.

As a stylistic ornament it invites very sparing use; it is potentially so florid, so portentous, that it lends itself all too readily to comic purposes. The orotund periphrasis of some commonplace noun or noun phrase is a stock-in-trade of the humorous writer. That mordantly brilliant Irish humourist, Myles na Gopaleen, refers to an election, for instance, as *the complex quinquennial gestation that culminates in an expression of The People's Will.* Such stylistic variants quite often occur in apposition to the noun they paraphrase; for example (na Gopaleen again) *that immaculate pectoral phenomenon, a clean breast, that indigenous culinary complication, the Irish stew.* Behind the comically inflated examples lurks a useful and serious function of periphrasis, as a method of identifying a person or making an explanation for the reader's benefit; a presentation of credentials, as it were.

Another function of periphrasis, and one that it shares with its neighbour-device of metonymy, is to present the challenge of a small verbal puzzle, a conundrum for the initiated. In this respect it becomes a means of involving the reader in an allusive and confidential relationship. If, for instance, we discuss the 1920s and the London literary scene, we may use the name *Bloomsbury* metonymically, as a compact reference to a group of people and their attitudes; and should we then allude to *the young author of 'Jacob's Room'* the periphrasis sets the reader a fairly easy riddle, with the answer 'Virginia Woolf'. Metonymic and periphrastic allusion can in fact be put to pleasant use in a confidential game of who-knows-what, played between author and reader – an old literary pastime, the sort of game played by Milton in referring to St Peter as *the Pilot of the Galilean lake*, or by Dante in calling Aristotle *the Master of them that know*. But Milton and Dante, poets in the grand style, could allow themselves to use such a device uninhibitedly; for the rest of us, apprentices in the craft of journeyman prose, some caution is indicated. It is in any case not so often that our ordinary ventures discover a name to conjure with, or an appropriate context in which to do it.

3.4 Text and texture: (d) multivalence

Many texts exhibit patterns of lexical structure that can hardly be accounted for in terms of reiteration or variation. They grow in a more sophisticated way, and the lexical points of intersection which knit their strands of meaning must be called multivalent rather than equivalent. These lexical items are not related to each other as synonyms or substitutes, but are associates in the sense that their fields of reference overlap, or have a metaphoric relationship, or are in some way semantically contiguous. In short, as the text grows, patterns of verbal association reflect and express its growth. This is much more difficult to illustrate than, say, the textual value of reiteration, because it cannot be consciously worked to a simple formula; the imagination burrows into the darkness of the theme, and the significant words are thrown up like so many tell-tale mounds. There is an element of blind responsiveness in the process, which the following passage may illustrate:

[6]   There are two different styles of painting that appeal to my imagination. In one, the artist achieves nothing less than a

suspension of time, and all tensions and conflicting forces find their resolution in the sempiternal calm of a jug, a table and chair, a commonplace pond, a not very remarkable field; in the other, irresistible energies are released to bombard the spectator with dynamic sensations of colour and movement, in restless testimony to the multiplicity, the gaiety, the fury, even, of common experience. It seems, in short, that I am drawn to what is perpetually still or what is invincibly in motion.

Certain kinds of still life or domestic interior, especially as practised by the Flemish masters, typify one of these effects. They are for me paradigms of stillness. Their peace grows endlessly full and round and hangs like a water-drop but never reaches the moment of falling. The glaze on the shoulder of a jug is an arrest in time; it leads the eye into a hypnosis, and in the heart of that reverie is an assent – this leads to a world, yes, and the world leads to this. The pattern on those tiles is a recipe for self-healing. Chairs and simple tables are signposts to the land of heart's ease. An ordinary room lies sleek on the surface of the canvas, but if you enter it with your eye you are ensconced in profundity, in a silence as mysterious and palpable as the long intervals between the pendulum strokes of a great slow-moving clock.

In the other kind of painting, the pigment itself seems unwilling to allow the spectator any moment of rest. It flares abruptly, swoops and veers along the contours of extra-ordinary compositional schemes, detonates grandly at some point where a run-of-the-mill painter might venture a timid highlight, infuses a sky, bathes whole tracts of middle ground in radiant cascades. This perhaps sounds more like the fun of the fair than the sober contemplation of a painting, but extravagant effects invite bravura descriptions; some pictures galvanise at first glance and never thereafter lose their power to exhilarate. They surge in their frames, and the eye, like an urchin daring the tide, scampers excitedly this way and that.

Here the style obviously has its ambitions; without venturing into judgements we can at least concede that this is a more intricate exercise than the examples previously used, and that its technical principles are not so simple or so easily summarized. Let us

concentrate on a single point. The passage evokes the effects
wrought on a spectator by two different types of painting; the first
paragraph states a general distinction – it is in effect a 'topic'
paragraph – while its successors elaborate respectively the themes of
stillness and dynamism. A quite casual survey of the second and third
paragraphs may suggest to the reader that the evocations of calm or
energy are prompted in the one case through a pattern of nouns and in
the other through a series of verbs.

To make the point in a fairly simple way means isolating certain
items, abstracting them from collocations in which they figure in
mutual effect with other words, and therefore misrepresenting the
character of the text as a complex of lexical gradings and shadings.
Bearing this admission in mind, let us nevertheless note the effect, in
the second paragraph of [6], of certain key nouns: *stillness, peace,
waterdrop, moment, glaze, arrest, time, hypnosis, reverie, assent, pattern,
recipe, self-healing, signposts, heart's ease, surface, profundity, silence, intervals,
strokes, clock.* These nouns, integrated into the text in various ways,
fall into thematically related groups; the relationship between
members of a group, however, is not such that each is a substitute for
the other, but rather that each is contingent upon another. Each
group is thus a range of semantic multivalents, not a set of
equivalents.

The groups are as follows:

(i) *stillness, peace, waterdrop, glaze, hypnosis, arrest, reverie, assent* (A
     complex pattern of associations, discussed below)
(ii) *pattern, recipe, signposts* (common meaning of 'directive')
(iii) *self-healing, heart's ease* (contingent meaning)
(iv) *surface, profundity* (association of opposites)
(v) *silence, strokes* (association of opposites)

The fullest of these groups, (i), illustrates most strikingly the
principle of multivalence, through associations which include
synonymy, hints of physical contiguity or semblance, reminders of
common contextual partnerships, and figurative or psychological
connotations. Thus while in this context *stillness* and *peace* have the
value of synonyms, there is a different kind of relationship between
waterdrop and *glaze* – the glaze, in the sense of 'glassy appearance',
being a characteristic of the waterdrop (as well as of the jug, of
course). But *glaze* in a slightly different sense is associated with
hypnosis, perhaps through common figurative descriptions of the

appearance of a hypnotized person ('his eyes glazed'), and *hypnosis* in its turn has a psychological link with *arrest*, inasmuch as the power of voluntary action is arrested in the hypnotic state. There are further semantic overlaps between *hypnosis* and *reverie* – synonymic relationship with 'trance' as the common core of meaning – and again between *hypnosis* and *assent* – the subject assents to, *ie* obeys, the hypnotist's suggestions. The word *hypnosis*, it must appear, is one of the most powerful lexical elements in the second paragraph, its multivalence being revealed through the networks of association which connect it with *glaze, arrest, reverie,* and *assent.*

The smaller groups are certainly not without interest. In (iv) and (v), for example, the matchmaking force is a counterpoise of opposites, a kind of antonymy. The *strokes* (by implication audible) of the clock are contrasted with the *silence* embodied by the painting, and the *surface* of the canvas presents a plane of organization which belies the *profundity* of aesthetic experience. This last example in fact makes the case for not isolating words from their supporting constructions. The antonymic balance here is not really between *surface* and *profundity*; a proper reading will contrast *lies sleek on the surface* and *ensconced in profundity.* There is a counterpoise of verbs every whit as important as the opposition of the accompanying nouns, and it is clear in this as in other instances that an understanding of the relationship between grammar and imagination can only be reached by exploring ways in which the thrust of the writer's creative energy shifts its pressure from one grammatical element to another. In a crude analysis, however, it can be said that the second paragraph of [6] reveals a mode of imaginative exploration through multivalent patterns of nouns.

In the third paragraph there is a discernible shift to verbs. They insist a little showily on their own importance: *flare, swoop, veer, detonate, infuse, bathe, galvanize, exhilarate, surge, scamper.* The first six of these have a common subject (*pigment*), and the next three also share a subject (*pictures*). Only the last item on the list has a subject to itself (*the eye*). In this paragraph, then, the topic of reference remains relatively stable, whereas in its predecessor there is a constant shuffling of subjects round the central theme. Now it is the verbs that are kept in apparently impulsive movement, each seeming perhaps to represent a casual and momentary choice; yet behind this ostensible spontaneity it is possible to discern lines of semantic patterning. There are diverse yet clearly overlapping elements:

(i) Explosive effect	*flare, detonate*
(ii) Fire	*flare*
(iii) Rapid curving movement	*flare, swoop, veer*
(iv) Massive/rapid versus light/rapid movement	*surge, scamper*
(v) Water	*infuse, bathe, surge*
(vi) Physical/mental stimulus	*galvanize, exhilarate*

Only the two verbs listed in (vi) appear to stand apart from a series of semantic interlockings, and even here an imaginative association can be traced between *galvanize* and *detonate*, as verbs which connote processes involving the powerful discharge of energy, whether electrical or explosive. Elsewhere the connections that take the questing mind from verb to verb are fairly obvious. Here again, however, we must be aware of complications in the lexical structure; themes are shared among parts of speech in much the same way that motifs are passed from one orchestral instrument to another. Notice, for instance, how the 'water' motif in the verbs *infuse* and *bathe* passes to the noun *cascades*. Notice further how the adverb *grandly*, in the phrase *detonates grandly*, is in textural play with the adjective *timid* in *timid highlight*, and how that phrase *timid highlight* in its turn makes a contrast with *radiant cascades*. These are specific examples of something that might be traced throughout this or any other text; the orchestration, it could be called, of the lexicon.

3.5 Text and texture: (e) the organizing metaphor

Patterns of multivalence, associative shifts in which meanings expand, splinter, and re-form like the coloured fragments in a kaleidoscope, often occur because the writer's mind is powerfully seized by some explanatory image or analogue (*eg* the implicit images of fire and water in the final paragraph of [6]). As long as we respond to these covert images without coming consciously to terms with them, their effect on the stylistic lexicon is complex and unpredictable; patterns of association are created, but they are schemes that only hindsight can reveal and analyse.

Such retrospect into the workings of the imagination may be contrasted with the foresighted structure of a text on the basis of some convenient metaphor – convenient, that is to say, in the sense that it provides a mode of explanation where technical language either fails the writer or cannot be presupposed in the reader. The basic figure is consciously extended until it becomes the scaffolding of the exposition, and by controlling the terms of the metaphor the writer is able to foresee the general shape of his text. Thus the first paragraph of the following example dictates the terms of the second:

[7] Entomologists tell us of a strain of ants known to science as the *sanguinea* – a species so martial and imperialist in disposition that they are commonly referred to as army ants, or soldiers. In the insect world their inroads may well be dreaded, as once the disciplined advent of the Roman was a signal of alarm to lesser peoples. For not only do they make war; they are also, it appears, slave owners who prey on unfortunate neighbour-colonies such as those of the wood ants.

When a slaving expedition is mounted, the attacking legion of *sanguinea* divides into columns, each led by a scout, approaching the hostile fortress from different directions. Once in sight of their objective they call a halt. Then, while the other detachments maintain a blockade, one unit is sent forward as an assault force. As a rule, these invaders easily beat down whatever resistance is offered to them. The wood ant defenders attempt to evacuate their positions, bearing with them the cocoons of their brood, but their line of retreat is cut off by the besiegers, who capture the fugitives while the storm troops continue to scour the fortification.

The informing metaphor of this passage is provided by the words *army* and *soldier*. In the first paragraph the figurative implications of these terms are tentatively explored. The adjectives *martial* and *imperialist* suggest two lines of development which intersect in *Roman*, and which move through *disciplined*, *make war*, *colony*, and *slave owner*.

The first paragraph therefore sketches a metaphoric plan which is systematically developed in the second. There is no need to point out the military terminology so assiduously worked into every sentence and so consistently developed from one sentence to the next. In this kind of writing there is legerdemain, perhaps, but no magic. Writer and reader, smiling self-consciously in the exercise of their own skills, know exactly what is going on. Yet subliminal and potentially subversive powers may still threaten to tug a planned image gently out of shape. We see, for instance, that the second paragraph begins with an attacking *legion* – undoubtedly a hint from *Roman* a few lines earlier – but ends with *storm troops*. The account of the soldiers' attack on the wood ants' nest is not consistently worked out in terms of a Roman legionary assault on a barbarian fort; reminiscences of a different kind of warfare usurp the mind and colour the pervasive image so effectively that the 'soldiers' begin their foray under the eagles and end it under the swastika.

3.6 Text and texture: (f) the subliminal metaphor

All lively writing has roots that run beneath the threshold of consciousness. Language itself is full of subliminal metaphors which often seem to come unbidden to the writer's aid, nourishing his text with a concealed power. For obvious reasons we cannot consciously construct a passage to illustrate a subconscious impulse, and the identification of such an event in someone else's work may be considered speculative. Yet there are instances in which the overt structure of the text seems to accord precisely with the perceived hint of a life beneath the surface. Here is a fine example from one of Bertrand Russell's essays:

> [8] Architecture, from the earliest times, has had two purposes: on the one hand, the purely utilitarian one of affording warmth and shelter; on the other, the political one of impressing an idea upon mankind by means of the splendour of its expression in stone. The former purpose sufficed as regards the dwellings of the poor; but the temples of the gods and the palaces of kings were designed to inspire awe for the heavenly powers and for their earthly favourites. In a few cases, it was not merely individual monarchs but communities that were glorified; the Acropolis at Athens and the Capitol in Rome showed forth the imperial majesty of those proud cities for the edification of subjects and allies. Aesthetic merit was considered desirable in public buildings, and, later on, in the palaces of plutocrats and emperors, but was not aimed at in the hovels of peasants or the rickety tenements of the urban proletariat.
> (From 'Architecture and Social Questions' in *In Praise of Idleness* by Bertrand Russell, Unwin Paperback edn, 1976, p. 38.)

In this, as in his other writings on social questions, Lord Russell asks of us no more than a sound mother-wit. In spite of the fact that there is a verse of Horace lurking behind the *palaces of plutocrats and emperors* and *the hovels of peasants*, he does not require his readers to be Latinists, and he certainly does not demand from them a taste for etymology. Yet something is given to the reader who notes that *edification* is related to *edifice* and therefore has the basic meaning of 'building'. This is one of those residual metaphors that are always waiting to show an unexpected colour, and it certainly makes an elegant figure in this passage. Russell's theme is that the purpose of architecture is partly to provide shelter and partly to build up a state of mind in the beholder. The word *edification* is therefore a key term, and if we reread the passage we can see how Russell works his way towards it, as to an instinctive goal, through a pattern of phrases combining the notions of 'mental state' and 'architectural form' (*impressing an idea upon mankind . . . by means of the splendour of its expression in stone; palaces . . . designed to inspire awe for the heavenly powers and for their earthly favourites*).

The pursuit of subliminal metaphors is perhaps the kind of Snark-hunting that should properly be left to literary critics. There is no way of foreseeing their occurrence, much less of planning their effects, but they are mentioned here because of their interest as symptoms of intention. They are most likely to occur when the mind has warmed to its subject and when the imagination is stretched to comprehend the most diverse nuances of meaning. To identify one of these fugitives in our own composition, as in retrospect we may often do, is to learn something about the versions and subversions of the creative process. While we write, our minds advise us in various ways; the subliminal metaphor is one of them.

3.7 The interrelationship of text and texture

Text and texture are involved in a counterchange which the writer must try to perceive and demonstrate; to combine textural appeal with an appropriate scheme of textual cohesion, in such a way that one supports the other, is a fundamental stylistic task. The text, however, has primacy; plot is more important than diction, though diction may be involved in plot. A text that has no scheme of cohesion (there is an example in Ch.2[4]) has no persuasive power and will not acquire it through the most elaborate texturing. Indeed, if the textual plot is disjointed there is no pattern to which the devices of texture can accrue.

It is for this reason that we give priority of consideration to syntactic cohesion – to the filling of the gaps between sentences. The lexicon, as our exemplary passages may have shown, can be a powerful auxiliary to syntax for cohesive purposes, but schemes of lexical cohesion involve distinct textural consequences. The examples in Ch.2[12] demonstrate in a fairly crude way the contrast between a simple text with minimum syntactic cohesion and a heavily textured variant constructed round a lexical pattern. In the present chapter, examples [2i], [2ii], and [3] show how the resources of the lexicon may be enlisted to control or modify textural effect. Those resources are numerous, almost bewilderingly so. They do not, however, present themselves to us as a thesaurus of single word-items, but rather as words conjoined with syntactic patterns; and those patterns often provide the clues by means of which, in our compositional searches, we discover the words themselves. Here, indeed, is a theme for a new chapter.

Chapter 4

Words in phrases

Words draw life from phrases, from the contexts in which as readers we perceive their value or as writers direct their power. This relationship was never better understood than by the classical rhetoricians with their figures of speech; a figure is a way of phrasing – a piece of text – in which a way of meaning – a sample of texture – is housed. The traditional figures have characteristic textual forms, often reflected in their classical names. *Zeugma*, for instance, means 'yoke'; it is a figure in which two nouns are brought under the government of a single verb or adjective – *eat your sandwiches and your words, with crooked grins and intentions*. The name *chiasmus* denotes a characteristic X-pattern, a structural crossover of the kind exemplified by a famous comment on *The Beggar's Opera*, that *it made Gay rich and Rich gay*. *Parison* is another rhetorical shape, a textual box with correspondent points in a symmetrical scheme; thus *To labour in a just cause is undoubtedly virtuous, to persist in a lost one is certainly foolish* presents a matching-in-parallel of *to labour* and *to persist*, *a just cause* and *a lost one*, *undoubtedly* and *certainly*, *virtuous* and *foolish*. Within the textual shape in all these instances there is a striking textural effect (an extension of meaning, a pun, an antithesis) depending on the location of significant items of vocabulary at key points in the syntactic design; the turn of meaning, the trope, follows the turn of phrase.

All this may seem to be a matter chiefly of antiquarian interest; yet figurative rhetoric is by no means a thing of the past. It appears daily in advertisements, sports reports, the speeches of trade union leaders and politicians, letters to various editors, and all manner of literary communications and bar-room pleasantries. Everybody relishes a well-turned phrase, and it is just in this process of turning, of giving meaningful shape to a short sequence of words, that figurative rhetoric and plain everyday grammar intermesh. A rhetorical potential is latent in common syntactic processes; the ordinary phrase, the necessary grammatical rule, can be turned and enlarged to figurative purposes.

4.1 Phrase types

The common practice of grammarians is to typify phrases by their heads – ie to name them in accordance with the grammatical category of the word that constitutes the indispensable centre or kernel of the phrase. Thus *a professor, a university professor, a charming university professor, a truly charming university professor, the one truly charming university professor, the one truly charming university professor with an infectious sense of humour* are examples, variously complex, of noun phrases each having the word *professor* as its head. The potential complexity and expansiveness of the noun phrase is one of the characteristics that make it a stylistic force. Another is its versatility in 'realizing' – or representing – different elements in clause-structure; in fact it may function in any role save that reserved for the predicator, the verb. In the following examples the phrase *a truly charming university professor* illustrates the point. That phrase might be the subject of a clause: *A truly charming university professor gave the lecture*; or the direct object: *Billy insulted a truly charming university professor*; or the indirect object: *Admiring colleagues gave a truly charming university professor their fullest support*; or a subject complement: *Slingby made a truly charming university professor*; or an object complement: *Everybody called him a truly charming university professor*. To become an adverbial (*ie* a verb-amplifying element) all it needs is an introductory preposition: *Mary arrived with a truly charming university professor*.

In their expansiveness and syntactic versatility these noun-headed constructions tend to predominate stylistically over other phrase types. Though adjectives and adverbs can and do function as phrase heads, their role is frequently that of subordinates in a hierarchy; adverbs occur as modifiers to adjectives (*eg: exquisitely* in *exquisitely beautiful*) and adjectives as modifiers to nouns (*eg: beautiful* in *quite exquisitely beautiful*). As elements in sentence-structure, adjective phrases like *very beautiful, beautiful as always, more beautiful than ever* are normally complements (*Our hostess looked very beautiful; her happiness made her more beautiful than ever*) or verbless non-restrictive clauses (*Our hostess, full of charm and more beautiful than ever, greeted us at the door*). To a limited extent they can also occur as clause subjects: *The very beautiful are often very happy, but the very happy do not need to be very beautiful.*

Adverbial phrases, too, can be sentence subjects – *eg: here and now, over there,* in *Here and now would suit me, Over there seems as good a place as any.* This, however, is a fairly unusual role. Such phrases commonly realize the syntactic element known (appropriately) as the adverbial, a role which can also be filled by prepositional phrases (*cf: with a truly charming university professor*). The stylistic interest, and at times the compositional difficulty, of the adverbial lies in the fact that it is a relatively mobile element and that several adverbials may occur in the pattern of a clause. Consider, for example, the sentence *Just then the old professor began to lecture, lucidly enough, quite fluently, and, as always, with considerable charm.* Here the subject (*the old professor*) and the verb phrase (*began to lecture*) form a fixed stem from which no less than five adverbials branch (*just then, lucidly enough, quite fluently, as always, with considerable charm*). The positioning of the adverbials in cases of this kind often presents syntactic and stylistic problems.

Verb phrases are generally simple in structure, with the result that their stylistic value may be all but obscured by the bulk of complex noun phrases (see, for example, 4.4 below). In its fullest extent, the finite verb phrase is a ruled sequence of auxiliaries preceding a main verb that might be phrasal in form; *eg: may (might, must, can, could, should, would, will, shall, ought to) have been setting up, may (etc) have set up, may (etc) have been being set up.* Non-finite (infinitive and participial) forms may realize the verb element in clause-structure and may combine with each other or with a finite verb in extended constructions: *He might have been trying to speak; The newcomers must have been hoping to avoid being recognized.* Such chaining of verbs is possibly more common in speech than in writing, where stylistic censorship tends to rule in favour of the compact verb phrase.

4.2 Complexity of phrasing

There is in any case more than one kind of phrasal complexity. Here, for instance, is a noun phrase extremely complex in structure: *the very first really reliable do-it-yourself fibreglass sailing dinghy with oars and a full suit of sails.* This shows syntactic complexity in the relationship of the phrasal head *dinghy* to the items which precede and succeed it. Those items have more than a syntactic interest, however; they also fill out a highly detailed pattern of reference. To interpret the phrase, a reader needs to know what is signified not only by the head, *dinghy*, but also by *reliable, do-it-yourself, fibreglass, sailing, oars, full*, and the idiomatic *suit of sails*. An elaborate noun phrase of this kind is systematically packed with lexical material, for which reason we might describe its complexity not only as *structural* but also as *lexical* or perhaps *referential*.

Now here is a fairly complex finite verb phrase: (*they*) *ought to have been getting shaved*. This by contrast is not packed with reference; it requires of the reader or hearer only that he should know what *shave* denotes. Its complexity is of another order, and has to do with the way in which, through a pattern of auxiliaries and through the inflection of the main verb, the phrase accommodates notions expressible in grammatical terms as mood (*ought to*), tense (*have been*), aspect (*getting* in *getting shaved* expresses action in progress as opposed to action completed) and voice (*getting* also expresses passive as against active). Because the semantics are of a different kind, because most of the words in the phrase do not refer to things, but express instead the abstractions of time, agency, obligation, etc, we might call this complexity *notional*.

The distinction outlined here is one that broadly affects our management of prose (see again the text and commentary in 4.4 below). The importance of the verb phrase as a vehicle for notional categories in no way detracts from the potential energy and vivacity of verbs as agents of reference; indeed, stylistic analysis may show in many instances that verbs can dominate the referential stage. However, there are different means of achieving precision and scope of reference.

4.3 Modification and amplification

Two such means – contrasting yet complementary stylistic resources – may be described as *modification* and *amplification*. *Modification* is a familiar term in grammar, particularly in reference to the structure of the noun phrase, in which items preceding the head are *premodifiers* and those following it, *postmodifiers*. Thus the head *woman* in *a profoundly intelligent woman* is premodified, while a corresponding postmodification is seen in *a woman of profound intelligence*.

One of the advantages of this pre- and postpositioning is that where lexical formations permit the option it offers stylistic alternatives for one and the same reference; *eg: a strikingly beautiful woman, a woman of striking beauty: a friendless man, a man with no friends: an irregularly shaped building, a building irregular in shape.* The alternations doubtless involve changes of focus, but the features to which reference is made remain the same. There are many cases, however, in which the option is restricted and the sequence of modifiers can only lie on one side or the other of the head. Thus the phrase *a man of great integrity* defies transposition (NOT *a greatly integrated man!*), and a construction such as *my old and incorrigibly rusty car* can only be turned about either by making a composite of noun plus non-restrictive relative clause – *my car, which is old and incorrigibly rusty* – or simply by apposing a verbless clause, *eg: my car, old and incorrigibly rusty.* Modification in the latter instance merges into something else, the amplification of one construction by another.

In noun phrasing, the premodifying array progressively closes the construction, narrowing step by step to the anticipated goal, the phrase head: *a; a profoundly; a profoundly intelligent; a profoundly intelligent woman.* The marshalling of the structure implies – at least as far as the reader is concerned – a kind of predictability. Postmodification on the other hand has a stylistic open-endedness that may be very elaborate and unpredictable in effect: *That fat man over there with the moustache that looks as though it had been trimmed by a journeyman barber in a passing fit of romantic melancholy brought on by recollections of a misspent youth.* In this last example, postmodification runs riot; what emerges is a highly complex structure with the syntactic value of a noun, built up through the incorporation of diverse elements. The elements that postmodify a noun might be prepositional phrases, for example, or non-finite clauses, or relative clauses: *the woman in white; an adversary to be feared; a horse wearing blinkers; the best dictionary for the student to consult; a reader versed in the rules of English; the man who has absolutely everything.*

The building of complex noun phrases is for any writer a major stylistic resource. We are able to construct patterns of multiple modification which dress the parent noun in many grades and shades of reference. Thus *the hat, the little red hat, the little red hat you bought last Friday afternoon in Oxford* represent burgeonings of a noun phrase in which reference becomes increasingly precise as it expands in scope; a cluster of informative items is systematically built up. For reasons touched on in 4.2 above, we cannot expand the referential scope of the finite verb phrase in this way, though possibly in the non-finite extensions of some verbs there is something analogous to the postmodification of the noun – *eg: swear to go on trying to uphold.* It is pre-eminently in the *amplification* of the verb by adverbs or adverbial phrases that we find something comparable, in 'informational' terms, to the pre- or postmodification of the noun.

For instance, noun phrases such as *hasty decision, eventual surrender, argument of great interest* may readily be translated into amplifications of verb and adverb or adverbial phrase: *hastily decide, decide hastily, decide in haste, eventually surrender, surrender eventually, surrender in due course, surrender at long last, surrender after a considerable lapse of time; very interestingly argue, argue very interestingly, argue to everyone's interest,* etc. The relationship of *hasty decision* and *decide hastily* or *decide in haste* is transparently obvious. It is simply a matter of making a syntactic switch while keeping the same lexical items. Less transparent is the connection between *eventual surrender* and *surrender after a considerable lapse of time.* Here the 'transposition' uses new lexical material, in a structure that could not be directly retransposed (*ie* we could not write an *after-a-considerable-lapse-of-time surrender,* though we might use the phrase *a considerably delayed surrender*).

The availability of alternative strategies in phrasing – call them, for the nonce, 'noun-aggregating' and 'verb-aggregating' – often creates a stylistic dilemma, leaving the writer to decide whether nouns or verbs should bear the weight of exposition. Compare the following sentences:

[1]i Freud encouraged his patients to reach into memory, thread with infinite care its troubled maze, methodically ransack the cluttered chambers of the mind, and in that groping fashion at last discover the corner from which neurosis darkly sprang.

ii Freud recommended to his patients a profoundly painstaking and systematic investigation of the depths of the memory, leading to the eventual discovery in the unconscious of the obscure origins of neurosis.

It may be evident that [1ii] is an attempt to redraft [1i], so that what is expressed in [1i] through amplifications of verb and adverbial is in [1ii] rendered by the noun phrase with its patterns of modification. Thus the successive 'verbalizations' of *reach into memory . . . thread with infinite care . . . methodically ransack* are collectively 'nominalized' in *a profoundly painstakingly and systematic investigation of the depths of the memory.* Similarly, *in that groping fashion at last discover* has its noun-phrase equivalent in *the eventual discovery in the unconscious,* and *darkly sprang* corresponds to *obscure origins.* Stylistic preference in this instance would have to be determined in the general context of composition; [1ii] makes a better abstract than [1i], but [1i] is more vivacious and it is worth noting how the verbs supply its figurative thrust.

4.4 Phrases in action: a text

The following passage illustrates the value of various kinds of phrase. The complex noun phrase is clearly in the stylistic ascendant, but the effect of other phrase types will be apparent at certain junctures:

[2]   Once more the football season has arrived, raising the usual prospects of broken windows, cracked crowns, and all the panoply of hooliganism. The police, undermanned as always, will nevertheless manage somehow to contain the idiot flow of so-called 'fans', the more enthusiastic of whom will in due course appear before a bench of affronted or contemptuous magistrates, who will impose fines remarkable either for their staggering leniency or their unprecedented ferocity, according to the social principles of the observer. We will certainly be assured that their alarming behaviour is a product of our sick society, and perhaps we will be briefly entertained by some new apostle of the social sciences who will inform us that the hooliganism of the football fan is really no more than a useful device facilitating the rehearsal of interpersonal strategies within the parameters of an ongoing situation of confrontation and stress. Our contesting voices will be raised, demanding that the hooligans should be fined, flogged and flung into jail or else be studied and cherished as a unique European institution, and in either event our demands will go unsatisfied. The football hooligan, nasty, British, and short, will remain unflogged, unflung, occasionally fined and sporadically studied, and we will simply have to endure his tribal practices until the long season ends.

Among the more elaborate noun phrasings in this text are *the usual prospects of broken windows, cracked crowns, and all the panoply of hooliganism; fines remarkable for their staggering leniency or their unprecedented ferocity, according to the social principles of the observer; a useful device facilitating the rehearsal of interpersonal strategies within the parameters of an ongoing situation of confrontation and stress.* In each of these constructions there is a luxuriant branching to the right, away from the phrase head (*prospects, fines, device*). The extravagance is particularly notable in the last example, a deliberate monstrosity that lunges parodically at the jargon of would-be sociologists and that might be regarded as the stylistic centre of the text.

The verb phrase, by comparison, might appear to be stylistically muted, the function of the verbs in the passage being mainly to put the argument on the notional stage of time, likelihood and option. Yet this is not wholly the case. If there is a point at which the elaboration of the noun phrase reaches a peak (*ie* in the 'sociological' parody mentioned above), there is also a moment of expressive prominence for the verb. This is in fact achieved by the coordination, alliteratively reinforced, of a series of verbs: *be fined, flogged and flung into jail or else be studied and cherished.* This is the basis for a further elaboration in which the same verbs recur, either with negative prefixes or else in amplifications of verb and adverb: *will remain unflogged, unflung, occasionally fined, sporadically studied and seldom cherished.* (Note how the adverbs now join the verbs in the pattern of alliterative cohesion.) The intermeshing of verb and adverb can be seen in other, less prominent instances: *will nevertheless manage, will in due course appear, will certainly be assured, will be briefly entertained, will simply have to endure.*

Though the adjective phrase plays the smallest of parts in this rhetorical drama, it has one spotlighted moment in the punning parenthesis of *the football hooligan, nasty, British, and short, will remain, etc.* *Nasty, British, and short* obviously makes skittish play with Hobbes' well-known phrase about the life of the savage, *nasty, brutish, and short,* but it has a double value in that the reference *British* is a counterpoise to *European* in the preceding sentence; in other words, the expanded argument might run, let us not dignify the football hooligan by imputing to him a continental status when he is all too lamentably a native product. Here is a convenient illustration of how a rhetorical turn may serve for something more than ornament and diversion; it may neatly encapsulate an allusion or a point in argument.

4.5 Phrase grammar and the rhetoric of phrasing

Sections 4.1–4.3 above make a background to the assertion in the introductory section that 'the ordinary phrase, the necessary

grammatical rule, can be turned and enlarged to figurative purposes.'
Something of this figurative potential may have been glimpsed in the
structure of the noun phrase, and here two points might be
recapitulated, as providing a basis for further exploration. We have
noted that the sequence of premodifying elements follows a scheme
of subordination, exemplified by *a truly remarkable book* (or *a profoundly
intelligent woman*, or *the very first really reliable do-it-yourself fibreglass sailing
dinghy*). Our native knowledge of the subordinating rules makes the
syntactic shape of the phrase generally predictable, in that we know
how it will narrow down to the head; however, we have some
rhetorical freedom to delay the narrowing down by introducing a
pattern of coordination into the subordinating scheme: *a truly
remarkable, well-planned, wise, scholarly, sensible, far-reaching, much-needed
and oh so abominably dull book*. Here the rhetorical figure of asyndeton
(see 4.6 below) is imposed on the syntactic process of premodification; the grammatical structure is as it were 'exploited' by a
governing trope.

While on the one hand we can predict the syntactic course of
premodification, postmodifiers on the other hand may elude
prediction, so that complex postmodification often proliferates
extravagantly, keeping the reader's attention stretched: *a book full of
possibilities that might be usefully explored by the kind of student who is ready
and willing to look beyond the basic requirements of a university first-degree
curriculum*. Such a construction, adding phrase to phrase, embedding
whole clauses within the master phrase, is not so easily predicted. Of
the various ways in which this freedom of development might be
turned to rhetorical advantage, the one that most commonly
recommends itself is to impose upon the growing construction some
form of symmetry: *a book designed to meet the particular demands of the
professional specialist and satisfy the general curiosity of the interested layman; a
book full of acute observation, brilliant insight, immaculate reasoning, and all the
scholarly virtues without the corresponding pedantic vices*. Once again,
figurative rhetoric rides on the back of grammar.

These examples raise the possibility of exploring some elementary
principles of rhetorical phrasing, founded on repetitions, sequences,
parallels, and antitheses. One generally important concept is that of
coordination, whether in pairs or extended series. A companion
principle is that of *counterpoise*, which involves the harnessing or
linking of phrases in contrapuntal schemes.

4.6 Coordination: (a) asyndetic and syndetic pairs

When items are paired in direct sequence, without a conjunction, they are said to be asyndetically coordinated. (*Asyndeton* is a standard figure in rhetoric.) Asyndetic coordination is a common pattern for two adjectives modifying a noun: *a pious, plodding writer of textbooks, a pale, downtrodden Doctor of Philosophy, a wild-eyed, inebriate grammarian.* It also occurs quite often in the pairing of adverbs – *deliberately, malevolently, the dog consumed a beetle* – but perhaps not so often in assembling pairs of nouns or verbs: *The room was full of professors, brutes; I shrank, recoiled from the unedifying spectacle.* In the last example the paired nouns are in apposition, with a clear implication that the second member of the pair defines the first; the apposed verbs are similarly related.

The syndetic (conjunction-bound) coordination of nouns, verbs, adjectives or adverbs is a primary stylistic device: *students and bronchitis are sent to try us; good secretaries neither simper nor whimper; a pious but plodding writer of textbooks; whimsically yet wisely Canute went paddling.* There is a wide range of coordinators (discussed below) with a consequent diversity of phrase structure that adds greatly to the stylistic interest of the syndetic type. One of its attractions is that, it is potentially text-informing; it can be used variously and recursively to build a text, thus:

[3]   He was the archetypally moderate man: neither impulsive nor calculating, neither a spendthrift nor a niggard, friendly yet never familiar, helpful rather than officious, eager for companionship if no less eager for privacy, sober and convivial, learned albeit simple, in every way a keeper of the middle course.

This is little more than mere word-spinning – the coordinations can be kept in shuttle as long as contrasting verbal colours can be found; the example does illustrate, however, how a simple syntactic device might be the seed from which discourse flowers, or – to shift back the metaphor – how words can only be spun when we have the right syntactic looms.

4.7 Syndetic patterns

Coordinators pattern the syndetic pairs in ways variously discernible as *addition, qualification, alternation,* and *equation.* Thus *and* is the familiar plus sign indicating that *B* makes a distinct addition to *A*: *an honest and intelligent man, the spread of poverty and disease, we must labour and rejoice.* Ostensibly each of the coordinates in such phrases should carry its proper meaning and not be a mere synonym or a rhythmic makeweight. The energies of composition, however, are rather easily absorbed in specious coordinations – *eg: honest and upright, poverty and deprivation, labour and endeavour* – which are meant to be additive but which in effect resemble the equational pattern discussed below. A special kind of 'addition' is represented by phrases like *mice and men, private and public, anybody and everybody, one and all,* where the coordinates are poles in a little world of inclusive meaning (*cf* the additive pattern of *not only . . . but also*).

Words and phrases such as *but, yet, if, but not, if not, yet not, and yet, though, although, albeit, without being,* yoke *A* and *B* in formulae of restriction or qualification. Different coordinators, and changes in the order of lexical items, vary the semantic colouring of these formulae. For instance, in *poor but honest, a tax inspector but a friend, painfully but cheerfully,* the 'positives' (*honest, friend, cheerfully*) plainly outweigh the preceding 'negatives' (*poor, tax inspector, painfully*). The phrases take an affirmative stance. Yet when the coordinators are changed to *albeit, though, if,* as in *poor albeit honest, a tax inspector though a friend, painfully if cheerfully,* the negatives outweigh the positives and the tenor of the phrases is now dismissive. (The honesty, friendship, cheerfulness, are of no real moment.) Then if the same coordinators are kept while the order of coordinates is changed – *honest albeit poor, a friend though a tax inspector, cheerfully if painfully* – the positives once more prevail, though the negative values are conceded.

Coordination with *or, either . . . or, neither . . . nor, whether . . . or,* generally implies a straightforward alternative – *pen or pencil, either write or print, whether fluently or haltingly.* A tendency towards the merely repetitive coordination occurs here, as in the additive pattern; phrases such as *investigate or analyse, ambitions or goals, objectionable or repugnant,* might be entirely meaningful in some contexts, but might equally well be quasi-alternations resulting from the writer's anxious fumbling for the precise noun, verb, or adjective. In some cases – and here again there is a parallel with the additive type – a polar contrast is implied (*death or glory, grave or gay, sink or swim*), while in others the phrasing suggests a sly but stylistically interesting option between supposedly comparable formulations, *eg: dancing or gyrating, timidly or furtively, teachers or pedants.* Such pejorative or ironic reformulations tip a disingenuous wink to the reader, who sees well enough how the author's intentions are to be construed. A similar and perhaps more explicit type of reformulation elaborates the coordinating element: *not so much dancing as gyrating, furtively or rather timidly, more of a pedant than a teacher.*

In certain instances the paired items appear to be coextensive, even synonymous, and there is something like an equational relationship between them. The formula is ostensibly *A plus B*, while the semantic effect is that *A equals B*. In common usage this may be the result of an idiomatic erosion, a blurring of the originally distinct import of one member of the pair. For example, everyday phrases such as *hale and hearty, well and good, right and proper, wholly and entirely, any shape or form, toss and turn*, are employed as lexical units in which there is no precise distinction of meaning between component items. Even when the import of the pairing is quite obviously 'both *A* and *B*', or 'not only *A* but also *B*', as in *an officer and a gentleman, a friend and counsellor, happy and glorious, completely and diametrically*, usage fosters the sense that the coordinated items are mutually attributive; psychologically the constituents of the phrase come to be equated – an officer *is* a gentleman, happy *is* glorious, completely *is* diametrically.

This equational pattern is often no more than a kind of stylistic stutter; however, in some forms it is not without aesthetic interest. Students of literary language will recognize in it a historically important device. Shakespeare, for instance, talks of *the dark backward and abysm of time* or *the catastrophe and heel of circumstance*, while Jeremy Taylor captures the effect of a bird's struggling flight in the phrase *the libration and frequent weighing of his wings*. In *hendiadys* (rhetoric's name for this equational-explanatory figure), one element is nothing less than a translation, gloss, or paraphrase in familiar terms of another, potentially less familiar; thus *backward* explains *abysm*, *heel* renders *catastrophe* and *libration* is translated by *weighing*. A rudimentary act of lexicography – necessary at a time when Latin and Greek words were being imported wholesale into English – is thus turned to stylistic account. Nowadays we have dictionaries to help us with the meaning of unfamiliar words, so that perhaps the gloss-by-equation is restricted to small essays in pedantic humour; one could, for example, describe the clientele at a pop concert as *trichomaniac and madly hairy.*

4.8 Elaborating the pattern

Many stylistic effects turn on the syndetic coordination. For instance, it may be the vehicle for bold, zeugma-resembling juxtapositions, *eg: this age of pollution and polymers; Nottingham, city of folklore and pharmacy; Blackpool, a prospect of bosoms and beer-mats*. It may sometimes form the nucleus of a text-pervading image: *the masks and counterfeits of political life* (suggests a description of politics as a masked ball); *our superannuated and arthritic tax system* (fiscal policy in the likeness of old age); *scholars prudently hedging and ditching their theories* (an agricultural metaphor for academic labours – with some incidental by-play on the meanings of 'hedging' and 'ditching'). This rudimentary textual device, it would appear, offers all sorts of textural possibilities.

The texture becomes elaborate as the text expands. To take a simple case, the straightforward coordination of an *A* with a *B* can make a platform for an extended construction of the type *xA plus yB*. Thus the formulae *adjective-noun plus adjective-noun, adverb-adjective plus adverb-adjective, verb-adverb plus verb-adverb* are commonly occurrent: *a gallant officer and a perfect gentleman; scrupulously honest and utterly sincere; labour long and think deeply*. The examples present compound structures of parallel and symmetrical pairings, *gallant* matching *perfect* while *officer* matches *gentleman*, etc. The box pattern thus created makes a frame for textural parallels or antitheses: *impudent masks and blatant counterfeits; prudently hedging and patiently ditching; large bosoms and little beer-mats; ancient folklore and modern pharmacy*. Frequently these symmetries and counterpoints are given a marked rhythmical or phonetic contour – alliteration, for example, is a common device in such cases.

In linking noun phrase with noun phrase the four-square pattern described above may be rejected in favour of a deliberately asymmetrical structure in which only one of the two coordinated nouns is premodified. (*ie* the pattern is either *adjective-noun plus noun* or *noun plus adjective-noun*): *the dark backward and abysm; a gallant officer and a gentleman; a prospect of magnificent bosoms and beer-mats* (in all of these the first coordinate is modified); *the libration and frequent weighing; an officer and a gallant gentleman; a prospect of bosoms and multitudinous beer-mats* (in these the second coordinate is modified). A comparable asymmetry may occur in the pairing of adjectives, where one or other of the coordinates is adverbially modified: *a nobly true and tender story; a remarkably voluble and spry politician; a true and poignantly tender story; a voluble and deplorably spry politician.* Though they are possibly not so frequent as coordinated nouns or adjectives, paired verbs allow the same stylistic manipulations: *to sink manfully or swim doggedly*; *to sink manfully or swim*; *to sink or doggedly swim.* In short, the basic coordination of *A* and *B* can be expanded, symmetrically or asymmetrically, in patterns which interlock (as it were) various parts of speech, building more intricate phraseologies.

4.9 Device and text

The elaborately developed phrase may intrude on the structure of the higher grammatical unit (the clause or sentence) so markedly as to affect its length, rhythm, and semantic focus. If the same kind of phrase-building recurs from sentence to sentence, whole stretches of text may bear a deep stylistic imprint. In [3] we have a brief example of a text constructed on the stylistic basis of the syndetically coordinated phrase. Here is a more ambitious example, with variations of phrase structure embodying both syndetic and asyndetic coordinations. The phrases containing the pairings are italicized to show the extent to which they invade the text:

[4] Canal boating is no pastime for *the impatient or easily fatigued*; it requires *serenity of mind and some durability of muscle.* Whoever lacks these qualifications, however great his *mental and physical skills* might otherwise be, will feel the want of them at the first long flight of locks. You cannot lock through *the Marple sixteen or the twenty-one broad locks at Hatton* with *a motorist's lounging speed and easy acceleration*; nor will *the stepped hill of paddles and balance beams* allow you to make your way with *the touch of a finger or the effortless flexing of a leg.* Paddles are *stiff or mysteriously jammed*, gates *budge groaningly and yield by inches*, perversely unwilling to move. As you work the flight, *half-charmed and half-dismayed* at the prospect of *white-painted heel-posts and gate beams* flagging out your *slow, strenuous progress* up *floors and escalations of water*, your sense of time is affected. You might have been at it for *twenty minutes or three back-breaking, leg-wearying hours*, there is no telling; you are *not so much the boatman as the mindlessly willing horse.* And yet, *punishing labour and creeping toil though it may be*, it offers *the simple though drastic* satisfaction of all drudgingly physical activities; a sense of achievement, a feeling that

whatever else is amiss in life, *this challenge and this resistance* will yield to *patient and methodical work.*

Here is a reasonably sensible and shapely piece of prose, written with a certain phrase-structure in mind (admittedly a perverse method of composition) and yet, despite the obvious loading of some constructions, not forced unnaturally into a stylistic mould. The italicized expressions – all coordinations – represent almost exactly one-half of the 229 words in this passage. The explanation of this remarkable collective bulk is that in all cases the simple coordinating formula has been elaborated, whether in linkages of phrase and phrase or in the expansion of modifying patterns within a phrase. Take, for instance, the construction *serenity of mind and some durability of muscle.* This is a case in which coordination goes somewhat deeper than the mere conjunction *and.* Two noun phrases are coordinated, each consisting of a noun head (*serenity, durability*) postmodified by an *of*-genitive (*of mind, of muscle*). These formal correspondences are reinforced by semantic parallels and antitheses (*durability* equates with *serenity, muscle* opposes *mind*) and also by phonetic prominences, *ie* the *m*-alliteration of *mind* and *muscle* and the suffix-chime (*-ity*) of *serenity* and *durability.* There is a comparable case in *the touch of a finger or the effortless flexing of a leg* – except that here the second of the two phrases has been complicated by the introduction of an adjective, *effortless,* creating an agreeable asymmetry of structure and a variation in the rhythmic balance of the phrases. Rhythmic effect also characterizes the intrusion of an asyndetic pair (*back-breaking, leg-wearying*) into a syndetic frame (*twenty minutes or three hours*), resulting in the elaborate flourish of *twenty minutes or three back-breaking, leg-wearying hours.*

These are some examples of a complexity of phrasing which persistently intrudes upon the structure of clauses, so that the expanded coordinations assume the role of clause subject (*the stepped hill of paddles and balance beams*) or object (*serenity of mind and some durability of muscle*) or complement (*stiff or mysteriously jammed*) or adverbial (*with the touch of a finger or the effortless flexing of a leg*) or of verb plus adverbial (*budge groaningly or yield by inches*). On to these textual stems the figurative textures are grafted – there are, for example, metaphoric variations on the theme of the staircase or ladder (*the stepped hill of paddles and balance beams; floors and escalations of water*) and implied personifications (*budge groaningly and yield by inches; punishing labour and creeping toil*) which give a dramatic colouring to the text.

4.10 Sequences: asyndeton and polysyndeton

The exemplary text in 4.9 above illustrates something of the stylistic potential of binary (*A plus B*) patterns of coordination. Other effects can be exploited by extending the coordination into sequences of three or more items. Such sequences may be constructed asyndetically – *a great, good, lofty-browed, calm-eyed grammarian; a book to be read quickly, light-heartedly, indulgently* – or they may be polysyndetic, *ie* linked by a series of coordinators: *a mellow and benign and altogether enchanting old grammarian; a work to be read gaily or earnestly but always attentively.* In a very common pattern the last step of an otherwise asyndetic sequence is syndetically coordinated: *this wise, witty, well-tempered and inexpensive textbook.*

Asyndeton in long sequences is a favoured vehicle for the denunciatory tirade – for example, Dickens' characterization of Scrooge: *a squeezing, wrenching, grasping, scraping, clutching, covetous old sinner!* One of the qualities of polysyndeton, on the other hand, is to suggest emotion beating at the gates of restraint: *dark and true and tender is the North* (Tennyson); *for there is neither work, nor device, nor knowledge, nor wisdom, in the grave, whither thou goest* (Ecclesiastes). In such examples the cumulative pressure of feeling issues powerfully, as if it were forcing its way out between the coordinators.

The longer the sequence, the more necessary it becomes to exercise some kind of rhythmic control over the verbal impulse. This is one reason for the syndetic linkage closing an asyndetic series – the coordinator in the final step 'cadences' the phrase: *beautiful, brilliant, ebullient, but bad; twist, shake, rattle and roll; slowly, wholly, intensely and precisely.* The presence or absence of that final coordinator may, however, be determined by the syntactic placing of the construction. The coordinator is a signal of completion, writing a more or less emphatic ending to the sequence, and phrases so completed are commonly occurrent in positions where they conclude or coincide with a superordinate grammatical process: *Solitude, alcohol, melancholy, and madness are the traditional destinations of the pedant* (the sequence defines the subject of the sentence); *When this book is finished I propose to eat, sleep, gossip, and booze* (the sequence completes the verb phrase and concludes the sentence). With a shift of syntactic role the pattern without the final coordinator becomes more appropriate stylistically: *Solitude, alcohol, melancholy, madness – such are the traditional destinations of the pedant* (the pronoun *such*, as appositional subject, now signals the emphasis of completion); *When this book is finished I propose to relax a little – eat, sleep, gossip, booze – until I feel compelled to begin another* (the sequence is merely a parenthetical expansion of the main verb).

4.11 Tirades and triads

The rhetorical swagger of an extended sequence puts paid to all textual restraint: *the cold, wet, cheerless, endless, dark, stark, ungodly, and deadly days of an English winter; politicians who smirk and simper and wink and twinkle, understanding and glad-handing and generally grandstanding the public.* Tempting as it sometimes is to ride a fine roller-coasting rage or a surge of humorous energy, such tirades nevertheless tug violently at the general shape of a text and indeed are a commitment to a density of texture that might be difficult to sustain. There is in them a stylistic posturing that becomes particularly evident when items in the sequence have some formal resemblance to each other – *eg* the participial canter of compounds in the following: *a deep-thinking, whisky-drinking, self-communing, Mozart-loving, Horace-quoting, rhyme-scribbling old teacher of English.* Matching rhythms, fortuitous rhymes, alliteration, and other phonetic grace-notes frequently enhance the effect of these inventions.

Less extravagant, and certainly much more amenable to textual control, is the triadic sequence, an arrangement so common as to have left its mark on the repertoire of documentary formula, catch-phrase and cliché: *love, honour, and obey* (from the marriage ceremony), *lost, stolen, or strayed* (a legal formula), *beg, borrow, or steal* (from Stevenson's *Kidnapped*), *bewitched, bothered, and bewildered* (caught into general usage from a song by Lorenz Hart), *lock, stock, and barrel, left, right, and centre. neither fish, flesh, nor fowl, good, bad, or indifferent* (common or proverbial phrases). This is stylistically a very attractive pattern. It effectively takes the polish of alliteration or assonance, and is often appealing as a rhythmic unit, a common stratagem being to open or loosen the rhythm towards the end of the phrase by prefacing the last coordinate with some word that makes a little eddy of unstressed or weakly stressed syllables: *blind, baffled, and utterly bamboozled; bread, circuses, and television broadcasts.*

It is also a climactic pattern, scaling a ladder of ascending degrees, and is therefore beloved of politicians and publicists seeking to evoke strenuous prospects of higher, farther, and ever-yonder: *tackle, contain, and finally defeat; the trade unions, the government, the entire population of this great country; voluntarily, consentingly, and full-heartedly.* In a mischievous variation on this pattern the reader is lured up two steps of the ladder only to be toppled into bathos on the third: *Thieves, vandals, and pedestrian acquaintances; wittily, eloquently, and somewhat inaudibly.*

4.12 Prominence and rhythm

In sequences of three the greatest prominence, or emphasis, is often claimed by the final item, so that in some cases the first two steps are of little more than supplementary importance – mere trestles to a superlative platform: *London, a busy, bustling, reverberant metropolis* (all the energy of the phrase breaks out in *reverberant*, to which the commonplace adjectives *busy* and *bustling*, with their *b*-sounds, merely serve to make a preparatory flourish, an up-beat); *the government has delayed, hesitated, and culpably procrastinated* (this says little more than 'delayed' three times over, but the adverbial intensification of the final item suggests prominence).

Such final emphases are underscored by the rhythmic shaping of the phrase. We have already touched upon the common device of loosening a tight prosodic grip by gradually adding to the number of unstressed or lightly stressed syllables: *the brash, booming, bombinating city of Chicago.* The impulse thus outlined is a sort of controlled unclenching, a deliberate lapse from a tight to a looser metre. An alternative is a gradual constriction of the rhythmic form as in *that bombinating, booming, brash town*: the preference for one prosodic arrangement or the other would have to be determined in the context of composition.

Rhythmic considerations are sometimes so pressing that it is actually necessary to find words with the right number of syllables to make up a prosodic pattern, one of the general constraints of verse being thus casually laid upon the writer of prose. Awareness of rhythmic appeal may underlie the choice of some phrase-enlarging adverb or adjective: *a large, lovable, and mildly eccentric lecturer; Tom, Dick and proletarian Harry; the endless burden of crises, prices, and crippling taxes.* The demand for such augmentations might result in a wording that is merely conventional (*crippling taxes*, for example, is a commonplace collocation) or on the other hand might nudge the writer into some nimbler invention (there is perhaps just a touch of burlesque wit in *proletarian Harry*). Rhythm at all events can have a directive importance, steering the writer towards a choice of words and perhaps occasionally prompting some happy stylistic discovery.

4.13 Figures: recursion and inversion

Each phrase takes distinctive shape in the mind of the writer as he ponders variables of meaning, sound, and syntax, and each shape is a piece in the general rhetorical pattern, requiring links and interlocks with other shapes. This is where figures based on repetitions or counterpoises begin to be useful, though they have their stylistic dangers. Used pervasively, such figures endow a text with a formal elegance or a bravura that may well suit its theme perfectly, but which on the other hand will show as pretentious artifice if the topic is inappropriate. In emotional or earnestly persuasive contexts they present themselves readily, as though they were the natural language of conviction, but otherwise their eloquence is treacherous and they need to be used with caution.

Many figures embody principles intuitively grasped by all exponents of verbal art and artifice, from cabinet ministers to copywriters: recursion, inversion, parallelism, and antithesis – principles which perhaps inform all aesthetic structures, musical and visual as well as verbal. The figures are most easily explained if we regard the text as a line, or, more elaborately, a set of potential alignments. Along this line the writer might, for example, set recurrent items which significantly mark a progress from phrase to phrase. Sometimes this recursion affects the first item in successive phrases: *prosperity for the housewife, prosperity for the manufacturer, prosperity for our country*; (*a picture*) *perfect in its proportions, perfect in its colouring, perfect above all in its sincerity of feeling*. In other instances it might be the last item in the phrase that makes the structural and emotional lynch-pin: (*life is*) *nasty, brutish, and short, painful and short, wasteful and short, wistful and short*. In yet another type, the last word of one phrase becomes the first word of the next: *Blackpool, a prospect of bosoms and beer-mats, of beer-mats and crowded boarding houses, of boarding houses and the loud, blond, vulgar beach*.

Such arrangements all have names in traditional rhetoric (the examples given above illustrate, successively, the figures of *anaphora*, *epistrophe*, and *gradatio*), though names are of little moment except perhaps as reminders of the antiquity of the art of composition. Long, long ago someone discovered that trick of turning the verbal line back on itself so that the figure comes full circle, ending as it began: *accuracy from first to last, always accuracy*; *paint mountains or apples or blotches, but paint*. (The figure is called *epanalepsis*.) In another kind of inversion the line is trained to a cross-pattern in which two or more words are repeated in reverse order: *politicians may make events, but events sometimes unmake politicians: be kind to your stomach and your stomach will be kind to you*. (The original name for this figure, with its well-buttoned air of proverbial wiseacreage, was *antimetabole*; later it came to be known as *chiasmus*.)

4.14 Antitheses and parallels

Antithesis is a major figure, one of the mainstays of oratory. It is not uncommon for items in antithesis to be given inverted roles in the syntax of successive constructions – *eg*: *youth* and *age*, *weak* and *strong*, in the following: *my youth fed on poetry, but grammar comforts my age*; *not all the prizes go to the strong, and the weak do not always suffer defeat*. On the other hand the antithetical pattern may be a box made by correspondent points on two syntactic lines, *eg*: *We submit ourselves to the discipline of grammar only to receive the freedom of poetry*. Here is a close syntactic matching of the significant items in the two clauses (*submit/receive, discipline/freedom, grammar/poetry*); the antithesis in fact dances on the points of the figure called *parison*. A very precise form of parison, in which the aligned constructions are of just the same length and syntactic design, is called *isocolon*. Modern examples are bound to wear their splendour a little absurdly: *Jovial scholars who frisk at midnight, quoting fine poems and gulping red wine, become joyless dullards who groan at noonday, nursing sore heads and sipping black coffee*. Fascinating though they may be to devise – and indeed they present a lexicological challenge – such creations are too dapper for the common thoroughfares of prose, and could now only strut their parts on some stage of deliberate bombast. In the history of literary English the classic case of elaborately symmetrical figuration is of course Lyly's *Euphues*, source-book of a stylistic dandyism that became something of a joke even in its own day. In this connection it is worth quoting a remark of George Puttenham, the Elizabethan rhetorician, concerning the use of antithesis: 'Many of our writers in the vulgar' (*ie* in the vernacular, in English) 'use it in excesse and incurre the vice of fond affection' (*ie* foolish affectation): 'otherwise the figure is very comendable.' This remains a valuable observation. The modern writer who over-patterns his text may indeed be reproved for 'fond affection', but a judicious figuration is nonetheless 'very comendable'.

4.15 Phrasing: a rhetorical display

In the composition of a text the writer explores the varieties of phrasal design, accommodating them to the rhythm and developing pattern of his prose, just as the graphic artist exploits the juxtaposition of various shapes in building up a picture. The process combines instinct and deliberation; the attempt to write creates a sensitivity, a nebulous but nonetheless reliable awareness of options in wording and construction, on the basis of which conscious craftsmanship makes its firm selections. Here – without further theorizing – is a display text. The attitudes it expresses are partly combative and partly devotional, a mingling of polemic and panegyric which encourages the parade of a bold, not to say grandiose, phrasal repertoire:

[5] Ever since Haydn declared him to be the greatest composer he knew, Mozart has been the musician's musician, a ruthlessly brilliant impresario of poignant feeling and matchless technical skill; yet there are so-called lovers of music – grave, judicious, amply-informed dullards – who dare to dismiss him as superficial. 'Light' is their word, as though this darling of the Muses and child of all the sorrows somehow lacked that fearful burden of passion and moral dyspepsia which alone can qualify a man for greatness. If Mozart had groaned a little more noisily, if only he had learned to throw his music into an uncivil tantrum or a strepitant fit, we should have been spared this talk of superficiality. We should have gained a trombonist and lost an angel.

But perhaps the dissidents speak better than they know. 'Light' is indeed the word, for what has more in it of light, of morning's elfin dazzle, of a calm nocturnal shimmer, than this lucid, vitreous, crystalline, sun-reflecting, star-refracting art, a superficial art indeed, an art of shifting surfaces, a multifoliate jewel, a flower of many facets? There are no impenetrable shadows in Mozart; there is grief, there is the knowledge of loss and disillusionment and death, but the discreet astringent modulations touch us with infinite courtesy, the lyric cadence breathes reconciliation and forgiveness, and in the experience of that gay, anguished, healing, heartbroken music we learn to suffer and yet rejoice. Mozart does not bellow at us from some cliff of Promethean torment; it is enough for him to address us decently in the streets and gardens of our sad humanity.

This is unashamedly rhetorical; it stands or falls by the blatant gusto of phrase-making techniques, some of which have been rehearsed in preceding sections of this chapter. Coordinations are frequent and often elaborate: *a ruthlessly brilliant impresario of poignant feeling and matchless technical skill; this darling of the Muses and child of all the sorrows; the fearful burden of passion and moral dyspepsia; an uncivil tantrum or a strepitant fit.* The enthusiastic defence of the subject finds expression in a use of asyndeton which verges on the extravagant. There are long asyndetic sequences, *eg: this lucid, vitreous, crystalline, sun-reflecting, star-refracting art;* in addition, phrases are linked asyndetically, forming appositional strings: *a superficial art indeed, an art of shifting surfaces, a multifoliate jewel, a flower of many facets.* The last example shows text and texture in busy commerce; note how the premodified noun phrases *a superficial art* and *a multifoliate jewel* are set against postmodified constructions – *an art of shifting surfaces, a flower of many facets* – and how within this syntactic alternation there is a lexical interplay in the correspondence of *superficial* and *surface* and the rather bold switching of *jewel* and *flower.* Figurative patterns are also used to mark boundaries in textual structure. Each of the two paragraphs ends with a parisonic figure – *ie: gained a trombonist and lost an angel* and (more elaborately) *bellow at us from some cliff of Promethean torment . . . address us decently in the streets and gardens of our sad humanity.* This was not consciously contrived, and the example points rather strikingly to a possible relationship between figurative rhetoric and the layout of texts. There must be many instances when, as here, a trope becomes in effect a device of punctuation.

4.16 The heuristic value of phrase patterns

Another aspect of phrasing is its heuristic value; the actual shape of the phrase is a clue to the discovery of the 'right' word, the word that combines precision of meaning and aesthetic power. It seldom helps, when at a loss for a word, to institute a casual search in a dictionary or a thesaurus. Just as a versifier looking for a rhyme will rehearse an alphabetical routine (*ash, bash, cash, dash,* etc) until he has sifted out a small number of candidates for a meaningful couplet or quatrain, so in writing prose we can use phrase patterns as a means of scanning and mapping the endlessly folded terrain of vocabulary. A symptom of this is the common habit of repeating over and over again, in a baffled mutter or in anguished inner monologue, the phrase into which the elusive word has to be fitted; changing the form of the phrase often leads to the discovery of the word. A small practical exercise may help to illustrate this fascinating but very complicated theme. Consider, then, the following set of variations on a grammatical frame:

[6] i A judge should be / (adjective or adjectives)
   ii A judge should be / (adjective) *and* (adjective)
   iii A judge should be / (adjective) *yet* (adjective)
   iv A judge should be / *both* (adjective) *and* (adjective)
    v A judge should be / *not only* (adjective) *but also* (adjective)
   vi A judge should be / *more* (adjective) *than* (adjective)
   vii A judge should be / (adjective) *rather than* (adjective)

Clearly, [6i] admits the greatest lexical freedom, and at the same time involves the greatest embarrassment of choice; it opens a possibly bewildering thesaurus of all the words that might denote adjectivally the qualities of a judge, *eg: fair, impartial, honest, incorruptible, learned, wise, shrewd, compassionate, sympathetic, humane, kindly, severe, strict, patient, painstaking, eloquent, lucid, articulate.* The range of possibilities is open-ended, or at any rate so wide that a writer trying to make the apparently simple attributive statement suggested by [6i] might find himself trapped and loitering helplessly in one of those back-eddies that all too frequently divert the compositional flow. Should he define his intention in one adjective or several? If in one, which of the many possibilities will hit his meaning best (and, indeed, does he know precisely what meaning he intends to convey, until recognition comes with the 'right' word?) If he is to use more than one word, then how many? And how are they to be interrelated semantically? Will they be synonyms, collectively defining the same general aspect of judicial virtue? Will they make, in concert, a phonetic or rhythmical pattern? In practice some of these doubts would certainly be resolved by appeal to the wider context óf composition, but the point of the present exercise is that the bare propositional frame *A judge should be . . .* offers in itself no directive clue.

In variations [6ii–6vii], on the other hand, the possibilities of lexical choice are delimited and brought into focus by the varying forms of phrase as set out to the right of the oblique stroke. They all imply a selection of two words, but indicate different axes of semantic relationship – extension, contrast, distinction, comparison, preference; variation [6iii], for example, might suggest *A judge should be firm yet fair*, or [6vii] *A judge should be strict rather than severe*, while other possibilities would be definitely ruled out – we would not expect *A judge should be eloquent yet incorruptible* or *A judge should be impartial rather than articulate*. The forms of phrase help us to survey and classify what would otherwise be a vague mass of dictionary items. To view syntax in this way, as a searching and classifying mechanism, is to understand perhaps a little of the ostensible paradox that a complex style is sometimes more easily managed than a drastic simplicity of expression. Simple syntactic structures offer few bearings on a required semantic object – the 'right' word has to come as a matter of inspired reckoning; whereas a greater degree of syntactic complexity may produce two or three points of reference, allowing the writer to take sightings from one word on to another.

4.17 Phonetic aspects of phrasing

There is a paradox with which amateurs of verse will be acquainted: the more rigorous a compositional scheme, the greater its heuristic power. Rules and conditions, that is to say, enforce discoveries. The demands of a rhetorical figure, or any kind of linguistic prerequisite, urge the mind to rehearse and methodically ransack its store of vocabulary. In this process, phonetic and kinetic (rhythmic) features may be compelling stimuli. Consider, for example, Edward Lear's comic denunciation of the monks of Mount Athos: *Those muttering, miserable, mutton-hating, man-avoiding, misogynic, morose and merriment-marring, monotoning, many-mule-making, mournful, minced-fish and marmalade-masticating Monx.* This joyous tirade clearly owes a great deal to the stimulus of alliteration, with perhaps the auxiliary impulse of that old invective soldier, the participial adjective. (A nice technical point is the placing of a coordinator – in *morose and merriment-marring* – to break the asyndetic flow with an eddy, a rhythmic swirl, before the torrent surges on.) Emotively charged phrasing is often characterized by phonetic bondings which are more than merely ornamental; they may be a symptom or even the source of the creative energy that has gone into the making of the phrase.

The mnemonic power of sound has subtle workings in the most ordinary compositions; it has affected not a few of the examples devised for this chapter. An interesting and typical case is the word *strepitant*, which occurs in Ch.4[5] in the context *an uncivil tantrum or a strepitant fit*. Semantic directives drawn from a wider context (*eg* the word *noisily*, which occurs a little earlier in the passage) must certainly have guided the choice of this unusual word, but in the immediate phrasal environment there are discernible phonetic promptings, *eg* the /s/ sound in *uncivil*, the cluster /tr/ in *tantrum*, and from the same word a more remote echo – a visual as much as a vocal impression – in the sequence /tant/. It may seem very remarkable that the mind in its creative probings should pick up these adventitious hints, but even the plainest texts will reveal, on careful examination, some striking examples of phonetic cohesion.

No less important are the effects of rhythm, several instances of which have been discussed in this chapter. There is an instinct that accommodates word-rhythm to phrase-rhythm to sentence-rhythm – which means that occasionally rhythm may be the ultimate arbiter in the choice of a word. Here, however, we find ourselves in the realm of individual preference. A writer's phrasing is like a painter's brush-stroke or a pianist's touch at the keyboard, a highly personal act, and sound and rhythm are possibly the ultimate expressions of personality in phrasing; through them the practitioner gains some sense of being able to taste and feel his own work, and knows the pleasure of trying a phrase on the tongue. Beyond the phrase, writing becomes ever more complex and abstract and the sense of physical contact with a medium is seldom so keenly felt.

Chapter 5

Sentences in texts

Through the practice of writing (as well as through studies in grammatical theory) we learn to consider phrases, clauses, and sentences in the dual perspective of forms that contain and are themselves contained. There is, as we have seen, a heuristic value in the form as container; the shape can help us to find the constituent pieces. There is also a directive value, inasmuch as the proposed form admits some choices and excludes others. The completed form, however, immediately comes under a higher directive. In constructing a complex sentence, for example, we need to determine a pattern of subordination, but once the pattern is complete, *or even while it is being shaped*, it must be related to the wider, comprehensive pattern of the text. It is to this aspect of composition, the adaptation of the sentence to the framing of the text, that we now turn.

5.1 Sentence into text: a preliminary exploration

Let us begin by looking at a list of sentences with a common ground of narration:

[1]1 The Sheriff of Nottingham imprisoned Maid Marian in the castle.
　2 He then announced an archery contest.
　3 He knew what effect these actions would have on Robin Hood.
　4 He wanted to trap in a pitfall of chivalric impulse this man who so defiantly eluded capture.
　5 The news soon reached Robin.
　6 He was leading a perilous, hardy, but not entirely unglamourous life as an outlaw in the notorious forest of Sherwood.

7   He and his followers were not men to disdain a challenge.
8   They never liked to fail a comrade.
9   They assumed heavy disguises and set out for Nottingham to rescue Marian.
10 What a sight they must have presented!
11 Imagine the scene.
12 It was a warm day.
13 The sun was blazing.
14 The townsfolk of Nottingham would hardly fail to notice the arrival of a company of perhaps fifty thickly-cloaked men with their hoods pulled about their faces.
15 Do you wonder that the Sheriff smiled as he made secret signals to his guards?

The sentences in this farrago are grammatically acceptable, and when read in sequence tell a coherent tale. The question is, however, whether taken collectively they make a text. If the 'tale' is set out in continuous form it wears a peculiarly lifeless look:

[2] The Sheriff of Nottingham imprisoned Maid Marian in the castle. He then announced an archery contest. He knew what effect these actions would have on Robin Hood. He wanted to trap in a pitfall of chivalric impulse this man who so defiantly eluded capture.

The news soon reached Robin. He was leading a perilous, hardy but not entirely unglamorous life as an outlaw in the notorious forest of Sherwood. He and his followers were not men to disdain a challenge. They never liked to fail a comrade. They assumed heavy disguises and set out for Nottingham to rescue Marian.

What a sight they must have presented! Imagine the scene. It was a warm day. The sun was blazing. The townsfolk of Nottingham would hardly fail to notice the arrival of a company of perhaps fifty thickly-cloaked men with their hoods pulled about their faces. Do you wonder that the Sheriff smiled as he made secret signals to his guards?

Considered as a *text*, this is surely a gross failure, despite its rudimentary narrative cohesion. The arrangement of the material in three paragraphs gives an appearance of systematic procedure but is hardly enough to redeem the shapelessness, the lack of contrastive emphases, the inflexible monotony of address. It moves fitfully from one sentence to the next simply because it has been *assembled*, item by item, and not *composed* with a view to harmonizing one item with another. It is a dead text, without harmonics and resonances. Even its small sporadic elegances of phrase are bent into awkwardness in the total lump.

Casual examination of this failed text suggests where some of the faults may lie. There is no attempt to fit sentence-length into an overriding rhythm; some sentences (11, 12, 13) are very short, to no apparent rhetorical purpose, while others (4, 6, 14) seem ponderous by contrast. A feeling of incongruity and disjointedness is provoked by the intrusion of exclamatory, directive, or interrogative sentence-forms (*What a sight they must have presented!*; *Imagine the scene*; *Do you wonder the Sheriff smiled* etc) into a generally 'declarative' context. It is all very well to address the reader, but surely not as abruptly and gauchely as this. Most of all, however, the sentences (with the exception of the three non-declarative types) are routinely patterned, beginning with a subject which is either a pronoun or a simple noun phrase, followed by the verb, followed by one or more items in predicative array. Thanks to this standardization of sentence-structure all sense of flexibility is lost, all nuances and highlights are obliterated, and the text is reduced to a flat recital.

Now taking the same sentences in almost the same order, and making only minor alterations in wording, let us attempt to compose something with the ring of a genuine text:

[3] Knowing the effect his actions would have on Robin Hood, the Sheriff of Nottingham imprisoned Maid Marian in the castle and then announced an archery contest. His object was to trap this man who so defiantly eluded capture; to lure him into the pitfall of a chivalric impulse.

The news soon reached Robin in the notorious forest of Sherwood, where he was leading the life of an outlaw – a life of peril and hardihood, though not entirely without glamour. Never men to disdain a challenge or fail a comrade, he and his followers set out for Nottingham, heavily disguised, to rescue Marian.

Imagination alone can suggest the sight they must have presented. On a warm day, under a blazing sun, a company of perhaps fifty men, thickly cloaked, with their hoods pulled about their faces, entered the city. Their arrival would hardly go unnoticed by the townsfolk; as for the Sheriff, small wonder if he smiled as he made secret signals to his guards.

This could hardly be called a distinguished piece of prose, but it does have in it some stirrings of life and persuasive power. Comparison with [2] must surely suggest that a few changes have wrought a vital transformation and that the text now begins to speak with a little authority and command some belief.

The version presented in [3] is thoughtfully composed and not merely assembled. The essential requirement of such composition is a reasonably skilful handling of a syntactic repertoire of incorporations, transformations, deletions, and additions. Here, with a few changes (*eg* the conversion of a verb, *imagine*, into a corresponding noun, *imagination*) the inconveniently short sentences of the original have been aggregated into larger units better adapted to the rhythm of the text. Further incorporations have taken place via broad transformations in syntax; *eg* the original sentence (8), *They never liked to fail a comrade*, has been incorporated with (7), *He and his followers were not men to disdain a challenge*, in a subordinate clause, *Never men to disdain a challenge or fail a comrade*. The value of such transformations lies not only in their incorporative possibilities but also in their contribution to a flexible sentence structure with potential variations of semantic focus. The opening of [3], for example (*Knowing the effect his actions would have on Robin Hood, the Sheriff of Nottingham imprisoned Maid Marian in the castle and then announced an archery contest*) not only incorporates the first three sentences of the original scheme, but also, through the front-positioning of the participial clause, imposes a perspective on the information conveyed. The perspective would shift slightly with a change in the position of the clause, *eg: The Sheriff of Nottingham, knowing the effect his actions would have on Robin Hood, imprisoned Maid Marian*, etc.

Without going into further detail (and several interesting points remain, *eg* the expansion of the original sentence (4)) we might say of [3] that it illustrates the importance of decisions or evaluations which the writer makes recurrently as he contemplates the relationship between sentence and text. In general terms, language nearly always offers two or more ways of saying and two or more ways of combining sayings; fluent composition therefore depends to a great extent on the ability to perceive and rapidly evaluate alternatives.

One kind of evaluation has to do with the length of the sentence; another with its complexity, or the complexity of one or other of its constituent elements; yet another with the mobility of sentence elements, *ie* with the possibility of rearranging the order of clauses or phrases; and still another with the power of the sentence to project simultaneously its own rhythms and the tempo of the text. All these factors are interrelated – length with complexity, complexity with mobility, mobility with rhythm, rhythm with length, etc, through permutations in which first one and then the other consideration dominates.

5.2 The long sentence

In quite properly encouraging their pupils to write simple, clear English, many teachers implant a prejudice against long sentences. There is no harm in this cautionary attitude, except when it hardens into the superstitious axiom that long sentences are always bad. A sentence is misconceived, certainly, when it is so rambling that we lose touch with the context of argument; when it is so intricately organized that we lose sight of essential syntactic relationships; when its constituent elements are so complex that the span of attention is stretched and our capacity to store information is put to the test; but not simply because it contains a large number of words.

Sentence-length is often governed by tactical considerations. If an argument is to be clearly and forcibly stated it may be advisable to enclose each stage in a separate and comparatively short sentence, achieving textual cohesion by means of connective devices of the kind explored in Chapter 2. On the other hand, points in exposition may be very intimately related, or the writer might want to create a perspective in argument, so that some points are brought to the fore while others more or less recede; in which case the long sentence could prove to be tactically more appropriate. Here is an example of a piece of exposition set out first in a series of short (or shortish) sentences, and then in a single long sentence:

[4]i The number of applications for arts degree courses has fallen recently. This is perhaps not very surprising. The prospect of going to a university is no longer as glamorous as it once was. Furthermore, young people are naturally anxious that there may be no job for them at the conclusion of their studies.

Nevertheless, the trend is disturbing. It implies a reduction in the status of the university as a guardian of humane values.

ii The recent fall in the number of applications for arts degree courses, though not very surprising in view of the diminished glamour of university life and the natural anxiety of young people about the prospects of employment at the conclusion of their studies, is nevertheless disturbing because it implies a reduction in the status of the university as a guardian of humane values.

Most readers will probably dislike [4ii] because of the length of a parenthesis (*though not very surprising . . . at the conclusion of their studies*) that cleaves the sentence, separating the principal subject from its predicate. Even were this long stretch of text to be placed at the beginning of the sentence, thereby reuniting the subject and predicate of the main clause, it would doubtless still seem burdensome. Version [4ii], then, is not an ideal solution to the expository problem. On the other hand, [4i] is far from perfect even though it has the advantage of putting the least possible strain on the reader. The best tactic would probably be to strike a compromise and present the material in two or three sentences. The one thing that might be said for the single long sentence in [4ii] is that it does draw an expository perspective – there is a syntactic foreground and background – and perhaps even shows a sly efficiency in making the reader hurry through the parenthesis, merely scanning its qualifying points. What looks like bad writing may in some cases amount to a wicked sleight of hand.

A sentence may be long for reasons of syntactic symbolism; because through its length it evokes a scene, a sensation, or a state of mind. Here is an example of a text consisting of two very long sentences. It sets out deliberately to construct an aesthetic relationship between subject-matter and sentence-length, and perhaps shows the strain of an attempted *tour de force*:

[5] To live far from the sea, to pass days, weeks, grimy urban months, without walking a beach, without hearing the surf, without feeling the strange comfort of that lullaby rhythm that marks the moonstruck lurching of our planet – this is to suffer a sense of loss, to be denied access to one of life's profounder joys, to be exiled, indeed, from the primal source of life itself. We wait and long for the day when the luggage is

crammed into the car and we make for the coast, cursing the traffic, counting the miles, until the road swivels round the last hill, and there below us slouches the good old monster, growling in his world-wide eternal paddock, ferocious, pitiless, yet so dearly and inexplicably remembered and loved that no one catching the first renewed sight of him can forbear an exile's happy cry of greeting.

As an exercise for reading *aloud*, this requires a sustained effort which (experiment will show) taxes the breath. In silent reading, however, its cadences merely imagined, the text fares better; it is written as it were for an ideal voice. In spite of its prolixity and occasional expansiveness of phrase (*eg: that lullaby rhythm that marks the moonstruck lurching of our planet*) it does not overburden the reader's interpretative and retentive capacities, and the chief reason for that is that it is meted out, presented in segments that are easily assimilated, not least because they *do* appeal to the aural sense, the feeling for what in Chapter 1 we called 'scoring'. The frequent commas are a symptom of this careful measurement. The passage is put under the control of a few simple grammatical and rhetorical devices, *eg* recursions and parallels (*to live, to pass, to suffer, to be denied, to be exiled: without walking, without hearing, without feeling*); the calculated break in the structure of the first sentence and the resumption of its wayward theme in the powerfully anaphoric *this*; the measured amplifications and appositions (*the good old monster, growling in his world-wide eternal paddock, ferocious, pitiless*); the generally asyndetic patterns of coordination that give contrastive prominence to syndetic sequences such as *dearly and inexplicably remembered and loved*. The intended effect of the resultant phrases, moving rhythmically in their long, fluctuating sentences (but here is a subliminal metaphor, for *fluctus* means 'a wave') is to evoke kinaesthetically an image of the sea itself, and at the same time to suggest the writer's emotional commitment to his theme. In this case, therefore, there are compositional motives to justify the considerable length of sentence.

5.3 The short sentence

It may be easy to write short and simple sentences, but it is far from easy to manage them sensitively in composition. One difficulty is that the plain straightforward text may verge on parody – of the nursery lisp, of the laconic fictional tough, of the tabloid journalist's glottal hop. Another problem is that simple sentences expose a theme baldly and mercilessly; less-than-convincing points and awkward qualifications cannot be conveniently recessed as they might be in the surbordinations of more sophisticated texts. A third difficulty is that a textual sequence of sentences each consisting of only one or two clauses, with little or no elaboration of phrase, leaves small room for those useful variations of tempo that give suppleness to a composition; the general evenness of sentence length makes the text move stiffly ([4i] above is an example of this).

Once again, the risks may be accepted if there are good compositional reasons for running them. Here is an attempt to compose, in short sentences, a text on a simple but emotive theme. The task is to curb yet emphasize the emotion, through the restraint of simplicity:

[6] Middle age is a time of despairing self-appraisal. Few men really like themselves when they are fifty. The young are engaged in an endless dance with their own images. The old are rapt in selfhood with a kind of purity. Only a middle-aged man dislikes what he sees in the mirror. He sees the testimony of failure and he knows he has to live with it. Young men hope, because they dare. Old men forgive themselves, because they must. But a middle-aged man knows neither hope nor reconciliation. He knows only the burden of responsibility. He is responsible for the life he has made, and he cannot plead excuses or look for sympathy.

Though there are one or two sentences here that threaten to break out into a modest complexity – the last, for example, runs to three clauses – the text as a whole reflects the self-imposed prescription to keep the sentences short. It consequently illustrates two of the difficulties mentioned above. The theme is flatly exposed to the critical eye of the reader, who is asked to accept some confidently sweeping assertions, eg: *Few men really like themselves when they are fifty.* Furthermore, the tempo of the piece is something less than subtle – a boneshaken rhythm of stops and starts.

It could be argued that these are defects which have been transformed into virtues. The short sentences check the impetus of this text, denying the possibility of a flowing discursive line and presenting instead a series of assertions which have the ring of maxims or gnomic 'wisdoms'. This is in tune with the attitude of naked appeal (or barefaced special pleading, according to one's response) which the text may be thought to convey. The driving force of this passage is essentially personal and emotional. No sociologist, philosopher, or other observer of the human condition could be expected to accept at an objective level the propositions made here about the ages of man; they are not of such a nature as to be supported or contradicted by statistics or logic. The only way to urge them upon a reader is as a set of quasi-poetic formulations, asseverations not requiring the subordinate apparatus of inference, development, and qualification. To this purpose the compact declarative sentences are quite well adapted.

Another feature of the text is that the short sentences have lent themselves admirably to the working out of a circuitous pattern in the rhetoric of the paragraph. The passage opens with a 'Stack' (see 1.5 [7]) consisting of: (a) a topic sentence couched in general terms (*Middle age is a time* etc); (b) a reformulation of the topic in particular terms (*Few men really like themselves* etc); (c) a sentence about the young (*The young are engaged* etc); (d) a sentence about the old (*The old are rapt in selfhood* etc); and (e) a sentence about the middle-aged (*Only a middle-aged man* etc), which is also the summary sentence completing a circuit back to the topic. However, this summary sentence (*Only a middle-aged man* etc) is the general topic sentence (a) of a second Stack, which now develops in exactly corresponding stages through (b) a particularizing of the topic (*He sees the testimony of failure* etc), to (c) a sentence concerning the young (*Young men hope* etc), to (d) a sentence about the old (*Old men forgive themselves* etc) and thence to (e) another summary sentence on middle age (*But a middle-aged man* etc). There is even a close similarity between the items – *only, but* – used to introduce the two summary sentences. The sentence *But a middle-aged man* now begins to repeat the pattern as the topic sentence (a) of a third Stack. The particularizing of the topic, (b), follows regularly (*He knows only the burden*), but then the pattern is interrupted or foreshortened, and what follows is the third, emphatically conclusive, summary sentence.

5.4 Variations of sentence-length: compositional tempo

Clearly there are relationships between sentence-length, theme, texture, and textual design which the writer must try to take into account, establishing norms of length that seem to fit the general demands of his material. This does not exclude the possibility – indeed, the necessity – of significant changes of pace. Compositional tempo often requires us to write long-and-short, in variations on a dominant length (all writers know the stylistic value of introducing an assertive short sentence into a context of longer items) and when the variations are successfully timed, the gain is twofold: the text is rhythmically pleasing, perhaps even exciting, and its message is contoured so that certain elements, crisply defined, come into prominence. Consider two versions of a simple narrative:

[7]i The companions called on dwindling reserves of strength to pitch their small tent, and having done so crept inside and there struggled to make themselves as comfortable as possible while they awaited the worst. Oates, however, apparently unresigned to waiting, left the tent, remarking that he would be outside 'for some time' – an action that drew no response from his exhausted colleagues, though they knew he was sacrificing himself to give them a better chance of survival and that he would never be seen again.

ii The companions called on dwindling reserves of strength to pitch their small tent, and having done so crept inside and there struggled to make themselves as comfortable as possible while they awaited the worst. Oates, it seems, was not resigned to waiting. He left the tent, remarking that he would be outside 'for some time' – an action that drew no response from his exhausted colleagues, though they knew he was sacrificing himself to give them a better chance of survival. He would never be seen again.

If the sole concern were to process the message so that its constituents (the pitching of the tent, the exhaustion, Oates' departure) are lucidly and unambiguously presented, then [7i] would not be noticeably inferior to [7ii]. A qualitative difference is felt only if we demand from the writing an editorial assessment of the information presented; it then becomes evident that the tempo of [7ii] is more adroitly managed. In [7ii] there are two short sentences (*Oates, it seems, was not resigned to waiting*; *He would never be seen again*) which cut a clear figure against the ground of the longer units, and in doing so give special emphasis to the information they contain. Furthermore, they may appeal to the reader on aesthetic grounds, as pleasing departures from the normal rhythm of the text. The flow of the longer sentences may be felt as the dominant, the norm, against which the tug of these shorter units is more or less powerfully felt. The contrast may not be violently exciting, but it makes a little stir not incommensurate with the epic theme. It would be possible to make one or two further changes so that the whole narrative would be cast in sentences with no very marked variations in length; but this would destroy a distinctive and significant compositional tempo.

5.5 Intensive complexity

There is obviously a relationship between the length of a sentence and the complexity of its structure. From a stylistic point of view it is useful to distinguish between two kinds of complexity: *intensive* and *extensive*. There is an expansion in the structure of the phrases that make up the elements in a clause – a matter discussed at some length in the preceding chapter – and this is what we shall call *intensive complexity*, a term suggesting that the elaborative tension of the sentence is built up within the framework of the simple clause elements.

If a sentence is intensively complex in all its phrasal constituents, then it may well be not only long but also unreasonably overstocked, a burden on the reader's attention because syntactic complexity brings semantic elaboration in its train. Let our basis of illustration here be a textbook example, *The farmer kills the duckling*. That sentence consists of three elements, each of which is very simply realized: a subject (*The farmer*), a verb (*kills*), and a direct object (*the duckling*). Now it is possible to elaborate the realization of these elements to such an extent that they considerably swell the bulk of the 'simple' sentence, and this is done by creating highly complex incorporative phrase-structures (*cf* 4.1–4.3 above). Thus our textbook sentence might be playfully expanded: *The only completely professional and therefore quite unsentimental farmer living in a semi-urbanized community of poodle-breeding stockbrokers and bucolic ex-teachers of Middle English will be wanting to start to try to kill the undeniably attractive little white duckling that has such appealing ways and such an awkward trick of hiding under the furniture at the very sight of a knife or the merest mention of gizzards.*

Here in facetiously inflated form we have the process of making a sentence intensively complex. The simple frame remains, but is almost obscured by the syntactic and semantic intricacy of its constituent elements, now realized as follows:

[8] *Subject*: The only completely professional and therefore quite unsentimental farmer living in a semi-urbanised community of poodle-breeding stockbrokers and bucolic ex-teachers of Middle English
Verb: will be wanting to start to try to kill
Object: the undeniably attractive little white duckling that has such appealing ways and such an awkward trick of hiding under the furniture at the very sight of a knife or the merest mention of gizzards.

The treatment of subject and object is particularly instructive. In the orginal sentence these are realized by simple noun phrases. In this revised version the words *farmer* and *duckling* remain as phrase heads with a considerably reduced semantic importance – they are mere categorical markers almost overgrown by the sheer sprawl of branching constructions. We have noted elsewhere (4.3, 4.5) the open-endedness of postmodification in the noun phrase. The process coaxes us away from the centre of reference denoted by the phrase head (*eg: farmer*) and draws us towards other points of meaning – *poodle-breeding stockbrokers, bucolic ex-teachers of Middle English.* In short, the elaborate construction has a distractive tendency, which may not always answer the writer's intentions.

These reflections raise a question of stylistic principle. Is it perhaps poor compositional policy to overstock a simple sentence by making too many of its elements elaborately complex? Some complexity there may well be within the simple scheme, but the writer needs to be equipped with a tact (or a cunning) that knows how to balance complexity and simplicity in adroit distributions. Here is an example that raises one or two interesting points:

[9] In a world made virtually uninhabitable by the noise of traffic, the din of popular amusements, and the dolorous rumblings of politicians, the library is a blessed haven. There I can meet, in decent silence, the amicable shades of those poets, historians and philosophers whose words have edified and consoled mankind and whose lives have been dedicated to truths which lie beyond the thrust of mass publicity, electioneering zeal, or

the accelerator pedal. The library is indeed my parliament, my highroad, the mutely clamorous playground of my imaginings. Its carpeted lanes of meditation, book-lined and gently bemusing, restore my soul.

Each sentence in this passage is basically simple, but each has an element of intensive complexity. What makes the complexity tolerable and even pleasurable is that: (a) there is only one such element, one problem-constituent as it were, in each sentence; and (b) that the syntactic centre of complexity keeps changing. Thus in the first sentence it is the adverbial (*In a world made virtually uninhabitable by the noise of traffic, the din of popular amusements, and the dolorous rumblings of politicians*) that makes an elaborate onset to what is otherwise a very simple subject–verb–complement construction (*the library is a blessed haven*). In the next sentence the heavily complex element is the direct object (*the amicable shades of those poets, historians, and philosophers whose words have edified and consoled mankind and whose lives have been dedicated to truths which lie beyond the thrust of mass publicity, electioneering zeal, or the accelerator pedal*). There is a discernible semantic cohesion between this complex object phrase and the extensive adverbial of the preceding sentence; thus *accelerator pedal* echoes *the noise of traffic, electioneering zeal* recalls *the dolorous rumblings of politicians,* and *mass publicity* is a reflex of *the din of popular amusements.* The *poets, historians, and philosophers* also have an implied place in the equation, as counters to traffic noise (vs poetry), political rumbling (vs history), and popular amusement (vs philosophy). In the third sentence, the complex element is the complement, with its apposed phrases (*my parliament, my highroad, the mutely clamorous playground of my imaginings*). Here again there are semantic bonds with preceding sentences: *parliament* (sentence 3) – *electioneering zeal* (sentence 2) – *rumblings of politicians* (sentence 1); *highroad* (sentence 3) – *accelerator pedal* (sentence 2) – *noise of traffic* (sentence 1); *mutely clamorous playground of my imaginings* (sentence 3) – *mass publicity* (sentence 2) – *din of popular amusements* (sentence 1). In the final sentence the centre of complexity shifts again, to the subject element (*Its carpeted lanes of meditation, book-lined and gently bemusing*). In this the semantic echoes have almost died out; they are appropriately 'carpeted'. There is perhaps a faintly suggested link between *lanes of meditation* and *highroad,* but the closing phrase, with its allusion to Psalm 23 and its connotations of 'green pastures' and 'still waters' significantly turns aside from images of urban life. Throughout this short text a semantic pattern is thus consistently developed, but it is plotted on a changing syntactic ground; the syntactically complex elements are in succession the adverbial, the direct object, the subject complement, and the subject.

Passage [9] then, suggests ways of exploiting the stylistic possibilities of intensive complexity so as to produce a shapely and even subtle text. The example prompts a comparison between the units in a sentence and the players in a game. The theme in this passage is like a ball which is passed from one player to another; only the verb appears to have no tactical role. Obviously (to continue the analogy) only one player at a time should make the running; to have two runners would be to spread confusion and break the purposeful flow of the game.

5.6 Extensive complexity

Our second kind of complexity, to be called *extensive*, is seen in what is customarily known as the complex sentence, with its chains and spans of principal and subordinate clauses. A sentence might be extensively complex because the writer is distracted by the sprawl of his own thoughts and afterthoughts, but preferably the complexity will be a result of careful calculation. In the following example the third sentence plays elaborately and riskily the game of keeping the reader waiting for a conclusion. The essence of the game is the combination of syntactic complexity and semantic density:

[10] There is one hour of day which is always pleasantly touched with minglings of expectancy and apprehension. This is the time when the morning post is about to arrive, bringing with it God knows what intimations of love, friendship, commercial advantage or downright legal menace. Though we may no longer actually station ourselves near the letter-box, as when in boyhood, agog with the excitement of our hobbies, we awaited the latest consignment from Eldorado, or as when in youth, our pulses hammering, we lurked to intercept thrilling, scented avowals from the most recent she, or even as when in maturer years we dared to hope that success and fame might yet come clattering into the house on the back of a postcard, still the moment is a glorious and an anxious one, and he must be a cold-spirited recluse who can calmly watch the postman

pass by his window, can indifferently contemplate a letterless doormat, and can accept with equanimity the bleak fact that there is no post for him today.

Here the first two sentences merely clear the ground for an attempt at an intricate virtuoso performance in the third. The first part of this truly episodic sentence has its syntactic foundation in the clause-sequence *Though we may no longer station ourselves near the letter-box . . . still the moment is a glorious and an anxious one*. This sequence is cleft, and the cleft is bridged by a huge 'suspended' structure in three spans, *as when in boyhood . . . as when in youth . . . as when in maturer years*. Two of these 'spans' are themselves cleft constructions, *as when in boyhood . . . we awaited* etc being interrupted by *agog with the excitement of our hobbies* and *as when in youth . . . we lurked* etc being broken by *our pulses hammering*. The aesthetic design of the sentence in this first part, from the beginning to the words *the moment is a glorious and an anxious one*, depends on a combination of 'successive' and 'recessive' constructions. The recession of span within span can be represented diagrammatically:

[11] *1st level*: A1   A2
       2nd level: B1   B1,B2   B2,B3
       3rd level: C1   C2

Where:

A1 = *Though we may no longer actually station ourselves near the letter-box*

A2 = *still the moment is a glorious and an anxious one*

B1 = *as when in boyhood . . . we awaited the latest consignment from Eldorado*

B2 = *as when in youth . . . we lurked to intercept thrilling, scented avowals from the most recent she*

B3 = *or even as when in maturer years, we dared to hope that success and fame might yet come clattering into the house on the back of a postcard*

C1 = *agog with the excitement of our hobbies*

C2 = *our pulses hammering*

The diagram presents the 'successive' structure in the horizontal plane, and in the vertical plane the 'recessive' structure, the pattern of recession and emergence the reader has to follow on his way from A1 to A2. At the deepest level of recession are the non-finite clauses (*agog with the excitement of our hobbies, our pulses hammering*) which interrupt the reading of B1 and B2. There is no such interruption in

B3, where the semantic role of these interpolations – they indicate states of emotion – is allotted to the verb phrase *dared to hope*.

The remainder of the sentence, from *and he must be a cold-spirited recluse* is less intricately patterned, the parallel growth of the three linked relative clauses being very readily discernible. Even here, however, there is a touch of stylistic calculation in the placing of these relative clauses after the completed main clause *he must be a cold-spirited recluse*, rather than in the clause-interrupting position after *he* (*ie: he who can calmly watch the postman pass by his window, etc must be a cold-spirited recluse*). The effective antecedent of *who can calmly watch, etc* is not *he* but *recluse*, and the succeeding clauses are appropriately worded so as to suggest a reclusive frame of mind (*calmly watch, indifferently contemplate, accept with equanimity*).

5.7 Mobility and presentation

The last example suggests that some syntactic elements enjoy a degree of mobility in sentence-structure, and that the positioning of these mobile components may be stylistically important. It clearly affects the way in which information is presented, and consequently the manner in which implications or special emphases are likely to be construed, but it has other important relationships – *eg* with sentence-rhythm and sentence-connection.

The first element in a simple sentence is commonly the subject; other items, however, may be moved for rhetorical effect into the sentence-opening position. Thus the placings of subject and complement may be reversed: *happy was the day, a proud man was Hector*. An object complement may be similarly fronted (*mad they called him*), or an indirect object (*to his wife Shakespeare left his second-best bed*), or even a direct object (*his second-best bed he left to his wife*). Such sentences are often described as having a 'marked theme'. In our examples, *happy*, *mad, a proud man, to his wife, his second-best bed* have assumed thematic prominence and have become quasi-subjects.

The mobility of complements and objects, however, is limited in comparison with that of one other element in clause-structure, the adverbial. The positional freedom of this element, and the consequent implications as to meaning and textual cohesion, may be roughly illustrated by the following example:

[12]i *The sorrowful mother laid her darling child on the doorstep.*

ii *The sorrowful mother laid on the doorstep her darling child.*
iii *On the doorstep the sorrowful mother laid her darling child.*

In these three versions of a statement there is a mobile adverbial, *on the doorstep,* the location of which must direct our reading of the sentence and its little drama. As the final element in the sentence (and assuming normal conditions of accentuation) it completes an information-giving process that would correspond to the question, 'Where did the sorrowful mother lay her darling child?' When, however, as in [12ii] and [12iii], another element is put in the position of so-called end-focus (see below, 5.8), the information is presented in a slightly different perspective. These versions would answer the question, 'What did the sorrowful mother lay on the doorstep?' Furthermore, [12iii] gives thematic prominence to the element that directly connects the answer to the implied question. Therefore [12iii] has a distinguishing textual (connective) mark as well as a semantic implication. A shift in the position of one component thus affects the whole pattern of relationships in a sentence, and the decision to locate a mobile feature at one point rather than another is an act of presentation taking into scope the interior design of the sentence and the external connections of sentence with text.

Such devices of presentation are by no means confined to highly rhetorical prose; here is a simple piece of narrative designed to show how a text can be shaped presentatively, in a way that quite unobtrusively 'stages' its action:

[13] Behind our living room was a short dark passage leading to an even darker cupboard, the cupboard under the stairs. Only rarely and on compulsion did I venture there; I firmly believed it to be tenanted by incalculably malevolent spectres. Such superstitions my grandfather was all too ready to exploit, for he enjoyed power in any of its forms and pleasurable indeed was the power a malicious adult could wield over the apprehensions of a child. To my protesting mother he would explain that it was all in fun, that I must learn not to be 'mardy'. 'Mardiness' was a contemptible affliction. To purge me of it, he would from time to time bundle me into the blackness of the understairs cupboard, my mother being out of the house.

If the passage is examined clause by clause it becomes apparent that the ruling strategy is presentative. Some clauses begin in normal fashion with the subject element, but these alternate (more or less) with others having a marked theme – *behind our living room, only rarely and on compulsion, such superstitions, pleasurable indeed, to my protesting mother*. These phrases refer mainly to locations (*behind our living room*), circumstances (*only rarely and on compulsion*) and states of mind (*such superstitions, pleasurable indeed*) – *ie* they present the setting of the drama, in a general sense, rather than its actors. Even the phrase *to my protesting mother*, which seems for the nonce to bring an actor to the forefront, is designed to present a feeling rather than a person – it is the mother's protest that is the object of presentative scrutiny, by contrast with the grandfather's pleasure and the child's superstitious apprehension. One thing that these presentations do, therefore, is to shape the text in such a way as to draw attention first and foremost to the narrative setting and its attendant emotions and only secondarily to the actors. They project for the reader an angle of vision.

They also have a purely textual role in that they affect cohesion between sentences or clauses. For example, the fronted object in *Such superstitions my grandfather was all too ready to exploit* makes a close textual linkage, taking the whole of the preceding clause into anaphoric scope. By contrast, the adverbial *Only rarely and on compulsion* actually postpones a linkage which is finally made with *there*. It would have been possible to write *There I ventured only rarely and on compulsion*, making the link immediate, but this apparent textual gain would have necessitated the sacrifice of a thematic marking of *Only rarely and on compulsion*. Another possibility would have been to write *I ventured there only rarely and on compulsion*, but that involves a double loss, of close textual cohesion and of the marked theme.

5.8 Sentence-process and text-process

Perhaps not every text is to be conceived in terms of dramatic actions and relationships, but in most writings there is nonetheless a carefully controlled pattern of changing prominences, a continuous processing of information through the variable plot of syntactic elements. This *text-process* (to risk a nonce-word) derives from the basic *sentence-process* (to venture another) that orders information in a communicative line. At the beginning of this process comes the *theme*, representing a topic or a basis of 'given' information. The theme often corresponds (but by no means invariably, see 5.7) with the syntactic function of subject and (but again, not invariably) with the semantic role of agent. (The components of a sentence can be identified not only in terms of information-processing and syntactic status, but also as *participant roles – eg: agent, recipient, affected item, instrument*, etc.) The informational line extends from the theme and finally homes on to an element identified in the spoken language by the *focus* of intonation and stress.

Elements representing 'new' information or matters of specific comment are therefore usually placed in this focal position at the end of the clause. In *Lord Nelson died at Trafalgar* the word *Trafalgar* would normally have accentual prominence; *Lord Nelson* is the thematic element and *Trafalgar* has the informational focus, as the item that finally brings the message home. A concomitant of *end-focus* is the *end-weight* that often tilts the clause on the predicate side – *eg: Lord Nelson died in the very hour of his triumph at the decisive battle of Trafalgar*. These are facts with important stylistic implications. End-weighting is often a matter of conscious contrivance – *eg* instead of writing *Our sympathetic neighbours helped*, we might prefer *Our neighbours gave their sympathetic help* or *Our neighbours were helpful and sympathetic*. To make a sentence front-heavy, as in *That Homer occasionally nods is a fact*, might be a deliberate stylistic choice, but it carries the risk of ungainliness. The usual tactic is to assign end-focus and end-weight, if necessary by reprocessing an awkward construction. The redesigning may take the form of a so-called *extraposition* (*eg: It is a fact that Homer occasionally nods*), or a *cleft sentence* (*eg: It is Homer who is said to nod occasionally*) or an *existential sentence* (*eg: There are people who say that Homer occasionally nods*). All these forms of focal postponement are discussed below, in 6.9.

In the routine processing of the sentence, information is more or less 'coolly' presented, without urgent nagging at the reader's attentions. A little stylistic heat is generated when the theme–focus relationship is disturbed by inversions and transpositions of various kinds. We have seen how the fronting of objects, complements, or adverbials changes the scheme of prominence with a so-called 'marked theme'. Such thematic shifts may be interpreted in two ways. In certain cases they create a double focus of information, on the shifted element, and on the clause-final item; thus *In the very hour of his triumph Lord Nelson was shot by a French sniper* might be regarded as giving focal prominence to the fronted adverbial, *in the very hour of his triumph*, as well as to *by a French sniper*. In other cases the purport of the shift might be to create a strong end-focus on some important element: note the variable prominence of *a good meal* in the two versions *Eat a good meal three times a day* and *Three times a day eat a good meal*. In the second version the forward shift of *three times a day* has the effect of 'shunting' *a good meal* into a position of sharper focus.

Among other modes of reprocessing information the passive is most notable. It reallocates items occupying thematic and focal positions (*cf: A French sniper shot the good Lord Nelson* with *The good Lord Nelson was shot by a French sniper*) and it also has the important function of reversing the participant roles of agent and affected (*cf: One of my students submitted an excellent essay* with *An excellent essay was submitted by one of my students*). The value of this is that it allows the writer to give end-focus and end-weight to an agentive item; between *Adam ate the apple* and *The apple was eaten by Adam* there may perhaps be little to choose stylistically, but if the agent is elaborately costumed, as in *The apple was eaten by foolish Adam and his equally gullible spouse*, there is an evident advantage in being able to use the passive and so avoid an awkwardly front-heavy construction. It is similarly valuable in reprocessing constructions introduced by a heavily weighted subject in the form of a finite clause; thus a cumbersome sentence such as *His determination to continue with the project regardless of the consequences to himself and his family astonished his colleagues* can be tolerably reshaped with a change into the passive voice: *His colleagues were astonished by his determination to continue with the project regardless of the consequences to himself and his family*.

In the text-process the writer tries to find the most effective combination of sentence-processes, working sometimes with the obstensible 'norms' of unmarked theme, end-focus and end-weight and sometimes with the stylistic variations of the marked theme, shifted or multiple focus, and fronted weight. Perspectives on participant roles keep changing: agency and theme might coincide in one case, while in another the thematic element is non-agentive or the agentive item has the prominence of end-focus. The aim is to manage a sequence of clauses and sentence-structures so that the information they contain is processed continuously, rhythmically, and with emphases that guide the reader in matters of cohesion and perspective. How a text might be well or badly processed is suggested by the two passages in example [14] below. Passage [14i] is a poor piece of textual management; in [14ii] the overall effect is somewhat less awkward:

[14]i *Poor*

That grandfather was so uncompromisingly religious as to bring decent fanaticism into disrepute was our misfortune. His sombre law proscribed all our recreations and simple pleasures, all those pastimes that could relieve the cares of an impoverished household. The devil's bible was what he declared cards to be. The consolation of her favourite game of whist was denied to my poor mother as long as he was present, and it was even a risky venture to play an innocent round of 'beggar-my-neighbour'. He regarded with considerable mistrust the radio, or wireless as it was known in those primitive times, and he frankly condemned as a satanic invention the gramophone. He could be provoked into denunciatory frenzies by one particular record, a setting of Browning's *Cavalier Lyrics*. With the wicked object of sending him stumping off to his room to simmer in Puritan zeal while the rest of us wallowed in our novelettes and dominoes, that record was sometimes played in sheer bravado by my mother. Alcohol of any sort, however, he most utterly detested, and my mother's greatest triumph in her long campaign against his joylessness was that she once managed to make him drunk with a sherry trifle. What he mistook for 'the gravy', to wit the residual liquor with all its headily fragrant sops, he had insisted on finishing, on the severe principle of waste-not-want-not.

ii *Better*

It was our misfortune that grandfather was so uncompromisingly religous as to bring decent fanaticism into disrepute. All our recreations and simple pleasures, all those pastimes that could relieve the cares of an impoverished household, were proscribed by his sombre law. Cards he declared to be the devil's bible. As long as he was present my poor mother was denied the consolation of her favourite game of whist, and even to play an innocent round of 'beggar-my-neighbour' was a risky venture. The radio, or wireless as it was known in those primitive times, was regarded with considerable mistrust, and the gramophone he frankly condemned as a satanic invention. There was one particular record, a setting of Browning's *Cavalier Lyrics*, that could provoke him to denunciatory frenzies. My mother sometimes played it in sheer bravado, with the wicked object of sending him stumping off to his room to simmer in Puritan zeal while the rest of us wallowed in our novelettes and dominoes. What he most utterly detested, however, was alcohol of any sort, and in her long campaign against his joylessness it was my mother's greatest triumph that she once managed to make him drunk with a sherry trifle. On the severe principle of waste-not-want-not, he had insisted on finishing what he mistook for 'the gravy', to wit the residual liquor and all its headily fragrant sops.

In some instances the blunders in [14i] are obvious. One sentence (*With the wicked object of sending him stumping off* . . . etc) is intractably front-heavy; another (*The devil's bible was what he declared cards to be*) is perversely ordered, taking as its theme the item that most obviously calls for focal prominence, and limping away under the hindrance of an awkwardly loaded complement, *ie* the noun clause *what he declared cards to be*. It would clearly be better to write *He declared cards to be the devil's bible*, or, as in [ii], *Cards he declared to be the devil's bible*. There are textual motivations for the fronting of *cards* in [14ii]. It takes its place in a rhetorical pattern marked out by *all our recreations – cards – the radio – the gramophone*, a pattern in which these items stand in the thematic position at the beginning of their respective clauses. The pattern is emphatically changed towards the end of the passage, when the word *alcohol*, instead of being presented thematically as might be expected (*eg: Alcohol was what he most detested*), is given the prominence of end-focus in *What he most utterly detested, however, was alcohol*.

Comparison of the two passages might further suggest that there is a certain hazard in assigning stylistic values to structures out of context; values are always relative to the immediate purpose or to the textual environment. For example, [14ii] makes effective use of an extraposition in the opening sentence (*It was our misfortune that* . . . etc), where the carefully organized postponement gives prominence to a paradoxical joke – that 'fanaticism' is preferable to a certain kind of 'uncompromising religion'. Example [14i] spoils the joke by embarking ponderously on a front-weighted structure with a long finite clause as its subject. Here, then, the postponing device of extraposition seems to be a useful tactic because it shifts weight conveniently to the end of the clause. Yet at a later point in the text, where [14i] uses an extraposition, *ie: it was even a risky venture to play an innocent round of 'beggar-my-neighbour'*, [14ii] is at pains to avoid it, with the delibrate front-weighting of *even to play an innocent round of 'beggar-my-neighbour' was a risky venture*. This is almost certainly an attempt to balance coordinated clauses by counterpoising the end-weight of the first (. . . *the consolation of her favourite game of whist*) with the front-weight of the second (*and even to play an innocent round of 'beggar-my-neighbour'* . . .). Obedience to the rhythmic pulse of the text might well be a reason for front-weighting.

Here and there the choice of a sentence-form is apparently open to argument. Though we have tried above to explain the use of the passive inversion in the second sentence of [14ii] as a pattern-setting construction, it is still possible that the corresponding active version, as in [14i] might be substituted without loss of tension in the text. Another debatable instance is the sentence reading, in [14ii], *There was one particular record, a setting of Browning's 'Cavalier Lyrics', that could provoke him to denunciatory frenzies*. Perhaps this is not greatly superior to the form in [14i], or to a reading *One particular record . . . could provoke him to denunciatory frenzies*. However, in [14ii] the existential construction *There was . . .* etc puts a primary focus on the phrase *one particular record*. The ensuing parenthesis (*a setting of Browning's 'Cavalier Lyrics'*) actually sharpens the focus by isolating the phrase from the clause it governs. That clause (*that could provoke him to denunciatory frenzies*) then follows its own pattern of emphasis and presents us with a secondary focus (as it were) on *denunciatory frenzies*. The sentence might well be cast in this form because it facilitates the dual focus, on two important phrases. It seems the strongest option at that point in the text, though of course it is not necessarily the one indispensable version.

5.9 Branching

It is evident that composition regularly involves choices of syntactic arrangement – fronting, transpositions, cleft constructions, etc. One recurrent compositional choice determines the arrangement of subordinate or attributive elements round a central core: the positioning of modifiers before or after a phrase head, the patterning of adverbials round the subject-verb node of a clause, the placing of subordinate clauses in relationship to the principal clause. The latter in particular is often denoted by the conveniently figurative term *branching*.

In the construction of a complex sentence, subordinate clauses may be left-branching from the stem of the main clause, or make a right branch, or be left- and right-branching, or even cleave the stem with a so-called mid-branch. The possibilities are briefly illustrated in the following examples where *the sheriff took no action* is in each case the stem of the sentence:

[15]i   *Left-branching:* Despite the reports coming in from all sides, the sheriff took no action.

ii   *Right-branching:* The sheriff took no action, believing that winter and rough weather would make short work of the outlaws.

iii   *Left-and-right branching:* Despite the reports coming in from all sides the sheriff took no action, believing that winter and rough weather would make short work of the outlaws.

iv   *Mid-branching:* The sheriff, believing despite the reports coming in from all sides that winter and rough weather would make short work of the outlaws, took no action.

5.10 Left-branching

The stylistic effect of left-branching is to make the reader wait for completed information. In some cases it may seem that the writer deliberately teases his reader by postponing the presentation of essential matter; at the same time, he forces him to bear in mind points of contributory information that accumulate as he works his way from branch to stem:

[16]   If they had all been captured, no hope of rescue would have remained. With this possibility in mind, Robin had posted half a dozen men near the town gate. Escaping into the forest, where small groups of outlaws were still lurking, this rearguard managed to summon reinforcements.

Here the branches in the first two sentences are simple, but in the third sentence we find a more elaborate example: *Escaping into the forest, where small groups of outlaws were still lurking.* This contains quite a lot of contributory information (they escaped – they went into the forest – there were outlaws in the forest – no large bands, only small groups – the outlaws did not show themselves openly, they lurked) and the reader has to keep this in reckoning while the construction homes on to the central point, *ie* that the escaping men were able to summon reinforcements. The fact that he is a *reader*, with a text conveniently laid out before his eyes, relieves him of what would otherwise be a burden of memorizing, of storage, as it were. Indeed, for this very reason left-branching is a device better adapted to writing than to speech.

Elaborate left-branching presents stylistic problems, however. Even though script or print relieve the memory, long left branches are still a psychological burden if they are not kept under close control:

[17] Knowing how popular Robin Hood was among the common people and how he could always slip quietly away into Sherwood where his pursuers would be hampered by their ignorance of the terrain and their inability to adapt to the conditions of guerrilla warfare, the sheriff decided to take no immediate action.

Obviously no effort of memory is required here, because a reader can at need retrace the course of the sentence; but that in itself is an annoyance, and the writer may want to find some way of putting the elaborately stored items into a more convenient order. One way of lightening the burden a little would be to make the whole of the left branch a pattern of complex noun phrases, asyndetically coordinated, and to lead this pattern to an appositional node, thus (the vital apposition is italicized):

[18] Robin Hood's popularity among the common people, his ability to slip away quietly into Sherwood, his pursuers' ignorance of the terrain, their failure to adapt to the conditions of guerrilla warfare – *all these considerations* persuaded the sheriff to take no immediate action.

The dramatic breaking off and resumption of the subject might not be to everyone's taste; some may find it too bold, others merely banal, an orator's commonplace. However, it does have the effect of bringing a little order into the store with a neatly arranged catalogue of items and a clear identifying label (*all these considerations*). One of the faults of [17] is that its subordinations (*where his pursuers* etc) lure the reader gradually into byways where the clear path of the sentence is lost. The ranked noun phrases of [18] eliminate this confusion. The parallel constructions trace and retrace the path, marking syntactic time until that decisive apposition gives the signal to move forward.

Parallel surbordinate clauses marked by a recurrent conjunction would produce a similar effect:

[19] Because Robin Hood was popular with the common people, because he could always slip quietly away into Sherwood, because his pursuers were ignorant of the terrain, because, above all else, they could not adapt to the conditions of guerrilla warfare, the sheriff decided to take no immediate action.

Here the phrase *above all else*, giving climactic emphasis to the fourth clause in the set, has something of the summary force possessed by the apposition *all these considerations* in [18]. It would in fact be possible to combine two methods, using the parallel-clause technique of [19] and the strongly defined apposition of [18]:

[20] Because Robin Hood was popular with the common people, because he could always slip quietly away into Sherwood, because his pursuers were ignorant of the terrain, because, indeed, they could not adapt to the conditions of guerrilla warfare – for all these reasons the sheriff decided to take no immediate action.

This gives two signals that the branch is about to join the parent stem – the first and weaker of the two in the disjunct *indeed* and the stronger in *for all these reasons*.

5.11 Right-branching

Right-branching sentences track outwards from the stem, in a procedure that to reader and writer alike may seem more natural, because more amenable to the habit of human thought than the left-branching arrangement. The left branch asks the reader in effect to store information; not so the right branch, which handles information cumulatively without imposing this burden of storage:

[21] My father endured the night shift for thirteen years, hating the inversion of his life, lamenting always the loss of good daylight hours necessarily given over to sleep, missing the company of his children, for we were off to school very shortly after he got home in the morning and off to bed an hour or more before he left the house at night. Yet 'being on nights' brought him some

kind of satisfaction, whether in the comradely sense of belonging to a special club, or because the more reflective types, the reading-and-thinking men, tended to gravitate to the night shift, or because the shipyard at night could at times be a strangely beautiful place.

Both sentences here have long right branches. The contrast between information carried and information accumulated will be apparent if we take the first sentence and rewrite it, following a left-branching scheme, thus: *Hating the inversion of his life, lamenting always the loss of good daylight hours necessarily given over to sleep, missing the company of his children, for we were off to school very shortly after he got home in the morning and off to bed an hour or more before he left the house at night, my father endured the night shift for thirteen years.* So arranged, the sentence presents a drama with a dénouement; we have to wait, patiently bearing all the details in mind, until the finale unmasks the mystery. With the right-branching arrangement there is a radical difference in the processing of information. The text as it stands presents us with a general statement (*My father endured the night shift for thirteen years*) followed by a sequence of items, a commentary as it were, providing the particulars underlying the statement. In a narrower sense, perhaps, we are given an analysis of the meaning of *endured* in this context – it embraces *hating*, *lamenting*, and *missing*.

The second sentence illustrates the tendency of the right branch to twine into thickets of reference. Though the tendency is fairly well controlled in this instance, there is always a danger that syntax will overgrow semantics, *ie* that the sentence will be allowed to run on when meaning might be better served by a break and a new sentence. This tendency can be countered if right branches are constructed in such an orderly fashion (through parallels, recursions, etc) that digressions are properly monitored. Severe formality is not necessary. The following example may appear to develop casually and digressively, but the branch is always under firm syntactic control:

[22] My car stands out there by the gate, nibbled with age, scabbed with rust, its chrome pockmarked, its paintwork begrimed, the nearside hubcaps dented in testimony to my approximate parking, the lid of the boot still bearing the scar sustained when the garage door – going up and over and finally coming off the runners – fell on it with a dull dismaying crunch.

The participial clauses between dashes (*going up and over and finally coming off the runners*) are symptomatic of a digressive tendency here. Indeed, at that point in the sentence attention is shifting from the present state of the car to an episode in its history, and it therefore might have been better policy to make a sentence break, say after *parking*. As the passage stands, however, participial clauses in successive manipulations and expansions have been made to take a cohesive grip on the whole, so that the sentence develops continuously, without awkward turns round corners of reference. The parallel clauses *nibbled with age* and *scabbed with rust*, with *car* as their antecedent subject, are followed by two further parallels, each with a new subject – *its chrome pockmarked, its paintwork begrimed*. The next participial clause again has a new subject, but adds to the pattern an extended predicate – *the nearside hubcaps dented in testimony to my approximate parking*; and in the next the predicate extends even more, into a cleft pattern of subordinate clauses, while there is a further innovation, the introduction of the present participle in place of the past participle – *the lid of the boot still bearing the scar sustained when the garage door . . . fell on it, etc.* It is this last and most extended development of the text-governing participial construction that makes a bridge between the part of the sentence that describes the car and the part that begins to describe what happened to the car. The example shows how it is possible for a long right branch to run on through a continuum of references, provided that its syntax is trained to some kind of directive framework.

5.12 Mid-branching: multiple (left- and right-) branching

Sentences may be designedly cleft by long interruptive (or suspensive) mid-branches, and sentence stems may have branches running to left and right. The following narrative illustrates these possibilities:

[23] Somewhere in southern Sweden, at the edge of twilight, in a terrain where the faint undulations of the land rock the traveller gently and bemusedly from one isolated farmstead to another, my car began to make signals of discontent. Swaying and fluttering in dainty wisps and fringes, a tassel of steam rose from the bonnet, changing presently into a ribbon and then

into a woolly white scarf that muffled the windscreen and flapped gaily on the passing breeze. I stopped the car and listened with painful intensity, searching the silence for the faintest excuse to leap out and make further observations from the shelter of some comfortably remote ditch. I am not in sympathy with motor vehicles. Being largely ignorant of their workings and deplorably unresponsive to their basic needs, I am inclined to regard them as malevolent wantons, nasty, perverse, rebellious, the potentially destructive offspring of dwarves and cantankerous fairies, ready at the merest whim to seize up or blow up. It did not occur to me, such was my presumption of the complex, violent, self-delighting and totally inexplicable waywardness of the internal combustion engine, that I had simply forgotten to top up the radiator.

Any floridity of style here arises from the determination to train branches to left, right, or centre, wherever branches might be persuaded to grow; however, this extravagance perhaps fits the orotund humour of the piece. One short sentence (*I am not in sympathy with motor vehicles*) eases the general density of texture. The remaining sentences are all complex stem-and-branch constructions. Mid-branching occurs in the first sentence and the last, where the protracted and teasing interruptions (*at the edge of twilight . . . to another; such was my presumption . . . internal combustion engine*) deliberately keep the reader in suspense, creating tensions that are humorously dissipated (*eg* by the banal conclusion *I had simply forgotten to top up the radiator*). One sentence (*I stopped the car, etc*) has an elaborate right branch; two others (*Swaying and fluttering in dainty wisps, etc; Being largely ignorant of their workings, etc*) are left- and right-branching, and it will be noticed how in these cases the right branch is the more elaborate structure, trained to a carefully devised syntactic frame (*eg* the pattern of expanding appositions in *nasty, perverse, rebellious, the potentially destructive offspring . . . ready at the merest whim to seize up or blow up*).

5.13 The rhythmic pattern of the text

An interesting feature of [23], and one that was certainly not foreseen in the writing of the passage, is that the sentences in their expansion or contraction obey something like a symmetrical impulse. The design of the text, unconsciously achieved, can be outlined as follows:

[24] sentence 1   mid-branching
      sentence 2   left- and right- branching
      sentence 3   right-branching
      sentence 4   simple
      sentence 5   left- and right-branching
      sentence 6   mid-branching

With one more sentence, a right-branching construction (or, with a twist in the design, a left-branching pattern) following sentence 4, the text would have been completely symmetrical in its distribution of sentence-types. Alternatively, the symmetry would have been complete had sentence 3 been omitted; but the awkward fact is that sentence 3 is necessary because it conveys an indispensable piece of information, *ie: I stopped the car*. In any event, the text as it stands has in it balance and regularity enough to suggest that even when writing to a recipe we instinctively try to adapt sentence-structure to the overall rhythm of a passage.

The rhythm in this example is created by the branches in their alternating positions. Word-counts present a crude but nonetheless interesting pointer to prosodic value; for example sentence 2 has a left branch of 8 words and a right branch of 23, while its correspondent in the textual pattern (sentence 5) has 13 words in the left branch and in the right branch an exactly equivalent 23. The right branch of sentence 3 is 22 words in length, and the mid-branches of the first and last sentences have 27 and 19 words respectively. (This tends to confirm a subjective impression that the mid-branch in the first sentence is just a little too long.) In short, the examples of respective types of branch are of more or less equivalent length, suggesting that the matching and differing branch-lengths operate in this text much as identical and contrasting line-lengths might operate in a piece of verse.

Of course such raw word-counts may reflect purely fortuitous symmetries. Yet they are striking enough to encourage belief in a kinaesthetic faculty, a censor in the mind, informed and trained by much practice, keeping watch over the prosodic development of the text, trimming or rearranging sentences to follow a rhythmic outline. Text rhythms are very hard to define objectively (other than by example) and present themselves in many variations; of the passages composed for illustrative purposes in this chapter, several have distinctive rhythms (*eg* [5], [6], [9], [10], [13], [19]) though it might well be difficult to identify their individual character in terms less impressionistic than 'flowing', 'staccato', 'even', etc. Nevertheless, examination of these passages should confirm that there is a relationship between the rhythmic procedures of a text and the supposed intention of its author to convey a posture, reflect or evoke a state of mind, echo sensory impressions, or otherwise express a personality in confrontation with a theme. In the choices a writer makes as he designs a text that confrontation is always apparent, and in the confrontation with a theme another encounter is implicit: that of writer and reader.

Chapter 6

The writer to his reader

Though the writer necessarily works alone, mumbling in fretful solitude, his writing, like any other form of communication, presupposes and audience; even the diarist in his self-communing has half an eye on that other self who will open the book tomorrow or next year and read his outpourings with the critical interest of a stranger. What is written may be destined to remain forever unread, yet we always assume a reader and put ourselves to considerable trouble for his sake. Confusions and ambiguities are patiently eliminated, connections are demonstrated, a programme of information is put into order. In short, the writer is at pains to make his work lucid and effortlessly intelligible, knowing that the reader cannot make use of those situational and personal promptings that help him through the transactions of speech.

This is a primary aspect of the writer–reader relationship, and what it amounts to is really a strict observation of professional courtesies; the reader's collaboration may be invited, but he cannot be expected to mend the defects of a shoddy textual fabric. There is, however, a further aspect of the relationship, and one that is of equal importance. The writer usually tries to establish a role and a tone of voice, suggesting to the reader a form of working agreement generally reflective of social conventions. If this rapport is successful, the reader can begin to 'understand' the writer in something more than a technical sense. He puts aside his resistance to the cold intrusiveness of the stranger-in-print, and responds to the appeal of a personality.

6.1 Roles

The masks in writing are many, but all performances can be said to be variations of four roles: the *informant*, the *instructor*, the *disputant*, and the *entertainer*. The following examples illustrate primary distinctions in role-playing:

[1]i *(The informant)*

As the name implies, watercolour paints require no diluent medium other than water. They consist of finely-ground pigments suspended in a soluble gum, and they have two notable characteristics that necessarily determine the painter's technique. One is that they dry very quickly, which means that the artist has little or no room for mistakes; watercolours cannot be corrected in the same way that oils, so long in the drying, can be corrected. The other is that they are transparent (in varying degrees), so that the picture is lit by the whiteness of the supporting paper, or subtly graded in tone by the overlay of one colour upon another. In classic watercolour technique, the picture is made by laying successive washes in broad outline. The watercolour landscape, with its near-and-far pattern of hedgerows and woods and hillside fields, may seem to be very intricately worked, but examination will often show that these effects are produced by simple washes of varying intensity.

ii *(The instructor)*

For a variety of effects – *eg* representing the texture of a roughly-plastered wall, or tree-bark, or the feathered edges of clouds, or the sparkle of light on water – the so-called 'dry brush' technique is invaluable. Practise this one some spare pieces of good rough-surfaced watercolour paper. First fill your brush with paint, and then shed the bulk of the water, either by gently pressing the brush against the palette or by very cautiously pinching and rolling it between the fingers. (The latter is not a standard method, but it provides an accurate if messy gauge of the wetness of the brush.) Next, drag the brush quite lightly over the paper, painting with the side rather than the tip. The 'de-watered' pigment will be deposited unevenly, taking those parts of the paper where the texture is raised, but not flowing into the depressions. Tiny points of untouched white paper or little patches of an underlaid colour then shine through the pigment, suggesting the glitter of the sunlit sea or the crumbling surface of that old wall.

iii *(The disputant)*

It is becoming fashionable to talk of a return to representational painting, implying that abstract art has been a profitless aberration. This implication is misleading, on two counts. In the first place, representational or figurative painting has never been wholly abandoned; in the very rage of abstraction there have always been some painters of landscape or still life or the human form, just as in periods of free verse there have been poets, and good poets too, who have preferred to continue exploratively the traditions of rhyme and metre. Secondly, and this is really the crux of the argument, there is no case for assuming that abstraction and representation are irreconcilable modes of painting. The position is, rather, that they are alternative accounts of the same set of phenomena, and are thus implicitly related.

A figurative painting may be 'about' spaces and intervals, for example, no less emphatically than an abstract. In the one case, however, the spatial rhythms (as the art critics might say) are conveyed through the positioning of human figures, natural objects, domestic articles, etc, while in the other the elements in composition are lines, geometrical shapes, irregular patches, with no apparent reference to the world of our everyday seeing. The figurative artist offers us a plot, as it were, in the reading of which we discover, if we are perceptive, an informing theme. The abstract painter, on the other hand, ignores the particular embodiment of a principle; grammarian or physicist rather than story-teller, he attempts to state in the simplest and most powerful way laws of perceptual and pictorial patterning.

The imagination is not thereby impoverished or limited. The viewer is still free to construct whatever plot he chooses upon the abstract theme, and for this reason alone abstract paintings which may at first seem coldly unpoetic, not to say trite, can wear rather well. They generate images in the mind's eye, they coalesce with certain archetypal symbols and evoke the feelings associated with those symbols. In these respects a good abstract can educate us visually and emotionally. By contrast, the figurative painting may go dead on the wall, inhibiting the imagination and limiting response by its very explicitness, unless the painter is able to achieve a resolution of many variables – of the abstract properties of shape, proportion, interval, angular and planar relationship, etc, plus the sensual properties of colour, light and texture.

iv *(The entertainer)*

It always takes a certain amount of nerve to settle down in a public place with your easel or your drawing board, but if you go painting in a waterside meadow on a bank holiday you need a lot more than nerve, you need a hidalgo's courtesy, a martyr's patience and a fine knockabout sense of humour. Let that field be never so empty when you pick your spot, by the time you have started to paint you will have an audience of grubby-handed children, resting their sharp little chins on your working shoulder and wanting to know if you are an artist. That is a difficult question to answer, since it usually brings ambition into abrupt conflict with truth. When the children tire of you their parents will come to peer benevolently and blankly at your work while they tell you all about the lovely Kodak they bought for twelve pounds, it makes lovely pictures and the colours are lovely, oh, absolutely lovely, and it's so simple, none of this messing with paints and water, of course they realise why you do it, it's because you're an artist. After that they send their dogs to knock over your water-bottle and snuffle around among your paints and get their eager muzzles bedaubed with yellow ochre and Payne's grey, and you can guess that those jaunty bow-wows are telling themselves what a fine thing it is to be an artist. The one extraordinary thing about all this is that you are the only citizen in the field whose privacy is not strictly respected. The lovers by the far hedgerow are treated with such delicacy that the very cows retire to a distant corner, and as for the fisherman, he enjoys a monastic seclusion so austere that no one dares to walk within five yards of him, let alone send a dog to trample among the maggots and the sandwiches; but the whole bank holiday world will actually leave its motor car and make a pilgrimage, on foot, across a field, to peer at you and prod you into conversation because it hopes you are an artist.

The affinity of roles in [1i] and [1ii] will be immediately apparent. To inform often implies a kind of instruction, and here, in [1i], the implication is clear; from the characteristics of watercolours some recommendations for use are inferred. However, there is no assumption that the reader will put the recommendations into practice, whereas [1ii] is based on the supposition that he has a practical interest in the matter and requires specific instructions on a detail of technique. Parts of [1ii] (notably the last sentence) suggest the informant, while parts of [1i] (for example the penultimate sentence) nod in the direction of the instructor; each passage, though, has a principal role which is not usurped by its corollary. A common characteristic of the two texts is that they assume (however tactfully) a dominance over the reader. The writer is the guide and counsellor who says, in effect, 'this is what I know and you do not', or 'this is what I can do and you cannot'. His position of authority is also apparent in a text like [1iii]. This conducts its argument as though conveying unchallengeably correct information; the disputant role is quasi-informant. In a sense the passage also instructs us, not in the performance of an act or process, but in the formation of our views. The message here is 'this is what I think and you ought to think' – a stance no less dominant than that of [1i] and [1ii].

In this respect (as of course in several others) [1i], [1ii], and [1iii] make a sharp contrast with [1iv], where the writer's posture is not at all dominant, but rather *appellant*. The entertainer (perhaps with some show of modesty) puts himself at the service of his public, declaring explicitly or implicitly that his only purpose is to distract, to make a hard world easier by putting on shows that will move the beholder to laughter or tears. Far from dominating his readers, he coaxes them into sharing his own reflections and discoveries, and if necessary casts himself in the role of the inferior, the victim for whom the reader may feel an indulgent sympathy. The entertainer always keeps this appellant character, even when he is strutting for all he is worth. As soon as the performance stops deferring to the reader, as soon as the jokes become deliberately sophisticated, the allusions designedly recondite, the imagery wilfully obscure, the writer begins to dominate his audience and the 'entertainment' becomes a distorted and perverse form of instruction.

Roles are reflected in details of language and style, though the indices by which we recognize them may also be the symptoms of 'tone' (see below, 6.3, 6.4, 6.5), or at any rate of tone-within-role. In [1] above, a few textual features can be identified as exponents of role. Passage [1i], for example, turns on constructions such as *they have two characteristics, one is . . . which means, the other is . . . so that, but examination will show,* constructions which are symptomatic of the author's 'informant' posture. The instructor writing in [1ii] uses the enumerative markers of a process (*first, then, next*); he uses imperatives, often heavily amplified by dependent constructions (*practise . . . fill . . . shed . . . drag . . .*); he makes use of the manner adverbials that characterize a recommendation (*gently, very cautiously, quite lightly*); and where necessary he formulates very specifically, either by adding or excluding alternatives (*pinching and rolling, with the side rather than the tip*).

The disputant attitude of [1iii] is most obviously reflected in terms expressive of listing, asserting, and contrasting: *eg: on two counts, in the first place, secondly, there is no case, rather, in the one case . . . in the other, on the other hand, by contrast.* The interruptive patterning of the text (on interruptives see above, 2.9) is clear enough. A subtler element, perhaps, is represented by the grammar of possibility and the vocabulary of seeming: *may be, may at first seem, may go dead on the wall, can wear rather well, can educate us, whatever plot he chooses, if we are perceptive, with no apparent reference.* There are two voices in the text, the one confidently assertive, imposing on the reader the structure of an argument, the other prudent and concessive, inviting the reader's assent, blandly hedging the writer's position. In other words this passage, like many samples of disputant prose, prepares a line of defence behind its line of attack.

The role-markers of example [1iv] are textural rather than textual; the passage depends on a jocular mimesis, the creation of a humorous masquerade. One typical symptom of this masquerading is the expression *a hidalgo's courtesy*; another is the reference to the fisherman's *monastic seclusion.* The reader is well aware that the fisherman is no more like a monk than the bank-holiday painter is like a Spanish grandee, but there is an appeal to him to accept the pantomimic incongruity, the comedy of postures. The verbal buffoonery (*jaunty bow-wows, the very cows retire, make a pilgrimage, on foot, across a field*) would scarcely be tolerable if the writer were appearing in any role other than that of entertainer; nor would the freewheeling swoops from a burlesquing of high-style syntax (*Let that field be never so empty*) to a deadpan-dandy turn of phrase (*brings ambition into abrupt conflict with truth*) or an impromptu flight of mimicry (*it makes lovely pictures and the colours are lovely, etc*). Here is a coat of many textures which only the would-be comedian can venture to wear.

6.2 Role shifts

The writer's task is frequently complicated by the requirement (no less awkward for being self-imposed) to play two or three roles simultaneously, or in rotations and overlaps. Passages [1i] and [1ii] above, for example, might occur in the same chapter of a manual on the elements of watercolour painting. Here is a text in which the writer commits himself to constant shifts of role:

[2] Charcoal (generally labelled 'willow charcoal') is sold in the form of brittle twiglets that leave their smudgy mark first on the user's hands and then, if he is not very careful, on the wrong parts of his drawing. Those who dislike having to work surrounded by cloths and cleaning tissues can buy their charcoal in pencil form, but experience may show that the clean pencil is artistically inferior to the grubby twig. The grade of charcoal in the pencil is normally harder than in the willow sticks, and that wooden case which so conveniently protects hands, clothes and furniture also has the inconvenient effect of limiting the technical range of the implement.

The twigs of charcoal have something of the versatility of the brush. They are in general rather soft, and respond sensitively (if at times friably!) to pressures which vary the thickness and intensity of line and shade. They are not pointed uniformly, like a pencil, but can freely be rubbed into tips of varying length and shape – indeed, the shapes change, tantalisingly and productively, as the work proceeds. They can, furthermore, be broken into short stubs of differing lengths, the whole stub being rolled or dragged sideways across the paper in broad sweeps. The charcoal stub may imitate the diffusions of the brush, or, at the user's will, can make the angled incisions of the pencil.

There is a peculiarly sensuous pleasure, a mud-pie pleasure almost, in making a charcoal drawing. The feeling of being in intimate contact with the work is very pronounced, possibly because the stubs of charcoal are so short and soft that the draughtsman has the sense of drawing with his fingers, or squeezing onto the paper those velvety gradations of tone. But this should never mean that the exercise becomes a self-indulgent romp. The drawing is built up carefully. A background is blocked in, using the side of the charcoal under

light pressure, to make bold shapes. This foundation can be
dusted over lightly with a clean cloth or tissue, or gently
smudged and 'sculpted' with the fingers or a scroll of card;
experiment will reveal ways of creating a misty softness
tenanted by shapes that loom or recede. The foreground is
worked in under harder pressure. Details are drawn as though
with a pencil, but broad tonal masses continue to be laid in
with the side of the stick. A plastic eraser is useful for picking
out highlights, and it is remarkable what a variety of effects
can be achieved, from the glare of a car's headlamps to the soft
gleam of light on a tree-trunk. Work boldly all the time.
Charcoal is within reason a forgiving medium, and mistakes
can be gently smudged away or taken out with the eraser –
though excessive correction will change romantic chiaroscuro
into dim industrial grime. Remember, finally, that because of
the instability of the medium the drawing will need to be
fixed; one of the modern aerosol fixatives will do this very
well.

The roles change, affably, from paragraph to paragraph, from
sentence to sentence, sometimes from phrase to phrase. The writer
begins as informant, telling us a little about the appearance and
properties of artist's charcoal. Behind some pronouncements,
however, lurks the shadow of the instructor; *eg: They are not pointed
uniformly . . . but can freely be rubbed,* etc, *They can . . . be broken into short
stubs . . . the whole stub being rolled or dragged sideways,* etc, *The charcoal stub
may imitate . . . or, at the user's will, can make,* etc. In these sentences,
which occur consecutively at the end of the second paragraph, there
are gestures of instruction, though the modals *can* and *may* suggest
that the role is still that of informant.

In the course of the next paragraph the instructor-spirit gradually
prevails, declaring itself openly in the imperative *Work boldly all the
time.* An important step in the direction of this clear imperative is
taken via constructions with the passive voice and the 'instructional'
present tense: *The drawing is built up, A background is blocked in, The
foreground is worked in,* etc. These have a curious ambivalence as
indicators of role, since they figure intermediately between the
potential-expressing modal (*The drawing can be built up, A background
may be blocked in*) and the command-expressing imperative (*Build up the
drawing, Block in the background*). One incidental point of lexical interest
is the apparent association of phrasal verbs – *build up, block in, dust over,*

work in, lay in, pick out, smudge away, take out – with the instructor role. Even in this final paragraph, however, the instructor does not altogether banish the informant, whose presence continues to be glimpsed in expressions suggesting option or potential, *eg: experiment will reveal ways of creating a misty softness, mistakes can be gently smudged away.*

Throughout the passage, while informant is gradually yielding to instructor, the entertainer makes frequent short entrances, appealing to the reader with turns of rhetoric, brief essays in mild humour, even touches of poetry. The passage begins, in fact, with a sentence that might well be the curtain-raiser to a piece on Messing About With Charcoal. Thereafter the entertainer appears sporadically, in bursts of phrase: *the clean pencil is artistically inferior to the grubby twig, respond sensitively (if at times friably!), may imitate the diffusions of the brush, or . . . can make the angled incisions of the pencil, a mud-pie pleasure, squeezing onto the paper those velvety gradations of tone, a misty softness tenanted by shapes that loom or recede, change romantic chiaroscuro into dim industrial grime.* It is more than possible that with such decorative turns of phrase the writer entertains himself as much as his reader; they express a pleasure in language that relieves the tedium of exposition. A further possibility however, and a very interesting one, is that they have a distractive function, like a stage magician's patter, tending to draw the reader's eye away from the essential process of the text, which is the transition from informant-posture to instructor-posture. Language is used to disorientate the reader for the reader's own good – a technique of kindly confusion that ought to be familiar to students of literature, though it does not seem to be much explored in writings on literary style.

6.3 Tones

The writer, then, may choose to vary and complicate his role-playing. A further complication is added with the choice of a style of address, a *tone* as we shall call it here. Let us consider first a passage in which the writer assumes the role of instructor, conveying his instructions in a tone that might suggest the easy give-and-take of everyday colloquy:

[3] You can't paint watercolours without knowing how to lay a wash, though anyone can learn the knack if they are willing to

go to a bit of trouble. People have their own fads about the drill, but my method seems to work as well as anyone's, so here it is.

You'll need plenty of paint, a good big brush (remember, sables are the best) and a heavy paper. If you're going to use a light paper, you'll have to stretch it first. Unstretched paper cockles, and that's the end of your flat wash.

Pin or tape your paper to the drawing-board – I always tape mine, it stays flatter that way – and then damp it *very* lightly with your sponge. (Some people don't do this, but I find it helpful.) Don't overdo this pre-wetting, and don't be so hamfisted with your sponge that you scrub the skin off the paper.

Hold your board at a horizontal angle of about 30 degrees, fill your brush, and run a broad, steady stroke across the top of your sheet. As soon as you do this you'll find that the paint starts to run down, but you'll see that it 'hangs' in a kind of long bead where the brush leaves off. Before that bead can break up, smartly fill the brush again and with your next stroke aim to overlap the first, picking up the bead and pushing it on down the paper.

You go on like that till you've reached the bottom, and that's all there is to it. When you first try, your colour will probably be rather uneven and tide-marked, but before long you'll be able to lay a perfectly flat wash every time.

In its directness of address (the pronouns are symptomatic) this is strikingly casual; it might, indeed, be a transcript of comments accompanying a demonstration lesson in the classroom. There is a warmth, an intimacy that depends on the mimicry of speech-style and an almost studied rejection of literary etiquette. It conveys an impression of the matter-of-fact and concrete, sometimes with a luckily precise phrase, *eg: scrub the skin off the paper*, and in other instances more fumblingly, *eg: it 'hangs' in a kind of long bead* – indeed, it has the casual colloquial habit of taking the hits with the misses. The level of casualness is however, quite carefully judged, and the breeziest expressions of colloquial intimacy are avoided (*Worried about laying a wash when you have to? No sweat! It's different strokes for different folks, but here's how I do mine*). The impression of planned informality can in fact be related to a quite complicated interplay of grammatical, lexical, and typographical features, but let us defer technical analyses and proceed to a second example, in which the instructor presents the same topic in quite a different tone:

[4] To lay a wash is a fundamental technical accomplishment which requires no more than a few hours' patient practice. As to method, though it may not answer in detail to the recommendations of some authorities, the following procedure is representative. Its prerequisites are a generous quantity of paint, a large brush of good quality, preferably sable, and either a paper sufficiently heavy to withstand wetting or one that has been stretched for the purpose. No wash can be laid effectively on a light unstretched paper, since the surface will be distorted by the first influx of watercolour.

The paper is pinned or taped to the drawing board, tape giving the better guarantee of an even tension, and a sponge is used to moisten the surface very lightly. In carrying out this helpful if not universally recommended preliminary, care must be taken not to soak the paper and not to damage a textured surface through excessively heavy applications of the sponge.

The board should be inclined at an angle of 30 degrees from the horizontal and the brush, charged with pigment, is drawn across the top of the paper in a single broad, steady stroke. Colour will immediately begin to flow down the incline, lying in suspension where the brush-stroke ends. While the flow is still suspended, the brush is quickly re-charged and a second stroke, slightly overlapping the first, sets in motion a further flow leading to a further suspension. Thus the paint is laid on in successive swathes until the process is completed. First attempts may well yield unsatisfactory results in the form of uneven and discontinuous areas of colour, but the skill of laying a perfectly flat wash at need will be acquired within quite a short time.

The contrast with [3] is marked in every sentence of this revision by formalities verging on the pompous. It is not only the vocabulary that has been academicized (*fundamental, recommendation, procedure, prerequisite, influx, preliminary, application, incline, suspension, discontinuous,* etc), giving the passage an air of the abstract and impersonal. The syntax also wears an academic look. Gone is the direct pronominal attack, and the text proceeds fastidiously through sequences of passive constructions. Gone too are the abrupt parenthesis and the trailing afterthought (*remember, sables are the best; I always tape mine, it stays flatter that way*); the instructor in this new version scrupulously contrives syntactic continuities and integrations (*a large brush of good quality, preferably sable; the paper is pinned or taped . . . tape giving the better guarantee of an even tension*). In sum, the text works efficiently enough at the task of instruction, but presents its reader-pupil with a face that is composed, ceremonious, and perhaps a little austere.

The slapaway casualness of [3] and the pallid formality of [4] represent extremes of tone. The writer's problem is generally one of finding a middle way, a stylistic compromise that will unite formality's careful composition and power of abstraction with informality's warmth and directness. There are doubtless many possibilities of striking a tonal mean; here is one attempt:

[5] It is not difficult to lay a wash, and no more than an hour or two of patient practice should be needed to acquire this basic skill. Methods may vary a little, but the one suggested here is a typical routine. For it we shall require a generous quantity of paint, a large brush of the best quality (which means, of course, sable) and a heavy paper, or one that has been properly stretched. Light unstretched paper will cockle, making the task of laying an even wash quite impossible.

The best way of fastening one's paper to the drawing board is to seal all the edges with adhesive tape; drawing pins are less satisfactory because they do not keep the working surface so evenly stretched. It is a helpful practice, though not one that is always recommended, to ease some of the resistance out of the surface by sponging it very lightly. In doing this be careful not to soak the paper, and at all costs avoid rubbing with the sponge. Rubbing will pulp the fine texture of a good paper.

Tilting the board at an angle of approximately thirty degrees from the horizontal, fill the brush and draw it in one broad steady stroke across the top of the paper. The paint will immediately begin to flow and will form a long rill at the bottom edge of this first stroke. As quickly as possible, refill the brush and with a second, slightly overlapping stroke chivvy the paint one brush-width further down the tilted sheet. A third stroke moves the rill yet again, and so we continue until the wash is complete. At first it may seem very difficult to paint evenly and not to leave brush-marks, but before long it should be possible to lay a perfectly flat wash whenever one is needed.

Here a prominent symptom of the instructor's clear wish to appeal to his audience as fellow workers rather than as pupils is the occasional use of the pronoun *we*. Further signs of this collaborative intent are that the vocabulary – in comparison with that of [4] – has come down off its high discursive horse, and that the idiom is generally more relaxed (*cf: methods may vary a little* with *as to method, though it may not answer in detail to the recommendations of some authorities*) and more concrete (*cf: chivvy the paint one brush-width further down* with *sets in motion a further flow leading to a further suspension*) without drifting into the approximations of the casual style (*cf: will form a long rill at the bottom edge of this first stroke* with *it 'hangs' in a kind of long bead where the brush leaves off*). The pleasant personal relationship which in this case the writer has tried to establish with his readers has not demanded a complete relaxation of the formalities of literary discourse. The writing is not without polish. There are no contracted forms, no typographical stresses and strains, the conventions of literary syntax are observed, the cohesion of the text is deftly organized. The instructor here may not be wearing full academic dress, but he is not exactly in shirt-sleeves, either; the style is lounge-suited, semi-formal, friendly without being presumptuous, punctilious but not austere. This *collaborative* tone is possibly the most difficult of all to achieve. The *casual* and *formal* tones are often merely self-indulgent; there are those who insist on writing as they speak, take it or leave it, and there are others, just as indifferent to the responses of their readers, who stubbornly hide themselves behind barriers of academic prescription. The collaborative manner is not self-indulgent. If anything (and herein lies its difficulty) it is self-aware. The writer who attempts it does so because he wants to consider his reader; but consideration of the responses of others makes us acutely self-aware and therefore deeply dissatisfied with what we do.

6.4 Tone shifts

Constant shifts of tone will occur in any text that reflects the presence of its author; writing without tonal nuances is like painting without varying intensities of colour. However, these shifts have to be carefully gauged in the context of role; certain latitudes are permitted to the entertainer that might not be conceded to the informant and the instructor. Consider the following example:

> [6] In human relationships language demands meticulous care and can never be so casual and unpremeditated as words like 'colloquial' might seem to imply. Colloquy is a game of some seriousness for the losing player. So much may turn on the happy or hapless choice of phrase – a salary, a friendship, the respect of a community – and phrases so often have a steely and irreversible finality. *Semel emissum*, the poet tells us, *volat irrevocabile verbum*: if you swear at a client there's no unswearing yourself, and once you've told the boss where to put his job you mustn't expect him to offer you a rise.

There is a sudden and potentially ludicrous shift of tone here, from the fairly formal to the noticeably casual; it sets in mischievously after the Latin quotation, and changes the whole complexion ('lowers the whole tone'!) of the passage. This is acceptable if we assume that the writer appears before us in the role of entertainer, in which case the tone-shift is perceived as humour, malapert perhaps, but not necessarily misplaced. On the other hand, if the writer's errand were to inform, instruct, or dispute, a stylistic shift as decisive and wide-ranging as this might very well be interpreted as a gross misjudgement. Shifts are not usually so violent; tone shades away into neighbour-tone. It is not uncommon, for example, for a long text to begin in formal style and gradually ease into a collaborative manner from which renewed excursions into formality may be made. (This book is perhaps a case in point.) But the changes are as a rule carefully and tactfully graded. Here is a passage that rides on fluctuations of tone:

> [7] A sovereign difficulty for the pianist whose ambition is to play Mozart is the absence of those specious commodities which are the refuge of the merely flashy player: the sonorous pedal, the densities of chording, the artful *rubato*, the general romantic freedom to 'interpret' a text. Mozart's piano scores are very spare and clear, and the player must risk exposure to that cool clarity. He has to draw that classic line, steadily and convincingly, without once fluffing it. There is no disguising a mistake or slurring a false accent, and if we must decorate, it

has to be done strictly in the style of Mozart and the eighteenth century. Decorations in the manner of Chopin won't do.

Playing Mozart, or hearing his music well played, can be a form of moral pleasure, because of his ineluctable demand for honesty. One of the beauties of classic art, and let us rejoice in it, is that it shines without mercy on the unjust. It finds them out. This isn't wholly a matter of technical skill. You can be all fingers and thumbs and still find some little bit of Mozart that you can manage to play. But God help you if you come at it with the notion of working it up to impress the neighbours. It will give you the coldest of cold shoulders. Mozart's music hates a faker, and there's a deep, crafty justice in that.

This ranges in manner from an almost archaic formality (*specious commodities*) to a modern intimacy (*God help you . . . working it up . . . Mozart's music hates a faker*). The tonal span might indeed be imprudently broad, but if the text nonetheless presents something like a uniformity of address it is because the shifts of tone follow, as it were, the impulse of the piece; there is an attitudinal wave, building and breaking in language of varying densities. Thus, the passage begins with a sentence in highly formal style, but after the next sentence (ending with the words *that cool clarity*) the formality relaxes noticeably. The shift is ultimately signalled by the *we* pronoun, but the transition from a formal to a collaborative tone effectively spans the lexicon of two sentences, beginning with *that cool clarity*, which is rephrased in *that classic line*, and ending with *fluffing it*. We 'fluff a line' in vocal or instrumental performance, or even – with the meaning 'blur' – in drawing; more remotely, 'clarity' might be said to be 'fluffed' in the sense of 'clouded'. The phrase *fluffing it* is thus a downshift in tone which nevertheless keeps the metaphoric continuity of the text. The paragraph continues in this collaborative or semi-formal tone, and at the close strikes a casual note with the contracted verb form (*won't*).

The second paragraph resumes the formal manner in its first sentence (*NB: ineluctable*), but in the next two sentences allows the tone to relax a little (*let us rejoice in it* is a symptom) and by the fourth sentence has slipped once and for all into the casual style. The definitive point of transition comes at *isn't*, in *This isn't wholly a matter of technical skill*. There are quite striking contrasts of vocabulary and idiom between the pre- and post-transitional halves of the paragraph (*moral pleasure, ineluctable demand for strict honesty, shines without mercy on the unjust* vs *all fingers and thumbs, some little bit of Mozart, working it up*). The reader's acceptance of this textural change may possibly turn on the placing of a short sentence (*It finds them out*) as a preliminary to the transition.

6.5 Indices of tone

In every text there are indices that collectively define the attitude of the writer to his reader (and, of course, to his theme). Some are in effect paradigmatic, *eg* the sets *you – we – the reader, I – we – one – this writer*, which offer choices synonymous in meaning but not equivalent in tone. Some are morphological, in the sense that they coincide with forms in the primary syntactic repertoire, *ie* commands, questions, exclamations, passive transformations, existential constructions. Some are stylistic, involving syntactic options such as the presentations and branchings discussed in 5.7 and 5.8*ff*. Others are lexical, appearing in the type or formation of words (learned words, technical words, slang, derivatives, compounds, etc) and also in metaphor, figure and image. Others again are typographical, often reflecting the special emphases, ellipses and intonations of speech.

We would hardly expect all of these characteristics to appear in any one text. Usually there are a few indices in stylistic company, and it is from the interplay of compatible features that we derive an impression of tone and a sense of what is tonally correct. Each of the following, for example, is correct in its own very distinctive manner:

[8]i The reader is invited to consider the following hypothesis.
  ii Here's a bone for you to chew on.

We might well accept these as formal and extremely informal variants in tone of the same directive. On the other hand, acceptance of the following would be questionable, to say the least:

[9]i You are invited to chew on the following bone.
  ii Here's a hypothesis for the reader to chew on.

These may be grammatically acceptable sentences, but we find them tonally incorrect (and metaphorically mixed!) because the proposed indices are simply not compatible. The tolerances within a single sentence are of course very strict. They relax a little as a text grows, –

necessarily, or it would be very difficult to make a shift of tone – but the writer still has to be careful about the rate of tonal change, the gradual discarding of some indices and the introduction of others.

6.6 Pronouns, personality, and address

Pronouns are a besetting problem, and the subject of many magisterial injunctions. The student who ventures to write *I think* may invite from his tutor a sardonic reproof ('Your whole essay is supposed to be what *you* think'). The luckless schoolboy who in simple enthusiasm for a theme commits himself to repeated assertions of *you* (*you can see, you feel, you wonder, you discover*) exposes himself to such red-ink ridicule ('Who? me?') that he may ever afterwards feel obliged to dress his Sunday observations in the genteel passive (*it can be seen, it is felt, one is led to wonder, the discovery is made*).

There is indeed a fairly powerful veto on *I* and *you* as pronouns fit for academic writing, the reason generally given for their exclusion being that scholarly expositions should be impersonal and objective. Subjectivity is forbidden to the academic disputant. If judgements are to be expressed, he expresses them at a becoming distance: not *I think Spenser's tough going, and so do lots of people if they're frank*, but *It is frankly conceded by many that Spenser is not the easiest of poets*.

Inasmuch as the scholar's tone must be quite formal, he is justified in deleting *I* and *you* from his code. However, there is no reason to exclude them under all circumstances. The role of instructor, for example, is most easily played in the casual tone, when *you* is readily permitted. The second-person pronoun keeps convenient company with the imperative (*eg: Don't wash the car with a pan-scourer, you'll scratch the paint*), whereas the exclusion of *you* might involve a formal excursion into modals, passives, and existential constructions (*The car should not be washed with a pan-scourer, as there is a danger that the paint might be scratched*).

The first-person pronoun is a necessary mask for the entertainer in a relaxed, informal style:

[10]   I'm not superstitious, but I don't believe in flouting superstition either. I walk under ladders when walking round them would mean stepping in front of a bus, but when the choice is less drastically governed I've no objection to going a yard or two out of my way. I see no harm in picking up pins

(but not on the Tube in the rush hour) and I knock on wood quite regularly, even though our plastic times are making wood ever less available for knocking on. In fifty years, I suppose, we shall be knocking on polyvinyl.

This passage with its casual tone (note the contracted *I'm, don't*) requires the first person. The *I* of the text is not necessarily the actual person of the writer; *I* is the mask, the costumed victim, the dummy to be laughed at and knocked about. The alternatives to *I* raise the discourse to a level of formality that makes quite the wrong kind of funny face: *This writer is not superstitious, but he does not believe in flouting superstition, either; One sees no harm in picking up pins . . . and one knocks on wood quite regularly.*

In 6.5 above, it is suggested that there are paradigms of written address, *I – we – one – the/this writer* and *you – we – the reader*. In each paradigm the successive terms correspond, very roughly speaking, to degrees of formality in tone, *eg: you* is casual, *we* collaborative, and *the reader* highly formal. The pronoun *one* is perhaps more formal than the corresponding middle term *we*; and *we* in any case is an ambivalent pronoun, belonging to both sets and hovering between the meanings *you, I,* and *you-and-I.* (*We should notice the importance of conjunctions*=‘more you than I’; *we have discussed this on an earlier page*=‘more I than you’; *we take pleasure in the style of Jane Austen*=‘both you and I’.) The nouns at the third remove in each paradigm are impersonal titular forms which are always used with the definite article, or, in the case of *writer*, with the demonstrative *this: the reader* ‘you’, *the writer, this writer* ‘I’. (*The writer* can of course also mean a particular writer as in *Sometimes in Juvenal's Satires it is hard to see what the writer means*, or writers in general, as in *The writer should always equip himself with a large waste paper basket.*) Without its article, *reader* is an appendage of familiar address: *You will ask, reader, how any textbook could be as dull as this.* Modifications elaborate the titular forms: *the discerning reader, the reader with a healthy aversion to academic hocus-pocus, this not inexperienced writer, the writer of this little treatise, this writer, who yields to none in his enthusiasm for Old English riddles.* Such elaborations tend to buttress the formality of address.

6.7 Imperatives, questions, exclamations

There is a stylistic compatibility, noted above, between the use of imperatives (*eg* in instructional texts) and the use of the familiar *you*.

Successive sentences in a passage of instruction might read: *Tape the paper to the drawing board. You can use pins if you prefer them.* It would be equally acceptable to write: *Tape the paper to the drawing board. Pins may be used if these are preferred.* The tone changes, and the level of formality is raised a little, but the imperative continues to 'warm' the little two-sentence passage with its directness of address. Note, though, how the warmth recedes when both sentences are passively constructed: *The paper is taped to the drawing board. Pins may be used if these are preferred.*

A regular concomitant of the imperative is the manner adverbial *eg: Sponge the paper cautiously,* or *Sponge the paper with caution.* Where adverb and prepositional phrase compete as adverbials, as in this example (also in *carefully/with care, hastily/in haste, stealthily/by stealth,* etc) they may possibly be regarded as indices of different tones. Compare, for instance, the following sentences:

[11]i Sponge the paper cautiously and you won't damage the surface.
   ii Sponge the paper with caution, thereby avoiding damage to the surface.

Cautiously and *with caution* are perhaps interchangeable in these examples with no marked effect on tone, but it should nonetheless be noted that in [11ii] there is an accord of grammatical category between *caution* and *damage*; noun matches noun. This if anything reinforces the impression that [11ii] is more formal than [11i], an impression rising in the first instance from a notable contrast between coordination in [11i] (*Sponge . . . and you won't damage*) and subordination in [11ii] (*Sponge . . . thereby avoiding*). Here again the lesson is that one stylistic choice meshes with another.

Questions and exclamations present quite delicate stylistic problems. They have, of course, a special and traditional use in narrative, where, with appropriate shifts of tense and mood, they may be used to reflect a character's self-communings. (*And Ethel? Did she love him? Bliss if she did! But if she didn't? Damnation! What would he do then, cut his throat? Join the Legion? Take a degree at the Open University? By Jove! The Legion! That was it! Better than the other two, eh?*) Narrative uses apart, they appear to be most effectively employed in two stylistic spheres: the formal-yet-warm rhetoric of dispute and the casual-personal style of instructional prose. In the following example a rhetorical question and an exclamation signal moments of con-spiratorial appeal from writer to reader:

[12] Violence surrounds us. Now as never before, it seems, our lives are violent, with the horror of the traffic accident, the fear of the hooligan, the menace of the criminal, of the terrorist. There seems to be no escape from it. Little girls are assaulted in green country lanes, newsboys are murdered in provincial farmhouses, football supporters die under the wheels of buses, husbands batter wives and women maim children in the seclusion of respectable suburban villas. And what are we to do about all this? It appears that we can do nothing, suggest nothing, almost feel nothing. Challenged to account for the triumph of the thug we say – oh how feebly! – that society must be to blame.

The passage is frankly designed to express and evoke emotion. This is what justifies the rhetorical question *And what are we to do about all this?* and the interjection *oh how feebly!* They appeal directly to the reader, willing him to share the writer's feelings. In such texts, the rhetoric of question and interjection is not misplaced; they become devices of formal elegance – whereas in other types of composition they convey an impression of extreme informality. Compare the following passages:

[13]i Eventually the steerer will need to turn, or 'wind' the boat, if necessary using one of the so-called 'winding holes', the wide ponds placed at intervals along the canal. The manoeuvre is not a difficult one. With the engine throttled back and the tiller put hard over, the boat is allowed to swing gently into the turn, due attention being paid to the fact that nowadays the winding holes are often badly silted at the edges. When the bow is as near to the bank as might seem prudent to the steerer, with the boat lying across the waterway and still swinging, the tiller is put hard over in the opposite direction and the engine is put astern. The boat should now begin to turn more or less on its own axis and continue its swing. The steerer must judge the moment to put the tiller over yet again and put the engine ahead, thus completing the turnabout. The whole manoeuvre is comparable to the three-point turn in driving, except that a boat is never stationary and the steerer must learn to harness the impetus of a moving vessel.

ii Then comes that moment when you have to turn the boat, probably in one of those wide ponds they call 'winding holes'.

A difficult manoeuvre? Not a bit of it! Come into the hole
quite slowly, put your tiller well over, and let the boat nose its
way towards the edge of the pond. Mind you don't go in too
far, though, some of these holes are badly silted! By and by
you'll find you've got the boat lying across the pond with the
stern still swinging in the direction where your tiller points. If
you'll then put your tiller over the other way and at the same
time shift your engine into reverse, you'll see that the swing
continues quite sharply while your boat moves slowly astern.
Before the stern hits the bank behind you (careful of that
rudder!) put your tiller over again and shift into forward gear.
The boat will go on swinging and complete the turn. Simple!
Just like doing a three-point turn in your car, isn't it? The one
big difference is that there are no brakes on a boat – you have
to watch the movement and make use of it.

The questions and exclamations suit the casual tone of [13ii], in which
the writer contrives a semi-dramatic presentation, a suggestion that
he is actually at hand while his reader-pupil (*careful of that rudder!*)
carries out the designated manoeuvre. The writer of [13i] makes no
such pretence, and in a text pitched at that level of formality (note
that passives are used rather than imperatives) the freely appellant
questions and exclamations would be quite out of place.

6.8 Passives: modals

The association of the passive with certain technical styles
('registers') is well known; every schoolchild writing a laboratory
report learns to say *A solution was prepared* rather than *We prepared a
solution*. It is also a matter of common practice that a passive
transformation changes the thematic balance (so to speak) of a
sentence, affecting the prominence of different parts of its message:
cf: The government suffered a defeat with *A defeat was suffered by the
government*. A further stylistic property of the passive is that it
noticeably cools the manner of address – *ie* it is an index of the formal
tone. Compare the following:

[14]i You can make a man fit seat-belts on his car, but you can't
make him wear one. The police can't (as yet) prosecute him.
Safety councils and other bodies may advise him, but that's all.
You can never pass laws to make people behave prudently.

ii Though seat-belts may be compulsorily fitted in motor
vehicles, no driver can be compelled to wear one. He cannot
(as yet) be prosecuted by the police. He may be advised, but no
more than that, by safety councils and other bodies. Prudent
behaviour can never be enforced by law.

The two passages convey the same message, [14ii] no less
forcefully than [14i]. The passive transformations of [14ii], however,
make the style formal and convey the impression of consciously
planned rhetoric rather than casually impulsive argument.

The modal auxiliaries *may*, *might*, *can*, *could*, *should*, *must*, often occur
in conjunction with the passive (they are, as it were, compatible
indices) and have the same distancing and formalizing tendency.
Contrast these two passages:

[15]i You think, perhaps, that the University is a bastion of
unshakable virtue? Misguided thought! We're a bit more
civilized, maybe, than the tribe at the gate, but like other
communities we have our villains. What do you say to thieves
in a University library? No, I don't mean people who steal
books – we call them unauthorized borrowers – I mean people
who steal purses, wallets, watches, fountain pens. We have
them. Granted, we don't yet have rapists in the refectory or
cut-throats in the common room, but give 'em time, it'll
come.

ii It might be thought that the University must be a bastion of
unshakable virtue. The supposition would be misguided.
Academics, it is true, may consider themselves a little more
civilized than the population at large, but wrongdoers are
nonetheless to be found in the University as elsewhere.
Though theft from a University library might be judged quite
inconceivable – other than by the unauthorized borrowing of
books – yet thieves, it appears, can lurk among the carrels, and
valuables in the form of purses, watches, wallets or fountain
pens are regularly stolen. To be sure, the refectory remains
unterrorised by the rapist and the common room unmenaced
by the cut-throat, but their invasion should only be a matter of
time.

There is a strong element of irony in both passages, but in [15ii] it
is cooler and more carefully formalized; [15i] shakes a harder fist,

[15ii] raises a blander eyebrow. The passives largely shape this formal posture, the ironic distance being most apparent in the final sentence, but a strongly contributory feature to the coolly thoughtful tone of [15ii] is the use in nearly every sentence of a modal (*must, would be, may, might, can, should*) making the whole text deal in potentials and hypotheses rather than in bold asseverations. This deprecating and elaborately formal manner is typical of much academic discourse.

6.9 Postponement: extraposition, existential sentences, cleft sentences

Another device that often conveys an impression of cool formality in exposition can be characterized by the general term *postponement*. (Often, mark, not always; postponement may be a means of planting a joke or of inducing narrative tension.) The term in fact covers a complex of structures, the common characteristic of which is that they more or less emphatically support the principles of end-focus and end-weight (see above, 5.8). The device of *extraposition* is commonly observed in everyday speech, *eg* in expressions such as *It's a pity to spoil it, It pleased me to see her smiling, It doesn't matter what you say, It seems he's out.* An anticipatory *it* fills the subject position and thus facilitates the postponement into predicative focus of a clause (*to spoil it, to see her smile, (that) he is out*) that would otherwise be awkwardly placed as subject. (Or, in the case of *It seems he's out*, unacceptably placed; (*That) he is out seems* is impossible; the nearest equivalent being the thematic inversion *He's out, it seems.*)

Here are some examples of the extraposition in a more academic–discursive style:

[16] *It is a mistake to neglect the practice of art in favour of the theory.*
  (='To neglect the practice of art in favour of the theory / is / a mistake.' Subject–Verb–Complement.)
It is purely by chance that some ancient manuscripts have survived.
  (='That some ancient manuscripts have survived / is / purely by chance.' Subject–Verb–Adverbial.)
It gratifies us to see others committing errors we have wittily avoided.
  (='To see others committing errors we have wittily avoided / gratifies / us.' Subject–Verb–Object.)
It must make a decent man angry to think how Mozart was allowed to sink into penury and illness.

(='To think how Mozart was allowed to sink into penury and illness / must   make / a   decent   man / angry.'   Subject–Verb–Object–Complement.)

*It has been remarked that Tennyson's preferences in music were naive.
(='That Tennyson's preferences in music were naive / has been remarked.' Subject–Verb (passive).)

It was thought unlikely that man could be descended from an ape-like species.
(='That man could be descended from an ape-like species / was   thought / unlikely.'   Subject–Verb   (passive)–Complement.)

The bracketed renderings show how the extraposition can be applied to different clause-patterns, and how, indeed, specific cases (see the starred item above) might require it for the sake of idiomatic elegance. It will be seen that considerable end-weighting is made possible by this device. Furthermore, it may sometimes imply (rather disingenuously) the authority of a widely accepted tenet. For example, there is a tactical difference, as far as the cunning of argument is concerned, between *Edward Fitzgerald remarked that Tennyson was musically naive* and *It has been remarked that Tennyson was musically naive*. The extraposition innocently leaves open the question of who and how many made the remark.

A related stratagem is the so-called *existential sentence*, represented in day-to-day language by formulae such as *There's something wrong, There's no one else, There's a visitor for you*. The rule for the formula is that the subject and verb of a basic pattern are inverted (*Something is wrong* becoming *is something wrong*) and are then preceded by a new, 'token' subject, *there* (whence *There is something wrong*). Certain existential constructions are primary, in the sense that they can hardly be interpreted as transformations of some underlying form, *eg* as *There is something wrong* may be considered a transformation of *Something is wrong*. They are, rather, asseverations basically cast in the existential form: thus *There is a God, There's never a dull moment, There'll always be an England*, rather than *God exists, Never a dull moment occurs, England will always be*. Akin to such 'bare existential' sentences are assertions of a quasi-proverbial or maxim-giving kind: *There is no stricter discipline than mathematics, There is a time for reflecting on what one has written, There is such a thing as an act of enlightened self-interest* (*cf: There's no fool like an old fool, There's a time and a place for everything, There's a divinity that shapes our ends*).

Normally the verb in an existential sentence is *to be*. Here are some examples, working from different clause-patterns:

[17] *There are many scholars investigating problems of grammar.*
(= 'Many scholars / are investigating / problems of grammar.' Subject–Verb–Object.)
There are dark storm-clouds on the horizon.
(= 'Dark storm-clouds / are / on the horizon.' Subject–Verb–Adverbial.)
There have been cynics calling Britain decadent for many years.
(= 'Cynics / have been calling / Britain / decadent / for many years.' Subject–Verb–Object–Complement–Adverbial.)
There may be some student reading this book with great interest.
(= 'Some student / may be reading / this book / with great interest.' Subject–Verb–Object–Adverbial.)
There was nothing left undamaged by the vandals.
(= 'Nothing / was left / undamaged / by the vandals.' Subject–Verb (passive)–Complement–Adverbial.)

In all these cases it will appear that the effect of the existential transformation is to put a focus on the subject of the transformed sentence – *ie* on *many scholars*, *dark storm-clouds*, *cynics*, *some student*, *nothing*. The structure may be further regarded as – in some instance at least – a recipe for multiple focusing. For example, in *There may be some student reading this book with great interest*, there is an initial focus on *some student* and a subsequent focus on *with great interest*. These points of successive prominence give the construction, potentially, a kind of projective depth, as though the reader, psychologically placed at the initial *there*, were looking along the sentence into a propositional distance. The impression is perhaps even more apparent in turns of literary style when a verb other than *be* is used:

[18] *There may come a day when we shall bitterly repent having so shamefully ignored the traditional architecture of our towns.*
In 1789 there occurred an event that was to shake the whole of Europe and deeply influence the history of the western world.
There exists a belief in the current activities and ultimate advent of a superlatively intelligent race of extra-terrestrial beings.

These examples show how the existential sentence can bear an appreciable end-weight; they may also suggest something of its value as a 'cooling' device, a method of donnish distancing.

Cleft sentences bear a superficial resemblance to extrapositions, in that they begin with the anticipatory *it*, but the ruling of the two structures is somewhat different. In the cleft sentence *it* is complemented (via the verb *to be*) by the noun phrase that makes the focal point of the construction; this in its turn is followed by a relative clause of the restrictive type. The construction is reasonably frequent as a colloquial form, *eg: It was John who told me, It was the food he didn't like, It was last Wednesday they came, It was on the beach that I lost it.* Examples in a more literary style will illustrate the value of this formula as a quite powerful focusing device:

[19] *It was Edward Lear who mistook a recumbent cow for a mound of earth.*
    (='Edward Lear mistook a cow for a mound of earth.' The cleft sentence focuses on a transformed *subject*.)
    It is to the USA that we commonly look for statesmanlike leadership.
    (='We commonly look to the USA for statemanlike leadership.' The cleft sentence focuses on a transformed *adverbial*.)
    It was the quartet form that Haydn fathered and perfected.
    (='Haydn fathered and perfected the quartet form.' The cleft sentence focuses on a transformed *object*.)
    It was an honourable man, if a poor one, that John died.
    (='John died an honourable man, if a poor one.' The cleft sentence focuses on a transformed *complement*.)

This is clearly an effective method of marking unambiguously the focus of information, and is therefore of value to the academic expositor whose conventions do not as a rule allow much 'scoring' (see 1.1) of the text. It might be added that the cleft sentence often implies a *contrastive* focus (*eg* 'It was Edward Lear, *not* Goethe . . .'; 'It is to the USA – *where else?* – that we look . . .').

The prose of unbiased report, of objective assessment, often seems to call for these postponing, end-focusing constructions; at the same time, their collective presence can suggest quite subtly a tone of pedantic irony that disclaims personal involvement in what is being said. In the following short passage the slightly tart manner, the air of holding a theme at arm's length, the frosting of donnishness or schoolmastery, may be attributed to the frequency of postponing constructions:

[20] It is sometimes argued that the system of proportional representation would be too complicated for the British

electorate to grasp. There would be difficulty, it is said, in making sure that the average voter understood the principle of ranked preferences and the permutative consequences of his vote. Since it is that same average voter who boldly unravels the intricacies of the weekly football coupon, the argument seems less than convincing. There is no evidence that the proportional system has been found too complicated by the inhabitants of Ireland or Sweden, and it is either insulting or disingenuous to argue that it would overtax the wits of native Britons.

From this arises the incidental point that postponements often do companion duty with modals and passives (eg: *It is sometimes argued that the system . . . would be; There is no evidence that the proportional system has been found too complicated by the inhabitants of Ireland*).

6.10 Frontings

In 5.7 we saw how the perspective of a simple sentence might be changed by fronting a direct object or a complement or an adverbial, and in 5.8 we considered the possibility of disposing subordinate clauses in different schemes of branching. These alternations of position in a syntactic structure were discussed mainly with reference to the problem of textual design, but frontings and other transpositions may be additionally important as indices of tone, or tone-within-role. Comparison of the following texts will illustrate the point:

[21]i Robin and his followers set out for Nottingham, being men who were never prepared to disdain a challenge or abandon a comrade. They were not foolhardy, though they were certainly brave, and they depended on routine provisions against failure when they set out on their mission. The reader may readily imagine what these were. A reserve force waited at the camp to effect a rescue if this should be necessary, and many a humble ally, ready to shelter a fugitive or carry a message to Sherwood, lurked in the city itself.

ii Never men to disdain a challenge or abandon a comrade, Robin and his followers set out for Nottingham. Brave they certainly were, but foolhardy they were not, and in undertaking their mission they relied on routine provisions against failure. What these were, the reader may readily imagine. At the camp a reserve force stood in readiness to effect a rescue should this be necessary, and in the city itself lurked many a humble ally, ready to shelter a fugitive or carry a message to Sherwood.

The sentences in [21i] are in the main constructed in accordance with syntactic 'norms' which dictate that the subject should be the first, thematic, element in a clause, and that a sequence of clauses should be led by the principal. Only in the last sentence has the writer struggled against this syntactic grip, permitting himself a cleft construction, a mid-branch (see 5.9) separating *ally* from its verb, *lurked*. This makes one rhetorical glimmer in a passage which is otherwise a flat report.

Passage [21ii], by contrast, is a sustained rhetorical gesture. Wherever the norms described above can be reversed, this is done; dependent clauses markedly precede their principals, complements precede subjects, adverbials take up positions of thematic importance at the beginning of sentences. This reworking is not strictly necessary for the sake of textual cohesion, but it noticeably and instructively changes the tone of the piece. Firstly, it seems to reflect a change in the writer's view of his role. He is no longer the mere informant; he tells the tale with something of the swagger of the entertainer. Secondly, while the frontings appear to give the text an air of formal rhetoric, their effect is not one of cold or remote formality; on the contrary, they have an appellant warmth, as though the writer, enjoying his own performance, were inviting the reader to share the ceremonious gestures and join the ritual caper. (For a comparable effect of 'warm' rhetoric, see [13] above, and the comments on it.)

6.11 Parentheses

In fronting, or in the inversion of any syntactic norm, there is thus an element of theatre; the attitude to the reader is that of the actor to his admiring audience. This posturing has its risks, of course, and the writer must be reasonably confident that his reader will enjoy the histrionics and assent to the masquerade. The parenthesis makes a slightly less theatrical effect. It can certainly convey the studied impression of the stage aside, but more often than not it is a reflection of the writer's confidence in the easy discursive relationship he has established with his reader. In such circumstances the parenthesis is a device for making disjunct qualifying observations of the type 'by the way', 'I should add', 'admittedly', 'You know':

[22] *The subliminal metaphor – an example can be found in 3.6 above – is the writer's bonus from a kindly Muse.*

The hours spent in typing (assuming that he is not skilled in the craft) add to a writer's burdens.

D. H. Lawrence's harangues on sex, and this is a painful thing for an admirer to concede, can be stupefyingly boring.

Browning was an adept at rhyme, but Tennyson was not without moments of burlesque agility (he once found an apt rhyme for the name Friswell).

The parenthesis can be used with witty effect as a form of typographical *sotto voce*, sometimes more striking than a conventional subordination in carrying a point: *Lord Nelson, a man of almost impeccably firm character (Emma was a pardonable indulgence) obliged the moralists by dying an exemplary death.* The parenthesis here is not really a throwaway; it is in fact a sly detraction and is much more subversive in this form than it would have been had it been presented as a subordinate clause: *Granted the pardonable indulgence of his affair with Emma, Lord Nelson was a man of impeccably firm character, who obliged the moralists by dying an exemplary death.*

The example will suggest that parenthesis is a mode of subordination (*cf* mid-branching, 5.9, 5.12); they may further suggest that it is a subordination with special characteristics and intentions. It can be a form of syntactic shorthand, and it can also be a symptom of the jostled thought that grasps at two assertions simultaneously. In some cases a dash or a bracket does duty for an omitted conjunction (*eg: the subliminal metaphor – an example can be found in 3.6 above – is the writer's bonus,* etc). In others the parenthetical clause has simply jumped its place in the expository queue (*eg: D. H. Lawrence's harangues on sex, and this is a painful thing for an admirer to concede, can be stupefyingly boring*). Such displacements can of course be corrected; we could write, for example, *D. H. Lawrence's harangues on sex can be stupefyingly boring, and that is a painful thing for an admirer to concede.* However, the distinctively familiar tone of the parenthesis, with its air of the urgency that cannot pause to consider literary niceties, may provide a reason for letting the construction stand. Moreover, a parenthesis may function as a focal reinforcement: *cf* the emphatic double focus in *It is wrong, and one says this in the face of all fashionable posing, to encourage mere rudeness* with the less emphatic *It is wrong to encourage mere rudeness*. In view of these stylistic properties it is easy enough as a rule to decide whether a parenthesis should be allowed to interrupt a sentence. What is sometimes harder is knowing how to present it, grammatically and typographically; compare, for instance *Tennyson – he once found an apt rhyme for the name Friswell – was not without humour* and *Tennyson (who once found an apt rhyme for the name Friswell) was not without humour*.

Behind such variations lies the fact that the parenthesis is not wholly a syntactic device. It is also a form of 'scoring' (see 1.1) and as such should imply a tone of voice. Syntactically there is no difference between *The River Soar, as benign a watercourse as you could wish to find on a summer's day, runs gently past my garden*, and *The River Soar (as benign a watercourse as you could wish to find on a summer's day) runs gently past my garden*: or between *This unpredictable river (it has burst its banks twice this year) is a rogue in winter* and *This unpredictable river – it has burst its banks twice this year – is a rogue in winter*. The difference is a matter of rhetorical presentation. The conventional signs of parenthesis, *ie* the comma, the dash and the round bracket, possibly indicate varying depths of scoring. A 'shallow' parenthesis, hardly breaking the flow of the sentence, may be placed between commas: *People who love chocolate roulade, and I am one of them, take unkindly to the regimen of slimming*. The flow is more definitely broken by the dash, the characteristic of the familiar aside: *Eat your chocolate roulade at weekends – Sunday afternoon is a good time – and abstain from Monday to Friday*. Brackets suggest the 'deepest' parenthetical level: *Forgo all sweets such as chocolate roulade (your health is surely important to you if your waistline is not) and learn to enjoy a nice apple*.

6.12 Coordination and subordination

Generally a tonal contrast is felt between texts which make extensive use of coordination and those which regularly subordinate their material. The contrast is between directness, intensity, simplicity of attitude – even naivety – on the one hand, and on the other circumvention, diffuseness of feeling, and sophistication of attitude – even pomposity or disingenuousness. Two passages in contrasting style make the point:

[23]i Writing a textbook can be the most insufferable donkey-work, your colleagues may praise you, your family may be proud of you, but it's donkey-work all the same, and you are the donkey. Dear God! Would a navvy put up with this? Would a dustman – cry you mercy, sanitary operative – sustain these grubby labours? It would break a coalminer's durable heart, the Trade Unions would pass indignant resolutions on it. What's more, it spoils your appearance, messes up your house and ruins your character. Write for two months and you're still a reasonably wholesome, tidy, sober man. Keep it up for another eighteen and you're King Lear with bags under your eyes, the floor of your room is littered with the crumpled remains of dead chapters, your discourse is unfit for babies, and you're down to buying cheap sherry or drinking diluted Martinis to keep yourself docile.

ii Though colleagues may voice their praise and families show their pride, the composition of a textbook is endlessly laborious, and the author must feel at times that he is a mere drudge. It must seem to him, in moments of blaspheming exasperation, that no manual trade, not road-mending, not refuse-collecting, not even coal-mining, can vie with writing as a form of toil the conditions and rewards of which would make a theme for many an indignant Trade Union resolution. Furthermore, it is an occupation that may have adverse effects on the practitioner's character and personal appearance, and incidentally disturb the serenity of his home. After two months of writing he may still present the appearance of one who is customarily well-groomed, sober, and neat in his habits. Should he however continue, day after day, for a further eighteen, some remarkable alterations will be seen; a tragi-comic figure, unkempt and foul-mouthed, he may then be observed among the carelessly-strewn remnants of his abortive works, drinking the cheap or much-diluted liquor which is the only means that poverty can afford to keep him in a state of compliance with his wretched task.

The two passages may remind the reader of the schoolbook contrast between *oratio recta* and *oratio obliqua*; and indeed, the writer of passage [23i] presents himself as spokesman, whereas in [23ii] he is merely reporter or commentator. The style of [23i] is in part mimetic of vocal address, *ie* there are questions, an exclamation and a parenthesis, all of which suggest the writer appealing to the reader as though in person. An additional symptom of this interpersonal appeal, however, is the heaping up of clauses in casual drifts of coordination, often asyndetic coordination. In [23ii] not only are the questions and other echoes of speech eliminated, but the syntax is changed so that material presented in [23i] with no apparent concern for connections and priorities is now arranged in schemes of subordination which sometimes make interpretations on the reader's behalf. Nowhere is this more apparent than in the last sentence; elements impressionistically presented in [23i], are in [23ii] worked into a carefully constructed picture. An important consequence of this difference in the handling of the material is that each passage presents to the reader a quite distinct tone; [23i] is personal, warm, concrete, grumpily humorous, while [23ii] is cooler, a little abstract, facetious rather than humorous, detached, verging on the pompous. The writer of [23ii] attempts the formal tone within the role of entertainer, a difficult combination at the best of times. Even writers who are adept at this clowning in the high style – Dickens comes to mind – sometimes fail to carry it off.

6.13 Cohesive devices

Devices of syntactic cohesion are to some extent reflective of compositional roles; the examples and commentaries of Chapter 2 may have shown how important the carefully demonstrated cohesion of a text can be to the instructor and the informant. To the entertainer cohesion is no less vital, but his patterns of textual structure are often complex and subtle, combining both textual and textural elements, and he is frequently at pains to conceal his cohesive workmanship. The reiterative and systematic use of certain ranges of syntactic connectors is therefore not so obvious in the prose of entertainment as in passages of information, instruction and analysis. The style of this book provides a large-scale example. Inasmuch as the author has adopted the postures of instructor and informant, the writing is characterized (at times, it seems, bedevilled) by expository devices repeated again and again in weary variants. Anaphora and cataphora – *above, below, the following, here, this, these, such* – occur on every page; enumeratives have been an obvious necessity; and exemplifications, inferences, reformulations, etc, occur frequently.

The rub of these systematic necessities has at times been so irksome that it has been a relief to be able to assume the entertainer's mask during the composition of one or two examples.

It is not only role, however, that devices of cohesion incidentally reflect. They can also be indices of tone. This again is a topic which Chapter 2 may be presumed to have covered. It should be obvious that, for example, enumerative expressions such as *to start with*, *for another thing*, and *what it all comes to* are casual variants of the more formal *firstly*, *secondly*, and *finally*; that *in addition*, *furthermore*, are not as colloquial *as on top of that*, *as well*; that expression-begging formulae of the type *as it were*, *so to speak* have casual equivalents in *if you will* or *what you might call*; and that the informal disjunct *I grant you* can be more formally expressed by *admittedly*. These are some examples of the way in which markers of textual structure may be coloured by the tone which invades syntax and vocabulary.

6.14 Vocabulary

Role and tone have their lexical aspects; indeed it is in the texture of a piece, as created by vocabulary and imagery, that the reader most often and most immediately feels its tone. As far as vocabulary is concerned, users of English are favoured and bedevilled by the facts of our linguistic history. Anglo-Saxon, French, Latin, Greek, have deposited layers of idiom and word-formation in which the contrasting colours of expressiveness are to be sought – the concrete and the abstract, the particular and the general, the homely and the remote, the common and the learned, the casual and the formal. With time and cultural change these distinctive layers have folded and bedded into one another, so that it now no longer follows, as once it might have done, that words formed out of Greek are exclusively scholarly and technical, that Latinate words belong mainly to the language of formality and abstraction, or that French words have the social advantage of their Germanic counterparts. (In the latter instance, the reverse may be true; to judge from the personal columns of some newspapers a *betrothal* is a superior event to an *engagement*.)

Nevertheless, this historical layering of the vocabulary has left its mark on stylistic values. Thus the writer may opt for a word of learned status, *eg: malefactor* (directly modelled from Latin), or he may look for a more familiar equivalent, *eg: criminal* (Latin mediated through French) or he might possibly choose something even more popular and familiar, *eg: crook* (Germanic). In such a series of options there is often a mean (*criminal*) between extremes of bookishness (*malefactor*) and colloquialism (*crook*), or between the abstract/general and the concrete/particular. Though most classical words should nowadays be no more 'difficult' than words of Anglo-Saxon origin, they tend to keep a certain mystery, for all but the accomplished classicist. Thus a word like *ingenuous* has an opacity which is in itself a tonal value, as compared with the transparent simplicity of words like *forthright*, or *frank*. The density of the classical word can be a barrier, sometimes deliberately raised, between writer and reader; or possibly a form of stylistic test. At the same time, words from the non-Saxon layers often have a useful power of superordination, holding several particular instances in their abstract grip. *Accommodation*, for example, may imply *house*, *flat*, or *room*, and can comically subsume *tent*, *hut*, or even *tub* (the simple accommodation of Diogenes).

A sense of provenance, a feeling for the status of the word as learned or familiar, a response to the opacity or transparency of its form, an assessment of its power to generalize or specify – these are possibly some of the criteria that provide bearings of usage and establish distinctions of tone. The vocabulary of the formal tone tends to be classicizing, learned, opaque, and general (*Sweeny Todd supplied the ingredients for some extravagant comestibles*) while the idiom of informality has a contrasting tendency to be non-classical, familiar, transparent, and specific (*Sweeny Todd cut the meat for some queer pies*). This much simplified statement is obviously vulnerable to criticism, and indeed the burlesque supporting examples show that the proposed criteria, crudely applied, produce crude oppositions. Formality of tone need not involve pompous verbiage, any more than informality need mean a trudge of monosyllables. In sensitive writing the vocabulary is in a constant play of tonal adjustments, here lifting into abstraction, there lowering towards the concrete and particular, now focusing attention on some learned word, now exploiting the warmth and intimacy of simple everyday speech. Here is a passage of descriptive writing, exemplifying tonal effects that result from a commingling of strains in vocabulary:

[24] When the river is in spate we watch its rising hour by hour, with interest, with excitement, and at last with an apprehension that knocks dully at the heart. It is one thing to sit in your

back porch at three in the afternoon, taking penny bets on the likelihood that the towpath opposite will be under water within the hour. It is quite another to lie awake at two in the morning, knowing that out there in the dark an implacable primitive is investing and pillaging the poor submissive fields, the traipsing hedgerows, the hangdog ranks of willows; that the flood is a mouthing beast softly rending and pulping your own garden. Will it carry the flower tubs away? Could it reach the boiler house? How safe are we? Your mind closes on the image of sliding brown water and opens again to the assurance that the house still stands high and mercifully dry. When you draw back the curtains, behold, a melancholy inundation, the whole valley lagooned; yet there is a grandeur in it, a bleak beauty – so long as the waters have done no more than rub off an inch or two of your soil in return for a deposit of beer bottles and brushwood.

The passage moves between different attitudinal levels: one, a relaxed and half-amused talkativeness, a raconteur's smiling account of the trials of flood-time, the other a mood of respect, verging on superstitious awe, for the brute power of the elements. These alternations (or complementations) of attitude are reflected in the vocabulary with its intricate meshings of the Latinate-Romance/abstract/portentous and the Germanic-Saxon/concrete/homely. The blend is perhaps most striking in the final sentence. Up to the word *beauty*, the vocabulary keeps a self-conscious elevation, with its greatest heightening in the denominative verb *lagooned*; thereafter it subsides to a level of mundane reference (*rub, inch, beer bottles, brushwood*) in which the Latinate *deposit* figures almost playfully. Juxtapositions of word-type are exploited throughout the piece – for example in the personification of the first sentence where *apprehension* (Latin, abstract) *knocks at* (Germanic, particular) *the heart*, or in the description *of the poor submissive fields, the traipsing hedgerows, the hangdog ranks of willows*, where the visual image of demoralization and defeat, expressed in the Germanic *traipsing* and *hangdog*, is as it were deduced from the Latinate generalization of *submissive*. In some instances, however, the provenance and affective power of individual items is of less moment than a collective effect; *eg* in *mouthing beast softly rending and pulping*, the actual origin of the lexical items (respectively Germanic–French–Germanic–French–Latin) is of no relevance to their evident stylistic function, which is to project corporately a sensuous image. Criteria of formality or informality lapse in such instances.

6.15 Metaphor and image

Figurative language (or in some instances the deliberate avoidance of it) is often an important component in the relationship of writer and reader. Metaphor has an explanatory power which circumvents the abstractions of technical and learned language, and also has an appeal, to experience and the sensations, that greatly reduces formality of tone. The cool detachment of very formal texts often seems to forbid the use of metaphor, as though it were a breach of etiquette. Texts composed in the casual style, on the other hand, make frequent use of the explanatory metaphor, though often in a random fashion that ignores the traditional veto on the mixing of figurative strains. This random image-making can be constrasted with a much more carefully stylized use of metaphor (for example, see Ch.3 [7]) in which a single image runs threadwise through a text. Here are three passages in illustration of non-metaphoric, casually metaphoric and consistently metaphoric (perhaps 'imagistic') styles:

> [25] It cannot be sufficiently emphasised that mastery in the art of composition requires among other things a familiarity with modes of conjunction in English. To the novice or amateur, this insistence on a study of the integrative devices of syntax might well seem both pedantic and trivial, but the professional (in fact or in spirit) knows how much of his time is spent in pondering the variables of phrase-, clause-, and sentence-connection. Not that a study of grammar and a detailed awareness of its resources can ever be enough to guarantee the unity of a text; for that it may still be necessary to rely on the imaginative vision.

All that can really be noted about this is the austere repudiation of metaphor. Such a denial of the figurative is in its own negative fashion an index of tone, compatible with the academic hauteur of the vocabulary and the studied formality of the syntax (*eg* the opening sentence with its anticipatory subject and its passive). Compare that hauteur with the casual and personal style of the following:

[26] One of the problems you will keep stumbling across as you write is the bother of always having to forge links. The books will tell you all about the words you can use as hooks and eyes, to clip one expression neatly into another, but a text isn't just *assembled* by rummaging through your technical stock-in-trade and finding the right part to plug into the proper socket. A piece of writing is like a castle in the building, and you need to be more than a crafty mechanic, you must also be the wise old architect. If you are doing your job properly, you can always see those invisible towers, and that should affect the way you go to work on these visible battlements.

Here metaphors rattle together like tools in a box – and indeed most of them have to do with the general notion of 'doing a job properly'. However, they are not very carefully organized, and they explain the craft of writing (perhaps confusingly, perhaps rather flatteringly) in the terms of several trades – foundrywork, dressmaking, mechanics, electricity, architecture. The metaphors turn up randomly, and only towards the end of the text, when the writer wants to make a distinction between technical competence and artistic vision, is an image developed in consistent terms (*architect – castle in the building – invisible towers – visible battlements*). The general casualness of the figurative language is matched by a casual style in other features of the text, *eg* the use throughout of the second-person pronoun. In the following passage, by contrast, there is a play of metaphor that is consistently related to one central source:

[27] In the anatomy of language, conjunctions are the very joints and ligaments; without them no argument could stand, nor could rhetoric flex its mucles. We say of a person skilled in speech that he is *articulate* – meaning that he can work the limbs and joints of language. Contrast this with that other word of approval for an easy talker – *fluent*. The two words are a brief commentary on the outward effect and the inward reality of linguistic skill. Good discourse must, to the reader, seem to 'flow'; for the writer it is meticulously 'jointed'. The movements of articulate discourse flow in the exercise of composition, but let a ligament be sprained or a joint be dislocated – let *for* and *whereas* fail in their function – then the grace goes out of it, and we limp and shuffle miserably.

In this passage there is a central comparison between the structure of discourse and the anatomy of the human body, a comparison which informs the language of the whole text. The pervading image is developed out of the etymological resource of one word (*articulate*: Latin *artus*, a limb, diminutive *articulus*; whence *articularis*, pertaining to a joint, *articulatus*, jointed). This teasing out of an inwound figurative thread presupposes the reader's lively interest in the process, and therefore is most compatible with the tone we have called 'collaborative'. It is certainly not as informal as the casual mixture of metaphors exemplified in [26], but on the other hand it exercises a warmer personal appeal than the aloof style of [25]; it is artificial, certainly (severer criticism might say artful) but the purpose of the artifice is to create a sympathetic communion of writer and reader. The use of the pronoun *we* and the casual occurrence of an imperative (*contrast this*) are symptomatic of the intended warmth of tone.

At the end of all these deliberations, some might say that the writer can appeal to his reader only by virtue of a personality that the collective devices of language generally reflect, perhaps occasionally distort, but never completely or permanently disguise; the style is the man himself, take him for what he is, peering out from his words as though from his portrait. Others might argue with as much conviction that the style is not at all the man himself. The style, they would allege, is the hypocrite in the strict etymological sense of that word; style is an actor, style represents the necessary hypocrisy of role-playing.

Authentic personage, then, or hypocritical presence? What is it that makes such a bustle in this black print? Let us try to reconcile the conflicting claims in these terms: style is first and foremost a relationship, the expression of an agreement between writer and reader, in the light of which a role is enacted and a personality finds play. Though time and space may separate the partners to the act, it is no mere huckstering with words to talk of an 'agreement'. The writer proposes the creation of a style and the reader gives his assent; style takes its effect only when the reader thus 'agrees' to it. Without his perceptions, his sympathetic attention, his intelligent connections and anticipations, all styles lapse into one, and all this care, this loving fretful labour in the strict syntactic field and the dictionary's enormous garden, must go for nothing. The writer is the stylist who creates, the reader the stylist who interprets; and the style of written things, from the humblest of scribblings to the most exalted works of literary art, is thus the lively expression of an accord reaching across countries or over centuries, framing one stranger's thought in the likeness of another's.

Chapter 7

Work in progress

So remarkable, then, is this act of writing that it apparently frees some part of us from the confines of calendar and atlas. Through it we reach to other times and other places; it passes the word to Whitsuntide and fetches an answer from Athens or Arkansas. Yet this, the wonderful liberty of the medium, is hardly achieved at a stroke. We begin by talking to ourselves, convincingly enough, maybe, but presently become involved in a long and laborious process of translation, a dull and often slavish imposition on the spirit. Suddenly language itself is strange, intractable, a material that responds lumpishly, a substance of stubborn grain that must be worked deliberately and in silence. Here is a speechless acquisition, a clenched and staring discipline. Here, indeed, is a trade, like metalwork or joinery; through practice we learn the craft, through learning we extend the practice, and always there is that charmed procedural circle, of doing and learning and doing, into which the initiate must break unaided. Demonstration is helpful, analysis is doubtless of great value, but who can teach the synthetic power of the creative imagination as it bodies forth some artefact – say a table, say a text? There are bounds, of course, to what theorizing can do; and so perhaps we have come in this book to a conjectural limit, beyond which all attempts at advice might be deemed presumptuous and futile. Once the making has begun, the maker must be his own apprentice and his own master.

Nevertheless something should be said, by way of summary, about the problems and strategies of work in progress. Three matters in particular invite commentary. One is the general question of 'blocks', ie of those baffling mental resistances that hinder the progress of composition. This is of course a highly speculative subject, but it can hardly be ignored in a book that otherwise has much to say about the elements of writing. Secondly, there is the process of self-monitoring – the writer's critical dialogue with himself, resulting in the choices and changes he makes as the work proceeds. Finally, comes the revision and correction of the completed text. These aspects of writing are presented here as though in an emerging order of objectivity, reflecting the gradual progress of the work from its conceptual origins to its printed conclusions. Seldom, however, is progress so simple and direct; reversions are frequent, and the writer must often run in vague circles to find his assured line.

7.1 Composition: inner and outer phases

The genesis of composition is a topic for conjecture. For most people there are periods of deliberation or creative daydreaming which alternate with active efforts at formulation; inner phases of imaginative exercise are followed by outer phases of technical exploration. The phases are interdependent, however, and in fluent composition it may be that we move more or less rhythmically from one to the other, sometimes letting technique follow the thrust of the imagination, sometimes training the imagination to the set of a technique. One process may in fact criticize the other. Formulation is a way of rapidly testing the feasibility of long-deliberated notions; deliberation in its turn assesses the value of what has been formulated.

Modes of alternation between phases must certainly vary from writer to writer, from text to text, and even from one part of a text to another. Sometimes the transitions between inner and outer are quite swift; the composition takes shape sentence by sentence, brief muttering fits of abstraction being succeeded by rapid forays on to paper. In other cases the writer will dash off whole stretches of text without much forethought, but devote long periods of deliberation to refining and correcting what he has written. Then again, pre-meditation on the work can occupy long hours, and not only those spent at the writing desk; household chores are bemusedly performed, daily travels pass as in a trance. These are some variants of a highly idiosyncratic process. Many practitioners are convinced that they follow one genetic method to the exclusion of all the rest; however, in writing as in other activities we are liable to self-deception about our own habits, and the production of any text must surely involve adaptive changes of compositional rhythm. For example, a long period of introspection might precede the drafting of a chapter, but then the shaping of some centrally important passage could impose a broken tempo of many brief deliberations and trial formulations.

Experience suggests that whatever the mode of composition may be it is important to keep inner and outer phases in some sort of supportive relationship. Too much introspection undoubtedly paralyses the will to compose; too much unpondered formulation produces an aimlessly wordy semblance of composition, a zombie prose from which the governing spirit has fled. Imbalance of the inner and outer phases seems, in fact, to be a primary element in the pathology of writing, and a potential cause of compositional blocks.

7.2 Blocks

The phrase *compositional block* suggests, perhaps, some chic professional malady to which idlers and literary hypochondriacs might be conveniently prone. These obstacles are real enough, however, and to achieve a piece of writing without stumbling into one must be a rare feat indeed. Each of us must find his own way of circumventing them, and it would perhaps be impertinent to offer advice on a matter so distinctly personal. Nevertheless, it might be useful to identify common difficulties, on the supposition that we approach the solution of a problem when we define its terms. Here, then are some recurrent forms of the doubts and puzzlements that bring composition to a standstill:

1 The most familiar of all difficulties is that of actually beginning, of putting the first words to paper; a reluctance amounting almost to a fear. (Amateurs of drawing and painting will recognize a comparable malaise; there is a dreadful timidity before the blank canvas or the large empty sheet of paper.) The symptoms are well known: a disposition to potter about, cat-nap, go for walks, read through notes, clean the typewriter, do anything to postpone the moment of writing. The cause of this initial block is most probably the intense and prolonged introspection that precedes the work; the more thorough the mulling over, the greater the first resistance, or so it sometimes appears. The writer is aware of the complex nature of the task he has undertaken. He knows how much he has glimpsed in thought, but the prospect of straining to

keep the vision steady while he translates it into writing, cogently and without loss, makes him faint-hearted. He is aware, too, of the treachery of the medium. With every sentence that is set down he will surrender a little of his original conception; the text will somehow assume control, luring him into formulations which misrepresent, conceal, even directly belie his intuitive strivings. He knows that his text will at best be a compromise between an ideal saying and what his desperate negotiations with language will allow him to say. There will be times when he will reject the compromise and may have to cancel whole pages and struggle painfully in revision to achieve some marginal improvement. With the knowledge that all this lies before him, he is not unnaturally reluctant to make a start.

What advice can avail here, beyond a bald admonition to say prayers and get down to business? The art of beginning, is, after all, only to begin – somewhere, anywhere – and perhaps not to fret if the order of composition at first is not the proposed order of the text. The important thing is to break the spell and put something on to paper. It may be an outline of the work, it may be one or two unrelated patches of text, it may be the framework of an opening paragraph, Whatever it is, it will doubtless be awkward and fragmentary. That need not matter; to make a few rough shapes is enough to remove the block. The process is analogous to that of beginning a jig-saw puzzle. With a thousand pieces scattered over the table the puzzle seems daunting indeed, but let a dozen of them be combined in a few pictorial fragments, and suddenly the possibility of completing the puzzle is not so remote. An idea of the whole is formed, and a working method is evolved.

2   There are junctures in composition when imaginative space and textual line seem irreconcilable; we run into what might be called a dimensional block. The work on the page is essentially linear; there is a sequence of events (topics, objects of description, points in argument, etc) set down in accordance with some articulatory logic worked out by the author. In the inner phase of composition, however, these same 'events' are not necessarily viewed in sequence; they will often be considered spatially, in changing perspectives and interrelationships. The evolving text presents one solution to a problem of arrangement; in the imagination, however, the configurations go on changing, disturbingly, in kaleidoscopic rotations. Inevitably there must be moments when

patterns seen in mental perspective resist the constraint of the chosen textual sequence.

Suppose, by way of simple illustration, that a student is set to write a critical dissertation on a series of short stories. In his musings he sees one story in the light of another, refers both instances to a third example, perceives numerous points of interrelationship in structure and style. Such global insights are very important, but for the purposes of his dissertation they must be brought – quite literally – into line. How, then, should the writer proceed? Should he consider each story in turn, commenting fully on plot, theme, characterization, structure, style, etc, or should he attempt to define certain governing motifs and treat the stories in thematic groups? Should he perhaps devote one section of his work to the general description of the stories, one to important themes, one to structure, one to characterization, one to style? Or would it be better to amalgamate some of these in major sections, perhaps combining theme with characterization and style with structure? Each of these possibilities projects a compositional line, and each line has its advantages and disadvantages, accommodating some of the 'spatial' relationships, but coping disjointedly with others. The problem is to determine the line that will permit the largest number of incidental links and meshes – the sequence that best allows for the play of non-sequential elements. This is so obviously a matter of choosing strategies to meet cases that perhaps nothing more can be usefully said about it here. When the chosen line is unsatisfactory, however, an inner voice will begin to say so, and will make its protests ever more frequently and insistently. The writer will want to ignore the voice at first, because he dreads having to dismantle substantial parts of his text; but in the conflict between the critic within and the artificer without, the writing is gradually blocked. It is best to heed the warning voice before the work goes too far, and consider a change of plan (on this see 7.3 below).

3 Problems of connection and transition are recurrent, and ultimately fray the writer's confidence. It is curious how the pen will scurry through an intricate construction or a closely patterned section of text, only to hover aimlessly when a boundary is reached. Sometimes it seems as though the whole process of breaking into the compositional act must be repeated from one sentence to the next, impetus failing with every full stop. Vague

ranges of meaning lie ahead, but these are only hazily discerned while there is no map of the territory in the shape of a proposed syntactic design. New routes may be suggested by experiments with alternative sentence-types, passive transformations, changes of focus, thematic frontings; or sometimes a standard cohesive device (*eg* enumeration) will set up a plan of connections sustaining an extended textual pattern. Sooner or later, however, the edge of the pattern is reached and the problem of transition recurs.

In effect there are two interrelated problems: that of devising transitions to facilitate *writing*, and that of demonstrating connections to guide *reading*. Though it may seem that they amount to one and the same thing, these are nonetheless different aspects of composition. The advantages the writer creates for himself do not always coincide with the amenities he provides for his reader; indeed, the construction of a text may often involve a subtle off-setting of the overt connections that mark out a path in reading and the covert transitions by means of which the writer guides the compositional flow. These matters are further discussed in 7.4 below.

4 If there were no other hindrance to easy composition, there would always be the bemused hankering for the elusive word, the expression that fits the immediate construction and also, perhaps, fills a place in the larger lexical scheme of interlinking references. We have all known the experience of sitting in a tense abstraction, mouthing not-quite-satisfactory possibilities, scratching at sounds and syllables that refuse to flare into meaning, taking random samples from a mental dictionary, struggling to establish a technique of rational enquiry, feeling bemusement harden into paralysis as the minutes go by. A possible way round this block would be to scribble freely in rough draft, leaving approximate choices for subsequent revision or even accepting temporary gaps. The perfectionist concern for accuracy, it might be argued, creates the mental tension that makes the block; thus one should postpone the hunt for precision while a jog through the text relaxes the mind. There are serious objections to this, however, the chief being that lexical dependences are created step by step of the way, and assurance in composition is based on the trust that each step is firm. If the choice of a word is so critical as to bring the writer to a standstill, it may well be because intuition is warning him that he has touched a nodal point in a pattern. Once choice

creates the conditions and directives for other choices; therefore
to choose approximately, or to evade choice, is potentially to
surrender firm control of a domain larger than the immediate
phrase or sentence.

A common procedure for tackling a lexical block is to use the
context, either immediate or precedent, as a scanning device. We
read and reread long stretches of preceding text in the hope that a
lexical pattern will emerge, that turns of phrase may provide
effectual definitions for the sought-after item (*eg* as *ups and downs*,
fortune's wheel, a turn for the better might point in the direction of
vicissitudes), that one word will cue another, or even that it may
prove expedient to borrow a word already set down and find an
easy synonym to fill the gap. The text thus becomes a large-scale
investigative matrix. A narrower method of scanning uses the
immediate syntactic environment, ringing the changes on clause
or phrase structure and making the construction act as pointer to
the word. (This strategy is discussed at some length in 4.17.)

If the form of the text will not elicit an answer, an appeal to the
form of the word may help. Intelligent reference to the elements
of word-formation, especially prefixes, yields the solution to
many problems. Notional formulations such as 'between events' or
'being informed already' might be precisely identified as *interlude*
and *foreknowledge* because the searcher has astutely translated
'between' and 'already' into the prefix-elements *inter-* and *fore-*.
There are people who are gifted with a dictionary sense, a feeling
for the structure of words, and who are particularly adept at this
kind of translation. The gift includes the power to make heuristic
use of etymological parallels; for instance, if *foreknowledge*
happened to be not quite satisfactory in a particular context, the
search might be taken a stage further by translating *fore-* into *pre-*
and *knowledge* into *science*, thus arriving at *prescience*. These
morphological clues may sometimes be reinforced by phonetic
hints, or, quite often, associations of sound alone may make
effective links from word to word; thus *intrusion* might be reached
via *interference*, because the two words begin (fortuitously) with the
same sequence of sounds,/int/.

5 Confidence in tone is important, and a mismanagement of tone
(see 6.3–6.5) will eventually block the progress of the writing.
Symptomatic of the block is a worried realization that the work
lacks all conviction and thrust; it rings false, and far too much

energy is wasted in posturing and pulling stylistic faces. If role and tone are properly conceived at the outset – if there is a balance in that precarious 'triangular' relationship between writer, reader, and theme – then often the text will acquire a self-sustaining momentum. It moves along purposefully because the writer is at ease with himself and has a clear view of his task. Initial uncertainty about role or lack of care in establishing a tone may mean that the writing straggles through page after page without generating any sort of impetus. In that case bold cancellation and wholesale revision may be the only resort.

This raises the general problem of discarding. The act of making an excision is in fact not so difficult as coming to the realization that something needs to be excised. The tone may be wrong, for one thing; for another, the pattern and direction of the work may be obscured by enthusiastic digressions, excessive illustrations, or prolonged analyses. These digressive passages are often most dear to the writer because they seem to embody his liveliest thought and best expressions. In fact they often betray an imbalance of compositional phases, a haste to formulate before the material has been thoroughly pondered. There is nothing for it in these cases but to strike out the superfluous text, stifling one's regret for lost time and energy. In the event, a resolute discarding can induce sensations of relief bordering on exhilaration; the removal of the offending passages puts an end to the aching puzzlement of feeling that the text is mysteriously deformed.

It is always a healthy measure to keep the text under review and to discard whatever can be shed without damage to the coherence and persuasive power of the whole. This need not mean stripping the work of all its embellishments, its playful interludes, its fun and ebullient finery. It does require, however, the discovery and rejection of passages in which the writer is performing showily for his private amusement, prosing uninformatively, presuming to instruct in matters that lie outside his competence, disputing points that were never in dispute.

7.3 Self-monitoring: (a) continuous planning

The text is reviewed in the light of a continuous plan. This requires in the first place the drawing up of a scheme of contents – as we are all taught in our schooldays – but the word 'plan' as used here indicates something perhaps rather more flexible than the traditional essay outline. There is a programme of topics to be ordered, expounded, and interrelated, and there are various pathways through this material. The choice of path will depend on the design the writer wishes to impose on the work, and the particular prominences and connections he wishes to bring out in his presentation. The scheme is not absolutely fixed; constituents may be added or deleted, shifted in order, incorporated or disjoined. In fact the plan may very well go on changing while the composition grows, and such change can be welcomed as a comforting symptom of vitality. Conversely, and paradoxically, it is necessary at every stage of the work to follow the currently relevant plan as though it were fixed once and for all.

In making the first programmatic sketches it may help to set out the constituent topics in propositional form, and then to link the items with connective words and phrases, *eg: thus, however, and so, in view of which, leading to, which means that.* This is a rough-and-ready way of testing the articulatory strength of the plan, a kind of skeletal proof of logic. What it may not do is guarantee the dimensional validity of the scheme (on this use of the word *dimensional* see item (2) in 7.2 above). The plan that seems strongest in linear logic may make very poor accommodation for all the spatial elements – the allusions and cross-references, the digressions and regressions, the parallels and contrasting perspectives – that give body to a complex exposition. In that case, the programmatic path must be changed and the constituent items of the text be regrouped (or in some cases discarded – see item (5) in 7.2 above). Such developments cannot be wholly foreseen at the outset; often it is only as a consequence of imposing a plan that the subversive shape of the work, straining against the imposition, begins to be apparent. In response to pressure, the work in effect displays its own inclination. The planning of a text is thus a continuous process. There is always a programme that is valid at any moment of writing, that channels thought and directs creative energies; yet the programme may be changed at any moment as its inadequacies are revealed by the very powers it has released. This is something rather different from the essay-planning which our schoolteachers enjoin upon us. Such planning is intended from the outset to give a secure overview of the development of the text. That kind of security is an illusion, however. We can never be absolutely secure in composition; we can only enjoy the relative security of having a plan that serves for a temporary orientation. As conditions change, we keep our security by making a new plan, perhaps not radically unlike the old one but different in some significant point of procedure, some addition, deletion, conflation, change of order, etc. We plan our compositions as we plan our economies, by trying always to face the treacherous facts.

7.4 Self-monitoring: (b) putting the text first

The uncertainty and mental strain of writing (to say nothing of its physical tedium) must be offset by some element of pleasure, some infusion of the maker's simple and secretive joy in his making. Without a little masquerading playfulness it is indeed weary work to sustain composition and bring it to a satisfactory close; the occasional turn of wit, the happy metaphor, the elegant solution of a tricky syntactic problem, the close and shapely bonding of a sequence of sentences – all such things awaken in the writer a pleasure that recompenses him for the necessary drudgeries of his task. On the other hand, when pleasure becomes sheer self-indulgence the task itself is put at risk and the work is sacrificed to wayward and irrelevant creative impulses. It should be an axiom, then, to put the text first, *ie* at every stage of its development to have in mind a programme, an audience, a role, and a tone, and to make that mental image of the work a constraint governing the exercise of pleasurable skills.

This is a complex and sensitive topic, and an illustration might be useful. Here, then, are drafts of an opening paragraph for an essay on *Germanic Heroic Poetry and its Audience*. A learned subject, this; some would say a dry one. Consider, therefore, which would be the better way of embarking upon it, assuming that one's role is principally that of the informant, that the tone should be one of easy formality, and that the aim is to present the elements of the subject for the benefit of intelligent but non-specialist readers:

[1]i For us, sitting in our comfortable, carpeted, well-lit, centrally heated rooms, drowsing the winter evening away with the poet's text passive in our laps and the TV 'repeats' busy in our ears, it is hard to imagine what the world was like for them. Their cold and their darkness were surely more oppressive than ours; sickness was a more terrible visitant; age and enfeeblement came earlier; they knew the condition of man as

we, in our technological cocoon, do not. Even in the houses of the great the wind gusted through the building, the terrified storm-blown bird fluttered in the rafters of the hall, the diners shrugged their cloaks about them, scowling blearily in the smoky light of the open hearth. The poet's harp jangled, the old heroic tales were mingled anew with praise for the All-Father and praise for the earl and praise for the bullies on the benches. Outside, night and the devil slouched across the chilly fields.

  ii At the little courts of Germanic kings and warlords, poetry had a function and an audience that shaped its conventions and established the principles of what was to become, in Old English oral and scribal tradition, a most elaborate verse-craft. The business of the poet was to record the deeds and sing the praises of a generous lord, whose name and fame would then go down to posterity. In this act of homage the listeners were profoundly involved, for such poetry, at least in its earliest forms, was a shared experience. It asserted their identity with a powerful leader, recited the legends of their folk-heroes, justified the actions of the great, affirmed common beliefs about life and conduct. Their use of poetry differed from ours, and it might be supposed that they judged poets by correspondingly different standards.

These are, as we have stated, drafts, and further working would make stylistic improvements in either version. The question is, however, which of the two is better fitted to its place and purpose in the proposed composition.

  In [1i] there is a firmly constructed paragraph design (of the stack type, see 1.5) and the cohesion is close and subtle, working through more than one device. The personal pronouns are an obvious source of cohesive tension, but note also how the syntax is used cohesively, in the subject-verb-adverbial parallels of *the wind gusted through the building, the terrified storm-blown bird fluttered in the rafters of the hall, night and the devil slouched across the chilly fields*. Lexical variants adroitly strengthen the cohesion: *cf: our comfortable . . . rooms, our technological cocoon; the houses of the great, the building, the hall, the benches*. Moreover, the passage exploits the stratagem of personification, with hints at the motif of 'encroaching movement' – *eg: visitant, came, slouched across*, in *sickness was a more terrible visitant, old age and enfeeblement came earlier, night and the devil slouched across the chilly fields.* This is, then, quite a close-knit, densely textured piece of writing.

Paradoxically, however, its principal virtue, its stylistic and structural tension, becomes a defect if we try to imagine the writing in relationship to a larger context. The paragraph is a little essay in itself – or a little patch of decorative imagery – and that final sentence strikingly shuts the passage down, offering no outcome. The text is left with nowhere to go; in his second paragraph the writer would still have to cope with the task of beginning the actual essay, leaving this introductory performance behind him as a sort of baroque prelude. The final sentence provides, incidentally, an example of the vivid invention that might have to be discarded. It is forcefully turned, and temptation might whisper that it is too good to lose, but the fact remains that it blocks the development of the text. Good rhetoric (in the sense of figuration) may be bad composition.

At times the rhetoric is in itself suspect – *eg: with the poet's text passive in our laps and the TV 'repeats' busy in our ears.* The nice symmetry of the figure possibly disguises the fact that *eyes* are more appropriate to TV than *ears*; but of course *with the TV 'repeats' in our eyes* would verge on the unidiomatic. The relish for the striking phrase is in general a little dubious. For example, *terrified storm-blown bird* alludes to an episode in Bede's *Ecclesiastical History.* Allusions may serve as signs of recognition between professional brothers, but perhaps in this case the allusion is not fair to the reader, the 'intelligent non-specialist'. Should a writer play this knowing game with an audience that supposedly looks to him for information, not for the passwords of the initiated? Indeed, the phrase might be subtly misleading, since the reader might not see in it a literary debt, but rather, a boldly original invention.

The gravest defect of [1i] however, is that it flouts the requirement to *inform.* It scripts the wrong role; the passage is high on entertainment and low on information (even though it might be said to inform implicitly or allusively). Consequently it fails to do its duty as an introduction. The opening paragraph in an essay of this kind should have the function of presenting the thesis, as it were, giving brief and clear indications of subject matter. It should be in effect a topic paragraph, and it cannot really be said that [1i] obeys that requirement. It teases the reader with its repeated *they* and *their* – much as a story-writer, following the conventions of entertainment, might legitimately keep him in suspense – but it disdains the sober informative task of saying who 'they' are and what 'their' importance might be in this context.

In [1ii], on the other hand, the informant role is quietly accepted and the task of setting out the theme of the essay is immediately undertaken, so that by the end of the paragraph we know more or less what ground the work will cover. It is much less strikingly written than [1i], and opens maladroitly; the first sentence stumbles through one coordination after another – *kings and warlords, a function and an audience, shaped the conventions and established the principles, oral and scribal tradition* – and ends with an awkwardly interrupted noun clause, *ie: what was to become, in Old English oral and scribal tradition, a most elaborate verse-craft*. There are signs here of that anxiety to amplify and qualify which often besets informative writing. However, [1ii] is not beyond hope stylistically, and is strongly constructed. It is developed out of the words *function* and *audience* in the first sentence, and a pattern of connectives leads skilfully if unshowily to a closing sentence which provides a point of departure for the next paragraph. This is technically useful; it is much easier to cross textual boundaries if, by a little forethought, we can build prospective bridges. (For further discussion of this, see 7.6 below.)

In short, [1ii], though inferior to [1i] as a stylistic showpiece, represents a much more realistic assessment of a project in composition. It puts the text first. Its style may leave much room for improvement, but there is one respect in which, through all his anxieties about wording, the author could be at ease; there need be no doubt in his mind that this is the right sort of paragraph for the job. Such simple assurance is not easy to win. The fiend is always ready to whisper that the writing is very fine, so clever, so beautiful, quite indispensable. Only the cheerful sound of crumpling paper will drown that wicked voice.

7.5 Self-monitoring: (c) the flow of the text

Composition is felt to be reassuringly effective when, in the common phrase, *it flows*, a quality sought through many revisions. This vital continuity depends to some extent on lexical features deep in the grain of the text; the passage on multivalence in 4.4 is a good example of the working of the lexicon in the continuum of a style. Rhythm is another factor, of obvious importance, and the sensitive writer responds progressively to the rhythm of his work as it develops from sentence to sentence. (There are some remarks on sentence rhythm and text rhythm in 5.12.) Of the very first moment, however, are connections and transitions, whether these take the form of syntactic changes of prominence facilitating and emphasizing sentence linkage (see 5.7*ff*), or devices of cohesion such as are reviewed and illustrated in Chapter 2. It is through these connective sleights that the illusion of flowing discourse is created. As experienced by the writer, composition is often a wretchedly discontinuous process; his text comes to him piecemeal, and he must not only search for the modes of association that best express his own thought, but also try to display a continuity for the reader's benefit.

This implies (as suggested in item (3) in 7.2 above) two complementary principles of textual structure; an overt connective pattern, including typographical layout – the reader-guiding structure – and a supplement of transitions that figure less obtrusively, though they may be of primary psychological importance. The text is moulded into form by the writer, who then presents it, in a form, to his reader. These two 'forms' will often coincide. Sometimes, however, they do not; they have a complex overlapping relationship, in consequence of which the continuity of the writing is strengthened.

It is in paragraphing that the alternations of writer-form and reader-form are most commonly observed. Topic boundaries are not always congruent with typographical boundaries, and there is a continuity of exposition, pulling hand-over-hand as it were, across the break. The effect is to lengthen the process of transition, so that there is perhaps a sentence or two that mediates between one paragraph and the next. Here is an example:

[2] To change the grammatical forms of a language is the devious work of time; all modifications are suspect and would be strenuously resisted by the community were it not for the fact that in their onset changes budge from the accepted norms by margins too trivial to be generally observed. Those 'accepted norms', furthermore, are derived from sources which are in themselves vulnerable to time and fashion. Writing is one type of authority that undoubtedly tends to fix the grammar of a language, but the status of writing as an arbiter is not the same in all ages, and the literary tradition may even be completely broken. Another kind of norm, no less mutable, is created by

social institutions and practices. Our modes of behaviour and our attitudes to each other can make or unmake structures in grammar, and leave their record in our linguistic history.

For instance, Shakespeare uses four distinct forms of the pronoun of address: *thou, thee, ye,* and *you.* In present-day standard English, we use only one of these forms, *you.* This reduction has not been imposed by any supervisory authority, with the aim of simplifying the language; it has been largely the concomitant of changes in social structure and attitudes. Shakespeare's testimony is particularly interesting, because in some scenes he observes very strictly the social differences of *thou* and *you* (and the grammatical distinction of *thou* and *thee, ye* and *you*), while in others he mingles the forms freely, with no apparent regard for persons or cases. His usage bears witness to a state of transition between the old and the new structures, in society and in grammar.

Ostensibly the connection between these two paragraphs is established by the *for instance* that makes an extensional link between the opening sentence of the second and the closing sentence of the first. Covertly, however, the transition has begun somewhat earlier – 'covertly' in the sense that the typographical organization here masks the real junction, the point of psychological shift, between one topic and another. The boundary is defined by the sentence beginning *Another kind of norm, no less mutable.* This sentence and its successor have the mediating effect mentioned above, presenting the continuity of the text in two perspectives. In one pattern of association they are linked to the *preceding* text, since they complete an exemplifying process stemming from *Those 'accepted forms' . . . are derived from sources . . . vulnerable to the time and fashion.* In another perspective they belong to the succeeding text, because *Another kind of norm* etc is effectively the topic sentence that heads a new development in the theme. In the flow of the text the word *another* locates the first moment of transition, the turning of a corner for the writer; the second moment, signposting the reader's way, comes with the typographical break and the connective *for instance.*

Conscious decisions govern paragraphing. Sentence-connection on the other hand, while never wholly automatic, is a process in which weary stylistic habits are sometimes evident. With so many larger problems to concern him, there is some tendency for the writer to deal with incidental difficulties of cohesion by resorting to the shorthand of one or two well-rehearsed connectives, thereby inhibiting the flexibility of his writing and potentially narrowing its discursive scope. Sometimes a little conscious effort to expand the connective range, restoring the awareness of a repertoire, may have surprising compositional results, because alternatives furnish keys to many possibilities. This is a difficult theme to illustrate compactly and substantially, but the following example raises typical issues:

[3]i Here in England the appearance of the sky changes from hour to hour. This presents a continual challenge to the painter.

ii Here in England the appearance of the sky changes from hour to hour. A continual challenge is thus presented to the painter.

iii Here in England the appearance of the sky changes from hour to hour, thus (thereby, consequently) presenting a continual challenge to the painter.

iv Here in England the appearance of the sky changes from hour to hour. Such mutations present a continual challenge to the painter (OR: present the painter with a continual challenge).

In [3i] there is a primary connection, a clear signal to the reader, in the form of the anaphoric *this*, and a secondary, somewhat less obtrusive connection in the semantic match of *from hour to hour* and *continual*. Versions [3ii–3iii] suggest ways of avoiding the hackneyed anaphoric and of exploring varied possibilities of connections. In [3ii], for example, a passive transformation turns the latently connective element into a thematic item; the relationship of *from hour to hour* and *a continual challenge* is made prominent by this syntactic rearrangement. The anaphoric role played, in [3i], by *this* is in [3ii] assumed by *thus*, but *thus* is a different kind of connective, suggesting an inferential bonding of the two sentences. Hence version [3iii], where the sentences are actually incorporated; there are times when the flow of a text is best promoted by such amalgamations. Example [3iv] works differently, keeping the sentences emphatically separate (there is something like a distancing implication in *such*) but reinforcing the elements of lexical cohesion (*mutations* refers to *the sky changes*, *continual* reflects *from hour to hour*). The connection is now semantically twin-stranded, and it is conceivable that out of this a text-sustaining yarn might be spun, threading a network of words denoting change or continuity. Though we can only speculate here, it is by no means impossible or unusual for an apparently simple sentence connection to be a point of origin for complex textural patterns.

7.6 Critical routines

After all these decisions and revisions the moment comes when all that remains, apparently, is the final draft, a work of mere copying. Composition goes on, however, even through transcription. So provocative and baffling is the attempt to formulate that to the very end we persist in making alterations and small innovations and are unwilling to let the text go. If beginning is hard, finishing is sometimes harder, especially when familiar labours have been so greatly prolonged that the writer, for all his eagerness to lay down a burden, is troubled by a prospective sense of loss. Sooner or later, though, the break must be made, and parting may be easier if valedictory musings can be translated into objective critical routines. Here, then, are some notes on the final exercises in self-criticism; because they can only represent an individual view (who would presume to lay down the general and immutable law in such matters?) they are addressed to the reader in personal fashion:

Sectioning

The work is presented in sections of various kinds, *eg* chapters, sub-chapters, paragraphs. These represent in the first instance your programming of the text, but they are also an aspect of the writer–reader relationship. Well-defined, clearly motivated sectioning guides the reader comfortably in his task of interpretation; hence the importance of numbering and titling, as well as the occasional value of explaining your procedures when such explanations can be conveniently and tactfully made – for example, at the end of a chapter, in commenting on the transition from one theme to another.

The apparent proportioning of your text is of some importance. You condition your reader to respond to certain conventions of layout and length, and you must therefore bear in mind that he may be disturbed when you stray far from your conventional norms. For example, he will fall into a rhythm of reading based on the length of your chapters or other major sections, and might be disorientated if you include without forewarning a chapter twice as long as the average. Similarly, awkward paragraphing may have an adverse psychological effect, and here there is quite a lot that can be done in critical revision, without having to attack the basic design of the work.

Inordinately long paragraphs, great-blossoming page-fillers, can be divided; it is usually not too difficult to find a line of cleavage and (perhaps with some adjustments of wording before and after the boundary) to make two paragraphs out of one. Respect the design of the text, however; if it will not cleave easily and proportionably, try some other tactic. It is often possible to reduce the length of a paragraph, while preserving its rhetorical pattern, by making syntactic compressions and excisions. Determine an average length, and look critically at units that seem excessively long or short. In Chapter 1 it is suggested that the paragraph is a viewfinder. Using another analogy we might say that it is also a balance or a measure, and that paragraphing is a way of hefting the text to judge its distribution of weight. As far as possible then, keep your sections in balance. If it is difficult to do this, then there may after all be something amiss with the programme and planning of the text.

Cohesion

Though cohesions should be monitored incidentally while the work is in progress, make a final check on the cohesive strength of the completed text. Look first at the transitions from paragraph to paragraph, bearing in mind the possibility discussed in 7.5 above, of making connective overlaps. Try to ensure that your overt markers of paragraph linkage are not crudely overworked. One of the most awkward types of transition is the heavy anaphoric linkage represented by such phrases as *the conditions outlined above* or *in view of the foregoing argument*; such old soldiers often have to be dragooned into service when fatigue or a temporary lapse of skill prevents the writer from perceiving a more elegant strategy.

Next, check the internal cohesion of each paragraph, keeping a censor's eye open for the awkwardly enforced connection and the phantom cohesion – the imposition of a *thus* when there is no compelling inference or a *nevertheless* when there is no clear counterpoise. (*Alfred burned the cakes. Nevertheless, he went on to beat the Danes.*) Such dubious connectives are generally a mark of lapsed logic or of some unhandy ellipsis in the process of exposition. (*Alfred burned the cakes. This might suggest a dangerous incompetence, since a man incapable of performing the simplest hearthside tasks could hardly be trusted to command an army in the field. Nevertheless, he went on to beat the Danes.)*

Syntax

The overriding problem of syntax in composition is that phrasing and sentence-structure have to be adjusted to multiple requirements, *ie* information-processing, focus and emphasis, textual cohesion, text rhythm, tone. Here the making of a fair copy is a valuable and more than mechanical exercise, for transcription suggests many re-appraisals; sentences are divided or incorporated, clause-structures are changed, phrasing is criticized. This is a chance to look carefully at branchings and parentheses (see 5.10*ff*, 6.11) to make sure that you have not weighted a sentence with encumbrances that needlessly obscure its informational pattern. An elaborately subordinated structure may of course be your deliberate stylistic intention, but still there may be cases where the integrative design of a sentence can be improved by relocating or even cancelling some heavily intrusive element.

Revision of the text will confront you embarrassingly with your own mannerisms in sentence connection, clause-structure, and, above all, in phrasing. Such mannerisms can be very stubborn – phrasing is often as personal as a thumb-print – but there are deletions and changes that can be made without doing great violence to meaning or much altering the set of your style. If, for example, you were to notice a large number of pairings with *and* (see 4.7*ff*), you might in a few cases be willing to delete a not-altogether-necessary coordinate, or else change the syntactic relationship of the two elements in the phrase; *his courage and endurance*, for example, might be reduced to *his courage*, or changed to *his courageous endurance*, or *the courage with which he endured*. Something may occasionally be gained by deliberately attacking a mannerism; our stylistic formulae are all too often put to work where a little thought might reveal a more effective solution. (On the relevance of this to sentence connection, see 7.5 above.)

Lexicon

Unless it is your preferred method to complete a draft first and attend to lexical precision afterwards, the struggle for the good word will have been protracted through the working of the text (on this, see item (4) in 7.2 above). Final revision may bring one or two second choices, but these are most likely to occur in connection with syntactic changes. What a critical reading of your draft will often reveal is a surprising number of clumsy repetitions and lexical mannerisms, many of them occurring (experience suggests) around and across topic boundaries or paragraph breaks. In coming to grips with the new topic the mind, it would seem, often draws on the vocabulary mobilized to handle the immediately preceding theme. It is therefore worth paying particular attention to junctions in your text, whether of 'writer-form' or 'reader-form' (see 7.5 above), in order to detect and cure this lexical stuttering.

Always ask whether a word is doing useful work (your criteria of usefulness will of course depend on your conceptions of role and tone), and do not hesitate to cancel supernumerary expressions, even at the cost of having to make a few syntactic repairs. Examine coordinations and sequences (see 4.6ff) and distinguish items that carry a real weight of meaning from those that merely pass the parcel of rhythm. There may be a case for leaving the rhythmic decorations alone, but that, again, will have to be determined in the context of your general intentions. Be aware, however, of the distinction between the indispensable and the additional, and be prepared as a rule to delete ruthlessly; indeed the last exercise on the text, the final manifestation of sincerity, is a willing purge of all things superfluous to your programme, your avowed role, your attempted tone.

Let three words make a brief finale, three words to define a spirit of composition. Firstly, pleasure: a *disciplined* pleasure in the exercise of a difficult but not unattainably remote skill. The writer's path is not always thorny with technicalities, and there are voluptuous moments when he enjoys, however briefly, the mastery of his material. Even in the composition of a business letter or a mundane report there can be a controlled playfulness that enlivens the commonplace task. Secondly, persistence: the determination to soldier on in the harness of routine, accepting any exercise, any drill, any dogged manoeuvring, this way or that, to cover difficult ground or capture a stubborn point. If this is ever pleasurable, so much the better; if not, it is still the way to competence, and to the distinction that lies beyond competence. Finally, and always, pride: pride in this, the mother tongue, and in the excellence of those who have used it well, for our instruction and delight. Let us be conscious of an inheritance, and while we work let us never lose a sense of homage, so respectful yet so importunate that in a lucky hour sweet English may show, even to us, a comely favour.

Exercises: Analyses and compositional routines

Note to the reader

The exercises follow quite closely the plan of the book from Chapter 1 to Chapter 6, with references which should help you to recapitulate a topic or find examples of a compositional technique. There are no exercises that relate specifically to the mainly retrospective and summary material of Chapter 7.

These projects consist partly of passages for analysis, correction, rewriting, etc, and partly of suggested themes for composition. Some of the texts are deliberate examples of poor technique, while others present a more competent face. In no case, however, has much care been taken to polish an example beyond the first draft. The aim is to give you a free hand, unrestrained by the considerations of politeness that might protect more distinguished compositions. If you are able to learn anything from these workpieces, so much the better; but in any case treat them as roughly and critically as you please.

Similarly, in attempting the compositional routines, work in a spirit of free experimentation. The literary competition, not the school essay, should be your prescriptive model. If the suggested topics occasionally seem naive, do not take offence. There is certainly no intention to insult you by asking you to perform childish tasks; what is important is the discipline of writing to a directive. Tackle the routines as zestfully as possible, writing and rewriting versions until you feel you have produced a satisfactory exercise; in the course of your experiments you may find that you make creative discoveries.

A: Paragraph patterning

REFERENCE: Chapter 1, Sections 1.4–1.8

Introductory comment

Section 1.4 *ff* discusses and illustrates a number of patterns discernible
in prose structure, specifically in the composition of the paragraph.
These patterns are described (for simple convenience and with *no*
intention of creating a terminology!) as *Step*, *Stack*, *Chain*, and
Balance. A summary reminder of their characteristics may be useful:

*Step: *A progression of discrete items*, either connected by
          enumeratives or merely reflecting the pattern of a
          reported situation. (*First*) *the barber laughed crazily.* (*Next*) *he
          sharpened his razor.* (*Finally*) *my whiskers fell.*

* Stack: *A recursive series* of illustrative or analytical comments on a
          proposed topic (A, a_1, a_2, a_3, etc). *Smoking is bad for you. It
          attacks the heart. It congests the lungs. It blackens the teeth.*

*Chain: *A progressive sequence*, each expanding its predecessor
          (A–B–C–D). *Smoking gives you bad breath. That makes you
          unpopular. Unpopularity leads to loneliness. Lonely people smoke
          heavily.*

*Balance: *An alternation* of proposition(s) and counter-proposition(s).
          *Smoking is bad for you. On the other hand, many people find it a
          comfort. Without some pleasure, life would be intolerable.
          Nevertheless we must control our indulgences.*

Few paragraphs of prose adhere to a single pattern; to quote the
text, 'a reader looking for the structures that inform a given passage
. . . will become aware of one procedure invading another, one
device abandoned in favour of another, one pattern begun,
interrupted, and perhaps resumed.'

Exercise A1

1 DIRECTIONS

The passages in (2) below are all examples of paragraphs constructed
in patterns that are sometimes complex or broken. The task is to
study them and try to define their procedures of patterning. It may
help, as a preliminary, to transcribe the passage chosen for study and
number the sentences. The following questions will be relevant:

*   Does the paragraph clearly split at any point – is there a fissure, as
    it were, in the contextual ground?

* Do the sentences fall into discernible groups? Are the groups clearly defined, or do they, in some cases, appear to overlap?
* What is the pattern-relationship of the sentences in each group? (Step? Stack? Chain? Balance?)
* How are the groups of sentences related in the total pattern?

It is sometimes interesting and illuminating to try to draw a complex pattern, using lines and rectangular shapes to represent sentences and blocks of sentences.

2 MATERIAL FOR ANALYSIS

(a) Most people hate fog, and with good reason. It is undoubtedly a treacherous and frightening thing for the road user. There is no more appalling sensation than to be driving a car, whether on a motorway or a winding country road, and to run into fog. All the customary points of reference are expunged and the driver is completely and terrifyingly disorientated, not knowing where he is in relation to the side and the middle of the road, to the next car, to the next bend. Even in towns it can be most alarming to drive in fog, especially when parked and unlit vehicles loom abruptly out of the murk and pedal cyclists drift perilously through the glaucous haze. Smoke and fumes make an urban mist particularly nasty and strengthen the conviction that fog is a totally hateful thing. On the other hand, a walk along a quiet lane on a foggy day can be an experience of great beauty. Mist, like snow, transforms a landscape. It swaddles the velvet-black trees and floods the white fields knee-deep. It changes perspectives; near things are vehemently nearer and far things mysteriously farther. Above all, it makes the world so silent, so still, so rapt, that the walker finds himself moving reverently, as if in church, and listening intently, as though for some annunciation.

(b) Under the floorboards my two-cylinder Lister talks to itself, to the steerer, to the river, to the whole English summer. Its voice is not the voice of any other engine. From the chatter of the Sabbs and the Petters, from the majestic enunciations of the rare and princely Bolinder, the emphatic dialect of the little journeyman Lister can always be distinguished. Its modes of address are many: the yelps and cacchinations with which it greets the morning, the self-satisfied prosing in locks, the thoughtful syllabics as the gears are engaged, the clergyman musings and rambling intonations on a long run – but always, always, that unmistakable accent, that characteristic rhythm. It is a sound once heard never forgotten, one of those impressions that never leave the mind, a dormant sensation that can wait for months or even years to be revived. You might wake from your winter sleep, wake on some ruined morning in Spring, hear those talkative stresses coming over the water from half a mile upstream, recognize them with a wry gladness, and think: this is England and that is a Lister and I am happy and soon I shall be eating my bacon and eggs and watching the other fools go by in their oilskins and waterproofs.

(c) Inflation is a word with which we are all uncomfortably familiar. It is hardly possible to open a newspaper without seeing it. Indeed, the journalists might even be blamed for promoting the phenomenon by circulating the word. They have been blamed for practically everything else it is possible to be blamed for, so to be saddled with this particular burden will hardly offend them. The accepted scapegoat, however, is the militant trade unionist. It is argued that were it not for his excessive wage demands prices would not rise, and that if prices did not rise he and his fellows would not feel obliged to make excessive wage demands. This is the process that used to be picturesquely known as the wage–price spiral. Against that, there are theorists who contend with equal fervour that inflation is not primarily traceable to high wages. On the contrary, they say, the solution to the problem lies in regulating the forces of the market. That is done by controlling the money supply, so that funds are simply not available to finance the workforce to demand the wages that put up the prices. The name for this cheerful nostrum is monetarism. On the one hand, therefore, we have the advocates of wage control, with their conviction that the curbing of wages must lead to the restriction of prices. On the other there are the monetarists, who support free collective bargaining for higher wages but cunningly refuse to finance free collective bankruptcy. There is something to be said for both sides and nothing we can do about either, so let us now turn to some truly interesting matter, such as the incomparable beauty of Schubert's great C Major Quintet, or the right way with greenfly, or the wondrous taste of lemon syllabub.

Exercise A2

3 DIRECTIONS

Compose paragraphs on the topics listed in (4) below, adapting the material to the designated pattern. NB: There is *no* mechanical relationship between pattern and topic. The patterning is an aspect of style, one way of treating the topic; there may well be others. These projects are therefore exercises in artifice. They will yield best results if they are based on a sound expository programme – *ie* if there are several good points to be made – and if they are tackled in an enjoyable spirit of free experimentation. It is a counsel of perfection, but the practice of composing several versions of a text does help to promote facility in technical routines.

4 MATERIALS FOR COMPOSITION

* Compose to the *step* pattern:

    A paragraph on *Making coffee*; or a paragraph giving instructions on any other common process.

    A paragraph narrating some precipitate event – an emergency, a quarrel, an unexpected occurrence or reaction, etc.

* Compose to the *stack* pattern:

    A paragraph on *The use of poetry*.

    A paragraph on *The Shakespearean tragic hero*.

    A paragraph on *The authority of parliament*.

* Compose in a *chain* pattern:

    A paragraph on *Reading in bed*

    A paragraph on *Roses*, or a paragraph on *Rice pudding*.

    A paragraph on *Official Secrecy*.

* Compose in a *balance* pattern:

    A paragraph on *Capital punishment*

    A paragraph on *Immigration*.

    A paragraph on *Official regulations and individual freedom*.

The intention is that the proposed topics should exemplify a simple pattern in a single paragraph. It is quite possible, however, that the material may spread into two paragraphs, or that the simple patterns may become complex and broken. Should that occur, the results may be worth analysing and the lesson may be instructive.

B: Textual cohesion

REFERENCE: Mainly Chapter 2; Chapters 1, 3–5 *passim*

Introductory comment

Chapter 2 is called 'The gaps between sentences', and deals almost exclusively with the syntactic instruments of sentence-connection. Remember, however, that there is cohesion *within* as well as *between* sentences. Remember also that cohesion is not solely a question of connective tags; lexical, phonological, and even graphological cohesion may be important in due place (see 1.9). A further point to bear in mind is that the cohesion of a text is partly a matter of *immediate* links and partly of more *remote* connections; the beginning and end of a paragraph for example, may be linked by syntactic or semantic features.

Exercise B1

1 DIRECTIONS
Study the passages in (2) below and try to identify the features that promote textual cohesion, bearing the following questions in mind:

* What are the syntactic devices that close the gaps between sentences?
* To what extent is lexical cohesion important?
* Do the lexical and syntactic cohesions appear to work in correlation with each other? Or as systematic alternatives? Or in random alternations?
* Are there devices apart from those of syntax and the lexicon that promote the cohesion of the text?
* Are there remote as well as immediate cohesions in the text? How are the remote links made?
* If there is more than one paragraph, are there textual links between paragraphs?
* How are methods of cohesion related to the *patterning* of the text, as studied under section A above?

2 MATERIAL FOR ANALYSIS
(a) In the corner of my new garden, near the garage, was a tall shrub.

It puzzled me for a long time, that shrub. My puzzlement was hardly remarkable, for I am a bleak ignoramus in horticultural matters and can just about manage to tell a japonica from a jasmine. Nevertheless I do like to keep a tally of my dependents, and after a while I had succeeded in identifying most of the bushes and blossoms under my dominion. The identifications were made partly with the help of a splendid gardening encyclopaedia and partly on the word of Jim's wife, an encyclopaedia in her own sturdy right. Indeed, I would back Jim's wife against a world of encyclopaedias if it came to a disagreement. Her scholarship is as broad as my ignorance is deep, and in the naming of flowery names she has more Latin than Virgil. She rattled off the right polysyllabic labels of this bit of greenery and that till I began to feel quite flushed with excitement, but when she got to the shrub by the garage the spirit failed in her. It wasn't that she failed to recognize the beast. Not at all; the shrub has yet to sprout that would pass unrecognized by Jim's wife. It was simply that she had forgotten its sacred name. She muttered something about the sea and the sky and said it would come out all blue in July. This I found poetic, but not informative. Next she began to murmur 'she, she' in a kind of trance, a quite extraordinary piece of behaviour for such a sensible woman. After that she retired in confusion, defeated and humiliated by a mere mass of twigs. I have seen that peeved and vanquished look on the faces of doctoral disputants in Scandinavia. She was quite right, though. The shrub *did* flower in July, in a dense and delicate pother of blossoms, small beaded globes of heavenly blue, cobalt blue. Shortly afterwards I at last discovered its name: *ceanothus burkwoodii.*

(b) Jogging, for which there is a current craze, appears to me to be a misguided enthusiasm. For one thing, I cannot believe that jogging is the slimmer's friend; the whole weight of scientific evidence seems to be against it. I have heard, for example, that a man would have to run 36 miles to take off one pound. THIRTY SIX MILES! In that case I would have to jog all the way to Edinburgh – TWO HUNDRED AND SIXTY MILES!! – to lose a little more than seven. Admittedly, Edinburgh is a fair city and well worth seeing many times over, but there *are* trains and I would prefer to use them thus avoiding the long historic jog over Carter Bar. Besides, if I ran all that way I would certainly be very hungry at the end of it and would probably eat enough good Scottish fare to put the seven pounds back. On top of which, there is the matter of good Scottish liquors, all those malt whiskies, fragrant and fortifying and cloyed with calories. So on the whole I do not think I want to jog to Edinburgh to lose a miserable seven pounds, or even to Aberdeen – THREE HUNDRED AND SEVENTY MILES!!! – to lose a touch over ten.

For another thing – turning from this pleasant talk of food and drink – there has to be something seriously amiss with a man who can get up in the morning, put on fancy dress, and go wheezing and gasping through the streets, to the pity and horror, not to say hilarious amusement, of milkmen and other professional itinerants. Such a man is in danger of abandoning all decency and self-respect. He is running to what vulgar folks call the funny farm or the laughing academy, a destination that for most of us is within COMFORTABLE WALKING DISTANCE!! Of course we need exercise, but a little unostentatious strolling will surely serve; alternatively, some discreet bending and stretching in the garden might keep the surplus poundage down and the mortician at bay. For my part, I prefer messing about in boats, if possible with a pretty woman. The boatman's pace is a little faster than a walk and a little slower than a gallop, and provided he has an attractive crew to work the locks for him he can enjoy the illusion of exercise without the painful inconvenience.

(c) Several excellent varieties of tinted paper are available to the pastellist. Many go under the generic name of Ingres papers, the best being those manufactured in Sweden (*Tumba*), Italy (*Fabriano*) and France (*Canson*). All these papers have an attractive grainy texture which the artist should try to turn to something more than decorative account. For instance, the shimmer of foliage, or the effect of light on water, or the detail of masonry can be suggested by letting the paper do the work. This is not unlike the 'dry brush' technique in watercolour painting. Indeed, it might be said that working in pastel is a compromise between drawing and painting, or a way of painting without a diluent. On the other hand, pastels have properties that in no way resemble those of watercolour, acrylics, or oils.

Unlike watercolours, pastels do not require immediate accuracy of touch. On the contrary, they can be corrected without too much trouble, using a plastic eraser, otherwise known as a putty rubber, or a stiff hog-hair brush. However, over-correction sours the texture, so to speak, by rubbing off the distinctive bloom of the colours. These pigments have a luminous brilliance that no other medium possesses. True, there is nothing like gouache for simple strength of colour, and with acrylics the modern artist can match the fine singing clarity of the old tempera painters; but pastels lie on the paper like the nap on velvet, with a sheen that takes the viewer's eye in changing lights. It is a unique effect, unrivalled in certain applications – in representing the texture of petals or fruit, for example.

Here, then, is a very attractive medium. For the comparatively inexpert, however, it poses some technical problems, the most notable being that it is difficult to superimpose one colour upon another. Watercolour permits the superimposition of wash on wash, and in acrylics or oils we can easily make 'glazes' of colour over colour. Acrylics are particularly suitable for this purpose. By contrast, pastels merely go lifeless and muddy when any substantial overlaying of colour is attempted. Furthermore, whatever the textbooks may say to the contrary, the beginner will find it difficult to work down to fine detail in pastel. This is perhaps a not very important limitation, and of course it can be circumvented by the skilled use of the pen, or carbon pencils, or those very convenient small 'carrés' manufactured by Conté. With such implements fine line-drawing can certainly be done; nevertheless pastel works best in broad application and the medium seems to require a certain scale to be most effective.

An incidental drawback of pastels is that completed pictures have to be treated with fixative and either put under glass immediately or else stored in such a way as to protect them from excessive smudging. Working with pastels can indeed be a smudgy business. The paper sleeves which manufacturers put round the sticks gradually become a nuisance; besides, many people dislike working with the whole stick and prefer to break off a small piece of pastel and work close to the paper. A cloth is therefore necessary to keep the fingers clean and so protect the drawing from accidental smears. As for the care of the pastels themselves, the following hints may be useful. First, keep them intact and soft by storing them, if possible, in a compartmented box on layers of foam rubber or some other cushioning material. This may sound elaborate, but in fact such a box is easy and cheap to construct. Second, keep them clean. This is perhaps more easily said than done, but one way of going about it is to take a handful or two of ground rice, put it into a small jar or plastic container, drop in a few pastels and shake up the mixture. The friction of the ground rice should clean the pastels without damaging them. A piece of rug canvas is handy for sieving out the rice; otherwise the pastel pieces have to be recovered by patient searching.

Exercise B2

3 DIRECTIONS

The text supplied in (4) below is so deficient in cohesion that in places it appears to contradict itself. A sensible and not inelegant passage can be produced from this material, taking the sentences in the order given and revising the text in the light of the following recommendations:

* Supply links between sentences. Links may be simple or compound. Look for good syntactic links, but do not ignore the possibility of lexical solutions.
* Where there appears to be a choice between 'inter-sentential' cohesion (the bridging of gaps between sentences) and 'intra-sentential' cohesion (the possibility of running two sentences into one) carefully evaluate the possibilities in the whole context of composition.

4 MATERIAL FOR COMPOSITION

This great library can overwhelm the newcomer with sensations of awe and suppressed excitement. It fills him with intimations of profound peace. Mingled feelings are natural. The voices of humanity, raised in moral and spiritual counsel, fill the air with the rumour of their debate, their triumphant doubts, their melancholy certainties, their final assurances of comfort. All is hushed and tranquil, like a church. Timeless calm and unwithering composure surround the devotee.

The library is a place of work, and hard work at that. It is possible to be idle. A fugitive is protected from the importunate business of the world. Friends and colleagues who would cheerfully invade the privacy of his home do not disturb him.

Sleep is strictly respected in the library, provided that the sleeper does not snore. No true scholar is idle. It appears that he spends most of his time gazing at the back of the librarian's neck. He is working to some purpose.

Note: There is more than one solution to this problem, and the meaning of the passage may be affected by a choice of different connectives (*cf* 2.1).

C: Lexicology

REFERENCE: mainly Chapter 3; Chapter 6, intro section and 6.1–6.5 *passim*, 6.14, 6.15

Introductory comment

Whereas each of the examples composed for Chapter 3 turns on one distinctive principle of lexical organization, the lexicology of most texts will be found to be diffuse and complex, affecting cohesion, texture (as defined in the introductory section of Chapter 3) and tone (see 6.5, 6.14). This complexity may be evident in the passages set for analysis in (2) below.

Exercise C1

1 DIRECTIONS
Study the passages in (2) below and try to define the lexicological principles that inform them. Consider in particular these points:

* Is there a major textural principle – *eg* reiteration (see 3.1), variation (3.2), periphrasis (3.3), multivalence (3.4), organizing metaphor (3.5, 6.15)? Or do such devices appear to enter sporadically into a not very clearly defined pattern?
* If there *is* a major device, do minor textural schemes enter the passage, supporting or extending or even subverting the governing stratagem?
* If there is *no* major device, can it be shown that the passage grows out of an interplay of two or more textural principles?
* What part does the lexicon play in promoting the cohesion of the text?
* What relationship, if any, can you perceive between lexicological devices and the tone of the passage?

2 MATERIAL FOR ANALYSIS

(a) Every morning of summer when I put back the curtains I see
something that never fails to please and fascinate: a view
patterned out of seemingly countless variations of green. Here is
something that could be painted almost exclusively in tones of
that one colour, an exercise in monochrome that would require
the most delicate management of the palette. Today, and at this
moment, the green of the pasture on the far side of the river is a
bleached and curiously abraded green, no more than distantly kin
to the rich vibrant green of the ash-tree that overhangs the water
on this side: and that in its turn is a sombre cousin, no closer than
that, to the luminous yellow-green of the saplings along the
towpath and the flickering green-silver of the willows. The
surface of the water is shifty with tenebrous moods of olive, and
the hedgerows and poplars which mark the distant bound of the
valley are a softly shadowed aquamarine. In two hours the light
will have changed, will change again before afternoon, will be
totally different tomorrow at this time, and all these values of
green will alter with it. A painter would have to go smartly to
work to capture this.

I would love to paint it, but my mind quails before the problem
of mixing all those greens, of making each accurate and totally
contrastive definition of colour. It is a challenge comparable to
the problem of identifying half a dozen different shades of
meaning in one complex word, except that semantics is an
abstract exercise, while mixing paint is an occupation with dire
practical consequences. It would be easy to fudge the problem, to
blur one or two definitions, to disturb the precise relationship
between tone and tone, then all that intricate plotting of
emerald, olive, beryl, would blend and coalesce in a mere
viridescent mass. The reduction of subtle monochrome to stupid
monotony would not only be bad painting; it would also belie the
character of our landscape.

For it is in no way monotonous, this midland countryside.
True, the folds of the land are unbroken by dramatic intrusions of
mountain or forest, but there is a significant modulation in the
changing pattern of the fields, a phrasing in the location of
nestling farmhouse or skyline coppice, and occasionally a starker
accent in a line of pylons or a group of cooling towers. There is a
sort of muted eloquence, a language which the stranger must

learn to read, an expressiveness to which at last he may acquire a lover's sensitivity. And always there are these rhythms and syllables and volubilities of green.

(b) At the first wink of changing weather, in come the tourists; the birds up from the south, and from the river those other seasonal folk, the voles. They are both welcome, the feathered crowd almost unreservedly, the furry bunch perhaps not so warmly. The one reservation about those wonderful crazy fliers is their habit of making a comfort station out of the cabin top of the boat. Some of the younger set, especially the swallows and the wagtails, seem bent on turning nature's requirement into an exuberant competitive sport, a form of aerial darts or acrobatic bowls, and the one thing we do not claim to provide here is a games area for the hooligan element among avians in transit. Apart from that, our guests are very pleasantly behaved and do credit to what we like to think of as a superior type of establishment. The rodents, it must be said, are less engaging; definitely a poorer class of resident, they tend to drive away the airborne trade. Putting out scraps of bacon on the lawn will bring them in like an advert in *Dalton's Weekly* – and they are *never* satisfied with the portions – but once arrived they stay and stay and stay and gradually bring in all their relatives in a sort of expanding package deal. What's more, they claim the run of the place. It isn't enough for them to have pleasant accommodation with all facilities under attractively decorated green and white flower tubs, they have to climb up one storey onto the scenic all-weather bird-table and dine *à la carte* from a menu designed for the more discriminating guest. That's the big drawback with these swimmers, their sheer cheek; the fliers may maculate your boat, but at least they don't come nosing up to the kitchen door looking for corned beef and cream crackers. And of course one hesitates to put a visitor to inconvenience by laying down Warfarin or calling in the Russian Blue from next door – a very efficient operative, certainly, but not renowned for his tact. In the long run, though, our clientele sort things out among themselves. When the voles grow numerous, the owls drop in and evict one or two of them. Permanently. And at night, with the minimum of fuss.

(c) If you walk along a bridle path or any broad track through a belt of woodland, and look up, you may have the momentary illusion that the sky is a river flowing high above the green bed of your path, lapping gently at the tops of trees whose branches and trunks plunge vertiginously down into the opaque element where you – well – what? – walk? – swim? – for suddenly you are looking at the world from a fish's point of view.

Now this, you may say, is nonsense, pure fancy, just the mind following the eye in a moment of silliness. No doubt; but there are some fancies that enable us to escape for a second or two from that most compelling of natural constraints, the instinctive assumption that the species (or nation, or class, or individual) is at the centre of the world and that all things else are creatures of the outer subordination. Such an assumption writes the programme of survival for non-human nature. Lions live in a world designed to supply food to lions, sharks in their ocean currents observe the ordinances of the shark. The spider crouched at the central node of her web might well suppose that the gentiles of the non-arachnid world merely contrive to affirm and serve the economy of her design. For a spider there is no other way of looking at it.

We, however, can always see the world not only from within the prison of man's necessary self-regard, but also, and however momentarily, from outside it. We build roads, navigate rivers, herd animals, catch fish, and in general manipulate a creation that seems to exist for our central benefit. At the same time, we are capable of strange intuitions of what might be a very different state of affairs; we take a hint, through some fortuitous image or some magically symbolic commonplace, that we ourselves are a creation's creatures, that we are in our turn manipulated, that we are fish in some aerial stream, herded animals in some cosmic field. Look up from the bridle path, look up at the riverine flow of air, and you might humorously fancy that a baited line will at any moment make bright rings in that silver surface and come snaking down towards you. Well, a little surrealism does no harm; it liberates the imagination from third-form physics. Consider, though, what happens when one such fantastic instant is associated with some other moment of topsy-turvy insight. Then you have the beginnings of myth. Institutionalise the myth and you have a religion.

Exercise C2

3 DIRECTIONS

In (4) below, some topics for composition are suggested. Do not write at great length; one paragraph or two, with a total length of no more than 250 words, should be your limit. Accept this restriction even though the topic you choose may seem to invite more extensive composition. The exercises are first and foremost drills in lexicology, but in performing them you should take incidental note of relationships between the lexicon and other stylistic features. If you have time and inclination, make several versions of each exercise and study your own work carefully and critically, always looking for the patterns that inform it. Do not resent the artifice of writing to a prescription; it is a necessary discipline and a very ordinary mark of technical competence. Remember the story of Brückner and Brahms. Brückner, a very devout man, is alleged to have said (in reply to an enquiry) that his slow movements were beautiful because they came to him direct from God: on hearing which, Brahms observed, perhaps not so piously but much more practically, 'mine are beautiful because my publisher likes them that way'.

4 THEMES FOR COMPOSITION

(a) Write a fourth paragraph for passage (c) in (2) above, taking your cue from the closing sentences of the passage as it stands. You will already have made a lexicological analysis along the lines suggested in (1), and you should make close reference to this in composing your additional paragraph. However, the exercise will almost certainly require the imitation of other stylistic features in the text, which means that you may have to extend your preliminary analysis; try to discover, for example, the principal indices of tone (see 6.5).

(b) Compose *short* texts on the following themes, experimenting with the lexicological devices indicated in each case. NB: These indications do not preclude the use of other devices in subordinate or contrastive patterns.

*   Topic: *Instinct and deliberation in craftsmanship.* (Use an organizing metaphor. See 3.5.)
*   Topic: *Weeding* OR *Eating.* (Write humorously or parodically, making free use of periphrastic variations. See 3.3.)

* Topic: *The liberty of the subject* (Make reiteration your principal device. See 3.1.)
* Topic: *Lawrence's narrative style* OR *Landscape and local character.* (Experiment with the technique of variation discussed and exemplified in 3.2.)

If in spite of all your efforts the suggested topic and the indicated technique simply will not match, compose your text without any preconditions and see if a lexicological principle emerges.

D: Phrasing

REFERENCE: Chapter 4

Introductory comment

Chapter 4 relates phraseology in composition partly to the grammatical classification of phrase types and partly to rhetorical patterns in the construction and combination of phrases (see 4.5). The exercises in this section reflect these two (complementary) aspects of phrasing. D1 is purely analytical, D2 and D3 call for the critical evaluation of alternative styles of phrasing, and D4 presents themes for composition in these alternative styles. In carrying out the exercises, do not forget the lessons that may have been learned from working on earlier sections in this programme; factors of cohesion and lexicological design will often be relevant to phrasing.

Exercise D1

1 DIRECTIONS

In (2) below are two passages for phraseological analysis. Passage (a) should provide an adequate display of different phrase types. Refer to 4.1–4.4 before making your analysis; then write an account of the passage, along the lines suggested by 4.4. Remember to include in your account some mention of:

* The noun phrase. Premodification. Postmodification.
* The adjective phrase, as a stylistic entity.
* Adverbs and adverbials. 'Amplifications' of adverb and verb (see 4.3).
* The verb phrase.

Passage (b) exemplifies something of the rhetoric of phrasing, in patterns of coordination or counterpoise (see 4.4–4.16). Take 4.16 as your general model of an account in which you should try to deal with the following points:

* What is the role of coordination (asyndetic or syndetic) in the phraseology of this passage, *ie* in the structure of phrases and combinations of phrases?

* Do the coordinates occur mainly in pairs, or are there any extended sequences? (See 4.11 on tirades and triads.) Do you see any stylistic significance, either in the general tendency or the specific occurrence?

* Are phrasal patterns elaborated, for instance by building coordinations into the structure of the noun phrase? (See 4.5, 4.9.) Are phrases symmetrically combined? (See 4.8.)

* Can you identify any figures of rhetoric, especially figures of symmetry such as parison and antithesis? Are they no more than casual ornaments? Do they grow naturally out of the general style of the piece? Do they have a structural value in indicating divisions, transitions, high points, etc?

2 MATERIAL

(a) The problem of translating titles – titles of books, plays, films – would make a pleasant theme for an essay. Something more than a linguistic difficulty is involved; there are questions of cultural compatibility, as it were, even of national character. Language in itself is rarely a great obstacle, though one of the best translation stories I know does happen to turn on a linguistic point. It concerns the showing, in Denmark, of the film *King Kong*. The word *Kong* happens to be Danish for *king*, so that to have presented the film under a direct translation of the original title would have meant calling it *Kong Kong*, an absurdity as manifest as *King King* would be to an English or American audience. The distributors cunningly evaded the difficulty, however, by simply reversing the component parts of the title, thereby Danicizing it in the form *Kong King*.

However, the general background of culture and temperament is often of much greater consequence than the immediate issue of language. Many years ago, when I lived in Sweden, it used to strike me that the titles of the films shown at my local cinema often contained words of strenuous, not to say violent, import; I remember that *uppror* ('uproar', 'turmoil', 'disorder', 'disturbance') figured with almost parodic frequency. My suspicion that there might be in the pacific Swedish soul the lurking shades of an inclination to baresark extravagance was confirmed when a film entitled in English *The Quiet Man* was shown in Sweden as *Hans vilda fru*, 'His wild wife'. A Swedish friend with some insight into the psychology of his fellow-countrymen explained to me that nobody would willingly go to see a film tamely entitled *The Quiet Man*, whereas a wild wife offered prospects of lively pleasure. The fact that the title was to a degree ironic, the 'quiet man' being an ex-pugilist growlingly portrayed by the fairly unquiet Mr John Wayne, was neither here nor there. There was no typographical wink or nudge that might conceivably advise the uninstructed passer-by of the intended irony; a film called *The Quiet Man* could only be a dull film, thoughtful, perhaps, artistic, possibly, shimmering with lyrical intensity, no doubt, but just not the thing for an evening's entertainment.

(b) Some books we read and re-read in seasonal acts of pious merriment and dutiful devotion: *Three Men in a Boat*, *The Diary of a Nobody*, *The Autobiography of a Supertramp* – everyone will have his own list. They are certainly not the greatest or the deepest of works. They are, perhaps, simply the kindest; the most unaffected, undemanding, unpretentious, charmingly common-place and sociably wise companions of our ordinary existence. They are not fashionable enough to be sold on station bookstands, not naughty enough to have been banned by the censor, not portentous enough to have been denounced by academic critics. They are quiet, self-demeaning and very extraordinary books; they belong to us as of ancient custom and patrimony, and we belong to them as to a club. Fellow clubmen recognize each other by the masonic emblem of an apposite quotation or a covert allusion, and instantly forge bonds of enduring trust and tolerance; a man may be forgiven for his major lapses of taste, he may raise Richardson above Fielding or prefer Meredith to Hardy, as long as in these smaller, simpler, sillier cases his heart is sound.

For myself, I am a *Diary of a Nobody* man. I have explored that text like a lover and a true scholar, I have always rejoiced in it and hope I may never tire of it. Talk of door-scrapers or painting the bath and my eyes glaze with a reminiscent pleasure; mention Cummings to me and I will tell you he is always Gowing; ask me 'What's the matter with Gladstone?' and I will answer, twinkling benevolently as though at the most egregious of jests, 'He's all right'. Fellow devotees of the immortal brothers Grossmith, hearing me thus affirm my right to be of their number, will chortle and hang (figuratively rather than literally, if they please) upon my neck; while the sullen and uninitiated bystander will turn away, wearily baffled at such antics, such childish enthusiasm, all for the sake of an old, obscure, trivial, supposedly funny book.

Exercise D2

3 DIRECTIONS

In (4) below are two passages on the same topic, following the same plan of exposition, and showing quite close similarities of wording. The major stylistic difference is in the phrasing, and particularly in the handling of the noun phrase. Make a comparative study of the passages, sentence by sentence, identifying differences in noun-phrase structure. Do the differences taken collectively make an appreciable stylistic contrast between the two texts? Have you an absolute preference, or do you find that each text has mixed features of strength and weakness? Experiment with the construction of a third passage, combining what is phraseologically preferable in these two.

4 MATERIAL

(a) All true-hearted and right-minded Englishmen are supposed to love cricket, though I confess I am beginning to find that an extremely irksome article of belief. Alas, I cannot be moved to rapturous enthusiasm by today's professional game. Lovely, lazy, inconsequential, summer-drowsy cricket did indeed once charm me, but this tedious gladiatorial spectacle bears about as much resemblance to that pastoral idyll as the Formula One racing machine does to a gently ambling pony cart. The fact is, I suppose, that I am sinking into a querulous middle age. I am not impressed by Chuckum's intimidatory speed or Blockum's impenetrable concentration; they are boring fellows both of them, and not a patch on the little heroes of my provincial boyhood. Nevertheless I must admit after all that I do listen eagerly to the Test broadcasts on my crackling transistor radio, and utter many a pious and exemplary prayer that clean-limbed English virtue may triumph over those coarse, sinewy, technically forceful Antipodeans.

(b) Cricket is supposedly loved by all Englishmen who enjoy the use of their faculties and whose hearts are in the right place; an article of belief which I must confess that I am beginning to find tedious in the extreme. Alas, I cannot be moved to raptures of enthusiasm by the game now played in our professional arenas. I was indeed once charmed by the kind of cricket that embodies, in its inconsequence and lazy beauty, the drowsy spirit of summer, but the tedious contest of gladiators that we see today bears about as much resemblance to that idyll of pastoral England as does a Formula One racing machine to the pony cart ambling gently down some country lane. I suppose that I must be growing middle aged and querulous. Bored alike by the speed with which Chuckum intimidates the batsman and the concentration with which Blockum defies the bowler, I find that neither of those worthies can vie with the men who in their own little way were heroes to me when I was a boy in the provinces. Nevertheless I must admit after all that I do listen eagerly to the Test broadcasts filtering through the crackle of my transistor radio, and pray with exemplary piety that the English in their virtue and cleanliness of limb may triumph over the sinews and forceful techniques of the coarse Antipodeans.

Exercise D3

5 DIRECTIONS
In (6) below are two short passages on the same theme, one depending for its expressive energy on clusterings of nouns and noun phrases, the other drawing its power from verbs or verb–adverb amplifications. For the background to this, see 4.3 and in particular example [1]. Compare the role of noun and verb in these texts. Which passage seems to you to be more successful, and why? Experiment with the possibility of a third version, combining the 'noun-aggregating' and 'verb-aggregating' techniques.

6 MATERIAL

(a) The gymnast mounts the apparatus with a hurtling leap that takes her in an instant to the higher of the two bars. There she swings into a series of gyrations so astonishingly supple as to draw from the spectator a murmur of pleasure that yields to an indrawn breath of apprehension when she appears to risk a precipitous fall. At the very brink of catastrophe, however, she takes a casual grip on the lower bar and resumes her parody of the jack-knife, the scissors, the centrifuge, until an abrupt cast lifts her once again to the higher position. More rotations, figurations, suspensions; a moment of masterly equilibrium, superb poise, every muscle vehemently still; then a prodigious back-somersault and a perfectly composed landing that once more exacts from the onlooker the tribute of an appreciative gasp.

(b) The gymnast explodes into action, hurling herself impetuously at the higher of the two bars, hinging her body at the hip, hoisting with the arms, surmounting and suppressing the bar, rotating from the pelvis, from the feet, from the wrists, flailing outwards till she topples precipitately, almost irrevocably, but clutches the lower bar in a safe grasp. Then again lunging, folding, twisting, changing her grip a dozen times, winding on visible and invisible axes, rocketing back to the upper bar; circling recklessly and vertiginously; balancing in a wonder of tension; and at last wheeling brilliantly backward to land composedly while the spectator still blinks and grunts in astonishment.

Exercise D4

7 DIRECTIONS

In (8) below are two compositional exercises which extend the ground covered by (4) and (6) above. Work in an experimental spirit, testing the value of alternatives. In the case of (a), write one short paragraph on a chosen theme. Bear in mind that the object of the exercise is to explore the stylistic possibilities of the noun phrase, but follow your own bent and do not attempt to force the style to a preconceived pattern. Study the structure and function of the noun phrases in the completed paragraph. Then attempt two further versions of the test, one in which as many noun phrases as possible are forced into patterns of premodification and another in which postmodification is the dominant feature.

In attempting the themes listed under (b) write, once more, a short paragraph on a selected topic, making either the verb or the noun the mainspring of your stylistic attack. There are models in 4.3 and in (6) above. Try both approaches – or even a mingling of the two if you feel that there is something to be learned from the experiment. Make a note of possible connections between the chosen style and a type of subject. Do verbs, for example, figure to the best effect in the writing of passages that deal with dynamic changes of state?

8 THEMES FOR COMPOSITION

(a) The noun phrase; premodification and postmodification.

* *The pollution of the sea*
* *What do examinations test?*
* *Hair styles and skirt lengths*
* *The smell of leather and the taste of raspberries*

(b) The stylistic role of verb and noun.

* *Ballroom dancers* OR *A concert pianist at the keyboard*
* *Reading Latin* OR *Looking at modern sculpture*
* *Landscape under snow* OR *Drought*
* *Children at play* OR *Cats in motion*

E: Sentence-structure and textual design

REFERENCE: mainly Chapter 5; Chapter 6 *passim*

Introductory comment

The exercises in this section conflate and somewhat simplify the programme of topics in Chapter 5. We begin with an exercise requiring the composition of a text from a list of sentences (*cf* 5.1), after which we proceed to brief studies of 'text process' (*cf* 5.8) and 'presentation' (*cf* 5.7). Several quite long passages are then presented for technical analysis, taking into account questions of sentence-length, complexity, and branching (*cf* 5.2–5.6, 5.9–5.13). The theory governing this necessarily brief rehearsal is that we move from the rudimentary task of composing sentences into a text to the more sophisticated matter of their interrelationships, schemes of prominence, rhetorical effects, rhythmic balances, etc.

Exercise E1

1 DIRECTIONS

In (2) below is a programme of sentences that make up a raw text (cf the examples in 5.1). Keeping the order of items as far as possible, but allowing yourself a free hand with incorporations and transformations, try to create a text that has some polish and fluency. Bear in mind:

* The possibility of having to incorporate several sentences from the list into one unit in the text.
* The possibility of having to make changes of sentence-type (eg from non-declarative to declarative).
* The possibility of having to break or rearrange a long sentence.
* The possibility of having to make some lexical adjustments in order to accommodate syntactic changes.
* The relationships of 'sentence-process' and 'text-process', as illustrated in 5.8.

2 MATERIAL

(a) Karin Boye wrote a prophetic fantasy called *Kallocain*.
(b) It is a lyric poet's essay in the craft of the novel.
(c) Her countrymen regard it as a prose classic.
(d) It is hardly known outside Scandinavia.
(e) Why is this?
(f) Handicaps of more than one kind have affected its chances as a candidate for international honours.
(g) It is written in Swedish.
(h) Swedish is a minority language.
(i) It evokes the doom of Mansoul with a grey despondency unrelieved by the humour that lurks in *Brave New World* or the horrific relish that vitalises *1984*, to name two comparable English essays in the genre.
(j) The writer is principally known as a lyric poet.
(k) Her novel may not be fully appreciated by readers not conversant with her lyric themes.
(l) She denied the existence of the slightest autobiographical element in *Kallocain*.
(m) Let us not interpret that too narrowly.
(n) Autobiography is more than dates, places and events.

(o) The events of *Kallocain* obviously have no correspondence with the facts of her outward existence.
(p) The book might still be an emblem of inner conflicts.
(q) Her personality was troubled and appallingly vulnerable.

Exercise E2

3 DIRECTIONS
Read 5.8, on 'sentence-process and text-process', with particular attention to example [14]. There two passages are compared, as 'poor' and 'better' examples of textual management, with particular reference to theme, focus, and weighting in the syntactic pattern of the constituent sentences. The passage in (4) below is awkwardly processed. Make a better version, keeping in view the aim defined in 5.8, *ie: to manage a sequence of clauses and sentence-structures so that the information they contain is processed continuously, rhythmically, and with emphases that guide the reader in matters of cohesion and perspective.* Be guided by these questions:

* If the clause-structure does not follow the common principle of end-focus and end-weight, is there a good textual reason for this?
* Are contrasts of focal prominence clearly defined?
* When a theme is marked, or there is some other form of syntactic inversion, *eg* a passive transformation, are there good compositional grounds for this? Conversely, are there points at which syntactic marking seems to be required, to bring out clearly a pattern of prominence?
* What is the relationship between the patterning of individual sentences and (a) sentence connection, (b) text rhythm?
* Do changes of syntactic structure imply changes in tone?

4 MATERIAL
Along with the elements of cookery and the basic procedures of motor car maintenance, a compulsory element in the school curriculum should be typing. Typing is a necessary adjunct to higher creative endeavours, and not only an honest and useful craft in itself. At some point in your strivings, whether you write novels or learned dissertations, you will need to use a typewriter. Gone is the day of the simple pen; typescript is what is now looked for by examining boards and publishers' readers. That

you may have a kindly friend who will type your work for you is quite possible, but even then the help of a professional who will naturally want to be paid for her labours may sometimes have to be sought. And make no mistake that they are labours; to her your work is no more than an object for dull transcription, though the vitality of its every word may charm you. Regret at having to forgo the right to complain may assail you if your obliging friend makes too many errors, and fear of losing her future services will make you hesitate to protest if your professional should overcharge you. If you knew how to type properly, and cook your own meals, and mend your own car, it would be better, all in all. You would have some measure of independence then.

Exercise E3

5 DIRECTIONS

Refer first of all to 5.7 and 6.10, then read the passage in (6) below and consider its textual structure with the following points in mind:

* In how many instances does a sentence or a clause begin with some element other than the subject – *eg* object, complement, adverbial?
* To what extent are these frontings related to the demands of textual cohesion?
* Do they help to present the theme of the text in certain perspectives (see 5.7), or are they simply indices of tone (see 6.10)?
* Do you attach any stylistic significance to those instances in which a sentence or clause begins with the subject?
* Are you in any way critical of the 'presentative' style of this text? What details, if any, would you wish to change?

6 MATERIAL

One of the finest, perhaps indeed the greatest, of Romantic poems is *The Rime of the Ancient Mariner*. Its lyric simplicity and majesty, its breathtaking wonderment at the unending beauty of all creation compel us (as the wedding guest is compelled) to suffer the terrible burden of the narrative. For a burden of suffering there certainly is, of pain and pity and terror. With his crossbow, with the reckless ingenuity of human contrivance, the Mariner brings down the Albatross. Idly, viciously, meaninglessly, the bow twangs and down fall the great white wings out of creation's ordered sky. From that wilful act of alienation springs all the Mariner's disorder of mind, his damnation; and from a spontaneous expression of blessing on creatures repellent yet beautiful in their vivacity comes the possibility of his regeneration. Coleridge presents us with a seaman's yarn transmuted into lyric verse of piercing beauty, and through the transmutation creates an archetypal tale of the lost and penitent soul longing for reconciliation with God and creation. In that tale we are all desperately involved.

Exercise E4

7 DIRECTIONS
Study the passages in (8) below, with particular attention to the structure of the sentences and the relationship of sentence-structure to textual design. Work critically through each text, keeping in view the questions listed below:

*   Is the length of the sentences generally appropriate? Is there any instance in which it might have been better to break a long sentence? Might textual rhythm be improved at any point by varying sentence length? (On these questions see 5.2–5.4.)
*   Are the sentences complex, and in what respect? (See 5.5 and 5.6.) Is this complexity well managed or does it hamper the text? If you find it cumbersome, what improvements would you suggest?
*   What instances of branching strike you as obvious and significant? Are the branches adequately 'trained', or would you suggest changes? (On branching, see 5.8–5.11.)

8 MATERIAL FOR ANALYSIS
(a) During the period of his laureateship, Tennyson's friends and admirers paid him the occasional compliment of rendering passages of his verse into Latin or Greek, an exercise which doubtless pleased him more than the parodies which could from time to time offer equally studied if less flattering tribute to his stylistic distinction. Hallam Tennyson's *Memoir* records, for example, the existence of several versions, by Gladstone and others, of the *Epitaph on Sir John Franklin* which Tennyson himself had proposed as a translation exercise for his sons, and the poet's

brother-in-law Edmund Lushington made translations into Greek of *Oenone* and *Crossing the Bar* which Sir Charles Tennyson described as 'almost as beautiful as the originals'.

Before this image of heavily-fobbed and sidewhiskered men of law, commerce and politics laying aside their professional concerns for an hour or so in order to render a stretch of highly-wrought Victorian English into a corresponding gobbet of pseudo-classical Greek the modern reader can only doff an admiring hat. Why did they do it? Was it a nineteenth century equivalent of the Ximenes crossword puzzle, a challenge to test the wits of the very élite? Or was it, perhaps, a very practical if exclusive form of literary criticism, a way of testing the text rather than the translator? Did they feel that a piece of English might somehow be ratified, receiving an ideal stamp of approval, if it could be put convincingly into one of the classical languages? There is an attitude of mind here, a set of assumptions about the classics, about English, about literature, even about patriotism, which we no longer generally understand and share.

(b) Virgil's *Eclogues* surely present a more faithful picture of pastoral life in his day than some commentators have been willing to allow. That they exhibit a great deal of artifice, that they are carefully stylised, that they draw freely on Theocritan models, that they are in some places clearly allegorical and in others downright mysterious, nobody would deny. They are nonetheless true pictures of the shepherd's life. In them we find the character and concerns of the smallholding farmer, the friendly rivalries and malicious friendships, the decent thrift, the loving care of crops and herds, the fear of natural mishap, the even greater fear of eviction in troubled times. There is artifice, certainly, a kind of bucolic theatre in the carefully-structured discourse of rustic lovers, contending poets, and admirers of beneficent Caesar's imperial sway. Yet if we knock away these trestles there still remains the real landscape that Virgil knew and loved. Here are the meadows with their irrigation ditches, here are the cypresses and the cicadas, here are the meres that lie unruffled in the windless evening; here above all is the heat, the hard, crackling mid-day heat that drives the herdsman to shelter under the spreading beech or the ivy-fronded rock.

(c) In his preface to the Old English version of Gregory's *Cura Pastoralis*, one of several translations which he put in hand for the benefit of his afflicted people, King Alfred describes the state of learning in England at the time of his accession. So abrupt had been the decline in literacy, he tells us, making his point with an interesting topographical distinction, that there was *not one single person* south of the Thames who could interpret a missal or manage to translate a letter from Latin into English. South of the Humber there were *very few* who might survive this simple test; and north of the Humber *not many*.

Alfred's remarks tell us something about the cultural history of the Anglo-Saxons. From embattled Wessex and from his immediate legacy and task of combating the Danish incursions, the king nostalgically evokes a golden age when 'men from abroad came to this land to seek wisdom and learning' – and not, he might have added, to burn churches, pillage monasteries and make the business of the soldier more urgent than the arts of the scholar. Despite his reference to the regions north and south of the Humber, Alfred's patriotic pride appeals to ethnic unity rather than to political and territorial divisions; thus he includes northerner and southerner alike in the word *Angelcynn*, the English race. However, the geographical allusion implies in himself and his reader an awareness that of all the English race it was the Northumbrians who in the 7th and 8th centuries established a European reputation for learning. The monastic foundations of Wearmouth and Jarrow, the international fame of Bede, the first great English historian, and of Alcuin the leader of the Carolingian Renaissance – these, surely, are the splendours recalled by Alfred as he mournfully reflects that 'not many north of the Humber' could in his day so much as gloss a rubric or translate a few lines of correspondence.

Exercise E5

9 DIRECTIONS AND THEMES FOR COMPOSITION

Rewrite any or all of the passages in (8) above, observing the following method:

* Read through the passage, noting the points of content which you think will be essential in your reconstruction.
* Make a list of 'content sentences', as in (2) above or 5.1. In framing these, try to use your own words rather than those of the original text. In fact, put the text aside at this point.

* Proceed, as in Exercise E1, to make a text which should reflect your own instinct for organization and rhythm.
* Analyse your reconstructed text (ie apply the criteria suggested in (3), (5) and (7) above) and compare it with the original.

For further exercise, apply the same routine – of devising a sentence-programme and then converting it into a text – to one of the themes listed below:

* *Restoration Comedy*
* *Superstition*
* *On being one's age*
* *Sport and Art*

F: Role and tone

REFERENCE: Chapter 6

Introductory comment

Our first exercise in analysis requires the evaluation of contrasting tones, and may show incidentally how difficult it can be to keep a tonal balance when trying to write in a pleasant semi-formal style. This is followed by a series of long passages, the proposed function of which is to provide material for the study of tone in all its aspects. Specific studies are limited to two short exercises, one on the syntax of postponement, the other on the tonal value of parenthesis. The programme closes with suggestions for compositional exercises in contrasting tones.

Exercise F1

1 DIRECTION

Study carefully the two versions of a theme in (2) below. Identify their respective tones in broad general terms, ie say whether you find them *formal* or *informal*, then ask these questions:

* Does each passage keep the same tone throughout, or are there tonal shifts, whether slight or marked? If you think the tone shifts, say where and how; identify the linguistic symptoms of the shift.
* Does either passage succeed at any point in striking a 'middle' or

collaborative tone? (This might be collaborative-formal or collaborative-informal.)

* How would you identify the role assumed by the writer – is he informant or entertainer? Does he take the same role in each of the two passages? Is it possible in either case that he himself is in two minds about his proposed role? As a general principle, do you think that uncertainty about role might account for stylistic failure?

* Which of the two passages do you find the more successful tonally?

2 MATERIAL FOR ANALYSIS

(a) When Catullus talks about kissing, he uses (as the commentators dutifully point out) the slangy *basium* instead of the respectable *osculum*: *da mi basia mille* says the lover to his lass. Translators cagily render this *Give me a thousand kisses*, and not only cagily but also necessarily, for there's a hole in the English language here. How else can we render the line, for goodness' sake? *Give me a thousand smackers? Give us a thousand smooches?* The language no longer makes serious distinction between the kiss reverential or salutatory and the kiss erotic or rumbustious. At one time we had the useful word *buss* (a descendant of Catullus' *basium*) to express the amatory smooch, the fine old carnal smacker. *Thou dost give me flattering busses*, says Falstaff to Doll Tearsheet; but Jonson, addressing Celia in courtly fashion, asks her to *leave a kiss within the cup* – a chaste *osculum*, surely, not a ripe and knowing *basium*. On the other hand, when Feste sings *Come kiss me, sweet and twenty*, it's a fair bet he doesn't mean *da mi osculum*, come and salute your old uncle, child. So even when we had two words for it, we seem to have bandied them about with our usual infuriating lack of consistency. Whatever happened to *buss*, though? Presumably it died somewhere along the strict road into eighteenth century correctness. A pity, because *kiss* now has to do as well for mother as for Mary Jane, for gallantry and gusto both.

(b) The commentators will draw our attention to the fact that in one of the most celebrated of his lyrics Catullus uses the vulgar *basium* instead of the more ceremonious *osculum*; the poet's words to his Lesbia are *da mi basia mille*. Timidly and necessarily, because of a defect in the vocabulary of modern literary English, translators render this line *Give me a thousand kisses*. No other rendering is possible since the modern English equivalents to *basium*, if indeed it has any, reduce a sprightly verse to lumpish absurdity. A distinction between *osculum* and *basium*, between the kiss as a salute and as an erotic manifestation, cannot be expressed in the vocabulary of present-day Standard English. The Elizabethans had recourse to the word *buss*, which is derived, ultimately, from *basium*. *Thou dost give me flattering busses* says Falstaff to Doll Tearsheet, thereby illustrating the meaning of *basium*; the sense of *osculum*, on the other hand, is contained in Jonson's courtly adjuration to Celia, *leave a kiss within the cup*. Sixteenth century English, then, could cope unblushingly with a distinction over which modern English must stammer and labour. Nevertheless, the distinction was not clearly and regularly observed, even in those fortunate days. When Feste sings *Come kiss me, sweet and twenty*, the context alone is enough to suggest the meaning *basium* rather than *osculum*. It is no doubt a pedantic vanity to demand that words should always be used consistently. However, when they are inconsistently used a rivalry for place between two will lead to the disappearance of one. This, presumably, is what happened to *buss*, and the loss is no doubt to be regretted, because we now have only one word to indicate the respectful and the intimate, the *vous* and the *tu* of kissing.

Exercise F2

3 DIRECTIONS

Examine the passages in (4) below, studying the writer–reader relationship in each case in the light of the following questions:

* What, in each case, is the apparent role of the author? Are there any indications of role shifting (see 6.2)?
* How would you characterize the tone of the passage? What indices of tone would you pick out to support your characterization?
* Do the same indices occur throughout, or do they gradually change? Are there localized special effects of tone, and how are these reflected?
* How would you assess the respective effects of *syntax* and *vocabulary* in expressing tone?
* Does the tone change at all, and if so for what purpose – *eg* are there sudden excursions into formality or informality that might

have a humorous effect? (You may have covered this in dealing with the immediately foregoing point.)

* Do you accept the proposed match between tone and role, or would you have pitched your writing at a different tonal level?

4 MATERIAL FOR ANALYSIS

(a) Interesting effects can be achieved by using watercolour, gouache or acrylics in combination with wax crayons. You need to have your whole design more or less in your mind's eye and to have worked out pretty accurately where you need to lay the wax and where you will want the paint to flow freely. If necessary, make a light pencil outline of your design or drawing, but do be careful not to score the paper with unerasable marks. If you're going to use a white crayon you may be particularly glad of a few guidelines, because it's quite hard to see how you're covering the paper.

Wax over the bits that you want to keep masked from paint. The wax is water-resistant, and when you come to lay in a wash, the paint where it meets the wax will retreat and break up into little beads which you can pick up on a dry brush or leave as random marks. If you wax lightly you will leave small unprotected patches and some paint will creep in, making quite a pleasant mottled or streaked effect. Wax heavily, and the patch will stay quite clear of paint. To suggest, say, the sheen of light on clothing you might rub a white crayon quite casually over that part of your design, but if your idea was to represent a cloud or a drift of snow the rubbing would have to be more thorough. Of course you don't have to use white crayon only. You can get all sorts of moods and textures by using other colours. For example, you can use wax crayons to mimic the play of colours seen through glass.

When you have made the wax-crayon part of your drawing, lay in washes of watercolour (or gouache, or acrylic thinned to watercolour consistency) in the usual way. Look for broad, simple colour effects, not a mass of fussy detail. What you are doing is drawing in highlights with the wax and then laying down the big tonal masses with your paint; the simpler you keep it, the more impressive it can be. In fact this is such a simple way of getting complex effects that your only problem might be to cure yourself of wanting to use it all the time. Try it at first with some fairly small pieces of stout watercolour paper, say about six inches square. The small scale will help you to judge the balance between wax and paint – also it's cheaper when things (as they will!) go wrong.

(b) Almquist's *Det går an* (the title is a common Swedish phrase which eludes translation by anything less approximate than 'That's all right' or 'It's acceptable' or 'It's done') is an entirely charming book; charming in the way that old diaries and 'travels' are often charming, with a redolence of provincial hotels, aproned waiters, the steamers that come and go, the long empty roads, the commonplace incidents that stay forever in the mind, the beautiful downright stunning ordinariness of travelling companions. That may be a sentimental estimate – the response of one remembering other journeys in other times – and in this particular book Almquist is a social realist, affectionate and indulgent no doubt, but a realist nonetheless, a traveller pointing his impartial camera at the scenes and personages of a journey. Yet all realism softens at last into nostalgic sentiment; yesterday's photographs in their sepia stillness trouble and charm the heart. So it might be said that the book is both realistically and sentimentally charming.

In its own day it was highly controversial, a polemic against the hypocrisies of bourgeois marriage and the subjection of women. Its heroine is no upper-class lady of leisure, dreaming of a romantic suitor and a fortunate match. Sara Videbeck is of quite lowly origins. Yet her behaviour, coolly competent and authoritative in practical matters, is not that of an underling. The other principal character in the book, a soldier perhaps more reflective by nature than most non-commissioned officers, describes her to himself as *ett mellanting*, a something betwixt-and-between. She is in fact a career woman of sorts, having taken charge of a glazier's business after the death of its owner, her alcoholic father. The sergeant and the businesswoman are brought into each other's company on a journey that takes them by steamer and chaise through central Sweden, and by the end of the trip Sara has succeeded in capturing Albert by the sheer force of a determinedly unromantic common sense. She is by no means the easy conquest his wishes may have looked for; 'to cut glass', she tells him, in her folkwise fashion, 'you need a diamond.' He wishes to marry her, but she has witnessed the devastations of an unhappy marriage and puts to him a counter-proposal: that they should live together under the same roof, each with an apartment, each with the right to withdraw from the arrangement without rancour. 'Is that all right?', she asks, and the sergeant agrees that it will do very well. Among Almquist's contemporaries, however, there were those who thought that it was not all right and would not do at all.

(c) Democracy is rarely considered as a state of mind or a personal characteristic, though this derivative sense (derivative because it is assumed that the rule of the people will lead to right behaviour) may be the only worthwhile significance left to the word. Its political credentials have been sorely abused; some of the most oppressive systems call themselves democratic, and we have come to suspect that the rule of the people is either a bad joke or a publicist's illusion. Never mind, let systems wither, the soul remains; there is a democracy seated in the skull and the solar plexus, a fair concord of reason, emotion and instinct, not the product of a political system but the very ground from which political systems arise. Democrats-in-heart are found under all flags.

So, alas, are autocrats-by-nature. The chief characteristic of the psychic autocrat is that he will allow only one faculty to rule his personality, and through his behaviour will extend that rule to others. Most commonly the dominant power is that of cold reason, tyrannising over thought to the exclusion of emotion, intuition, instinct – all things to be swept aside as sentimental and irrational. There are other varieties of the condition, however; the emotional or instinctual autocrat can be as tyrannous as the stubborn rationalist. The essential feature is an obsession with one way of interpreting and managing experience, an obsession which hardens at length into a cruel stupidity, a set of principles which stiffen into a remorseless jargon. The autocrat-by-nature denies his own humanity, on principle, and on the word of his own artifice tries to repress the humanity in others.

On this definition no one, of course, would confess to being an autocrat-by-nature. Yet the temptations to be one are great. This inner life is easy; it can look so much like faith, like unswerving devotion to a cause. The democrat-at-heart has a much harder time. Listening patiently to the pronouncements of the intellect, hearing the cries of emotion, catching the whispers of instinct and intuition, badgered, indeed, by the whole parliament of personality, it is difficult for him to come to any conclusion except that conclusions are dangerous. He lives necessarily in indecision, takes the issues on their merits, rejects nothing, files everything in the cabinet of his doubts, and to autocratic eyes appears to be the ineffectual victim of events. Yet out of this apparent ineffectuality, out of this patient groping for the truth of the moment, out of what Herbert Read has called in another context the 'wavering wandering grace of humble men' comes the real strength of experience and the real hope for a well-ordered society.

(d) Have you ever had the appalling social experience of completely forgetting someone's name? I don't mean the name of an absent third party, some author or actor or blessed politician, I mean the name of the fellow you are actually talking to, a chap you know quite well and see nearly every day of the week. The misery of it is, you only discover you have forgotten his name when someone joins you and introductions are needed. 'This is . . .' you begin, or 'May I introduce . . .', and that name promptly scuttles away like some offended rodent and skulks in the mental undergrowth. 'This is Ken,' you say, brightly resorting to forenames and trying to look like one of those breezy modern spirits who believe in breaking down barriers and can't be doing with stodgy old surname-using reactionaries. 'Ken, this is Mr Barrett-Browning' for of course you then realise that you don't know Mr Barrett-Browning's forename. Mr Barrett-Browning holds speech with Ken, addressing him occasionally as Stan and sometimes as Ron, while Ken manfully tries to keep up with Mr Barrett-Browning, calling him by turns Mr Barrett, Mr Browning, and 'sir'. It isn't a happy arrangement. You have put Ken in a forelock-tugging posture, so to speak, and have obliged Mr Barrett-Browning to dispense little penny-pieces of conversational patronage.

Meanwhile you hunt desperately for that fugitive name. Where in all the forest of your uncertainties could it have got to? Out with your mnemonic hunting-kit, and as a first resort try a cast through the alphabet. That undergrowth makes a promising rustle, somewhere around P – Plack? Posnett? Pantelides? – then all is discouragingly quiet. Very well, try the association game. Parts of the body, say. *Kenneth Leg? Ken Toenail? Kenneth J.*

Oesophagus? No, no, all the branches hang heavy and soundless in the stilly heat of a summer-long oblivion. All right, put the man into a setting, remember some previous encounter, some exchange. *I saw Ken Boat on the river last Sunday? It must be two weeks since we ran into Ken's wife, Mrs Groceries?* Hopeless, not so much as a flicker in the grass. Come now, don't attack it so directly. Look away. Turn your mind to something else, then whip round suddenly and you might catch it. This is better, there are shy little peepings from behind distant tree-trunks: *Lai-, Far-, Dow-,* once or twice you almost have it, but the thing is so damnably agile. At last, in the car on the way home, nearly ramming a lamp-post in the crazy lust of the kill, you run it down: *Milner!* What on earth made you think it might be *Boggs* or *Salamanca?* See how the poor thing lies motionless and unresisting in this moon-bright glade, a mere Milner, the easiest of quarries. What took you so long?

Exercise F3

5 DIRECTIONS

Refer to 6.9, where the relationship between tone and syntactic postponement is discussed at some length. In (6) below are two passages, one embodying a fairly large number of 'postponing' constructions. In the other, the device is not used at all. Compare the two texts, with reference to the following questions:

* What are the distinctive tonal indices in each passage? Do they have any indices in common?
* In your view, which passage is the more successful tonally?
* Would it be possible to combine some features from each text to make an improved third version?

6 MATERIAL

(a) It is not good practice to part from your manuscript without much afterthought. There are always errors and blemishes to be discovered, and it has been known for authors to rush into print only to wish they might rush out of it again. If there is time for second thought, it is as well to give yourself the full measure of that time. It was Horace, after all, who recommended the aspiring poet to keep his epic for nine years. That may possibly be a little too long for your convenience, but there is no harm in giving a month or two to careful revision. There may well come a day when you will bless yourself for your own prudence.

(b) To part from your manuscript without much afterthought is not good practice. Errors and blemishes can always be discovered, and authors have been known to rush into print only to wish they might rush out of it again. Take all the time you can for second thoughts. Horace, after all, recommended the aspiring poet to keep his epic for nine years. That may be a little too long for your convenience, but a month or two spent in careful revision does no harm. You may one day bless yourself for your prudence.

Exercise F4

7 DIRECTIONS

Section 6.11 deals with tonal aspects of parenthesis. Below, in (8), is a text in which parentheses disrupt every sentence. Attempt to rewrite the text after considering the following questions:

* Are the parentheses in all cases easy to rewrite?
* Are you willing to let any of them remain?
* If so, given the disruptive effect of the parenthesis, what dramatic/narrative/tonal grounds do you see for keeping it?
* How, if at all, would you change the notation (the 'scoring') of the parentheses in this or in your revised passage?

8 MATERIAL

The beginning of term – especially the beginning of the Autumn term – is for many of us a time of hope and cheerful anticipation. All the wrongs of last year will be put to rights (we fervently hope and grimly determine to ensure) and our liveliest plans, a little jaded and crestfallen in the late summer, will soon be set on foot again. We shall give – or, as academic status dictates, attend – that brilliant course of lectures. Our tutorials, graced alike by gifted student and able tutor, will be a total success. That book we have always been vowing to write (if only the publishers of this country were not blind to all considerations other than commercial advantage) will be gratefully – nay, grovellingly – accepted for publication, and the critics, that heartless and hard-headed crew, will receive it with cries of happy acclaim (or something like that).

Exercise F5

9 DIRECTIONS AND THEMES FOR COMPOSITION

Choose one or more of the themes listed below and compose two versions, attempting in the one case a fairly easy-going informal tone and in the other a rather greater degree of formality. In assessing the results of your work (an important part of the exercise) refer to these questions:

* What indices of tone have you tried to exploit? To what extent was this a conscious process?
* Do you notice shifts of tone in your own writing, in either of your versions? Can you explain and justify such shifts, or are they perhaps simply the result of a temporary failure to control the tone?
* Is there any case in which you think it might be quite easy for you to strike a collaborative balance as you write? Is this because some roles or some themes prompt the collaborative tone more readily than others? As a general rule, would you say that a role or a theme virtually dictates a certain level of tone, or is the writer always free to impose his own terms?
* Of the versions you produce on each theme, which satisfies you most, and why?

Themes (no more than 400–500 words in any instance):

Instruction (*Cf* Ch.6[1ii]: Write two versions of an instructional passage on *Papering a wall* OR *Baking bread* OR *Ensuring that the car starts easily* OR any domestic and practical matter you may care to choose. NB: Remember that your principal role is that of *instructor*. It is temptingly easy to use the informal style of instruction on topics such as *Papering a wall* as a vehicle for humorous entertainment.

Information (*cf* Ch.6[1i]): Write versions of informative passages on *Culture in the reign of Charles II* OR *The character of Lincoln* OR *The story of 'Pride and Prejudice'*. Change the names (*eg to Henry VIII, Disraeli, Tom Sawyer*) if the proposed topics strike no responsive chord.

Argument (*cf* Ch.6[1iii]: Write versions of an argument against *High rise flats* OR for *Better public transport* OR for *The bicycle* OR against *The fitness craze*. If you prefer to change *against* to *for* and *vice versa*, do so.

Entertainment (*cf* Ch.6[1iv]: Write versions on *Sales talk* OR *The telephone* OR *Eating your words*.

Bibliographical notes

For purposes of reference, or for further discussion of matters raised in the present text, the following works may be helpful. The appended comments are an attempt to define the value of the listed items as accessories to the study of composition.

A: Reference grammars

1 CLOSE, R. A. (1975) *A Reference Grammar for Students of English*, Longman: London.
2 LEECH, G. and SVARTVIK, J. (1975) *A Communicative Grammar of English*, Longman: London.
3 QUIRK, R., GREENBAUM, S., LEECH, G., and SVARTVIK, J. (1972) *A Grammar of Contemporary English*, Longman: London and New York.
4 QUIRK, R., and GREENBAUM, S. (1973) *A University Grammar of English*, Longman: London.
5 SLEDD, J. (1959) *A Short Introduction to English Grammar*, Scott Foresman: Chicago.

Comment: For a writer, the principal function of a good reference grammar is to promote a lively and creative sense of syntactic *repertoire* – to display the constructions that serve different aspects of meaning, and to set them in a pattern of formal and semantic relationships with other constructions. Such a grammar is a source of ideas and a map of expressive highways and byways. In the above list the master-item is undoubtedly 3; this is now the standard grammar of the language, the most comprehensive of recent descriptions. Based on the *Survey of English Usage*, it presents a great wealth of examples, including regional and stylistic variants, yet from this diversity draws a clear account of the 'common core' of English grammar. Item 4 is a concise version of item 3, a filial text, as it were; it is less expensive and may be more conveniently sized for those who like to work with reference books at hand on the desk. In organization it matches the chaptering and sectioning of the parent text, and of course uses the same descriptive language – *ie* the terminology of traditional grammar, adapted to the insights and definitions of modern linguistics.

Item 2 is also a derivative of item 3, but its organization differs from that of the foundation study. Like item 1, it is a grammar written with the foreign learner in mind; however, its arrangement should appeal to anyone interested in the connections between grammar and creativity. It concentrates on the *uses* of grammar, and in particular on 'types of meaning' and 'ways of organizing meaning'. In effect, it is a grammatical thesaurus. Together with items 1, 3, and 4, it represents a school or a current style in descriptive grammar; in spite of differences of presentation and emphasis, the four books might be described as stablemates. Item 5, an outsider, is included here because one of its avowed concerns is the creative potential of syntax; it contains a section entitled 'Applied grammar: some notes on English prose styles'.

B: 'Rhetorics', manuals of composition, guides to usage

1 BROOKS, C. and WARREN, R. P. (1979) *Modern Rhetoric* (4th edn), Harcourt Brace Jovanovich Inc.: New York.
2 GOWERS, SIR ERNEST (1978) *The Complete Plain Words*, revised by Sir Bruce Fraser, Penguin: London.
3 GRAVES, R. and HODGE, A. (1943) *The Reader over Your Shoulder: A Handbook for Writers of English Prose*, Jonathan Cape: London.
4 KINNEAVY, J. L. (1971) *A Theory of Discourse*, Prentice-Hall Inc.: New Jersey.
5 YOUNG, R. E., BECKER, A. L. and PIKE, K. L. (1970) *Rhetoric: Discovery and Change*, Harcourt Brace & World: New York.
See also below, C1, C4, and comment.

Comment: 'Composition is so clearly the stepchild of the English department . . .' complains the author of item 4. If this is true of American colleges, whose students appear to be well supplied with excellent manuals of rhetoric, then it must apply with even greater force to university departments in Great Britain, where the study of composition is not so much the stepchild as the unmentionable absentee. Composition (as distinct from stylistics, but see the comment on section C below) is seldom studied and taught as an academic discipline; on the other hand, books on 'correct' English are in some general demand, and are produced by journalists, poets, freelancing scholars, and civil servants (two of these categories are represented in the list above). Such books usually stress the need for clear, logical, and concise exposition; they are freely prescriptive and sometimes make dictatorial (not to say arbitrary) pronouncements about style. Item 2 is the current edition of an old favourite, a book that has achieved something like classic status; item 3 has fared less prosperously, but is nevertheless an interesting example of the genre. It contains a section called 'Examinations and fair copies', in which the authors – poets turned pedagogue – minutely analyse the faults of selected passages of prose by distinguished writers, and present corrected versions, or 'fair copies'. It is a useful if at times exasperating exercise to follow these examinations step by step, (a) in order to appreciate the strict principles on which authoritative criticisms can be made, and (b) at times, to discover the broader grounds on which mere authoritarian nagging ought to be ignored.

Items 1, 4, and 5 are examples of composition manuals written for use in American colleges and universities; probably 1 is the best known. All develop their practice out of an underlying theory of composition, and all contain numerous and useful exercises. Item 7 deserves particular mention as an ambitious attempt to relate rhetoric and linguistic theory – in this case the tagmemic model associated with Kenneth L. Pike. The attempt to present theoretical bases for the practice of composition is entirely laudable, and suggests a distinction between the kind of text that is called a 'Rhetoric' and another kind that might be designated, for the nonce, a 'Usage'. The tendency of the 'Usage' is to impose rules, and hence to make its readers blindly dependent on the authority of prescription. The tendency of the 'Rhetoric' is to describe the varying conditions and aims of composition, and thus to suggest principles and techniques which the reader may independently develop. 'Rhetorics', furthermore, have a close and sometimes *interlocking* relationship with works on stylistics (see section C below, especially items 1 and 4).

C: Works on stylistic analysis, the structure of discourse, etc

1 CHRISTENSEN, F. (1967) *Notes toward a New Rhetoric*, Harper & Row: New York.
2 CRYSTAL, D. and DAVY, D. (1969) *Investigating English Style*, Longman: London.
3 HALLIDAY, M. A. K. and HASAN, R. (1976) *Cohesion in English*, Longman: London.
4 TUFTE, V. (1971) *Grammar as Style*, Holt, Rinehart & Winston: New York.

Comment: It is possible to study stylistics without giving much thought to the subjective problems of composition; it is also possible – and indeed very profitable – to approach the study of composition through the comprehending discipline of stylistics. Items 1 and 4 in the above list are most valuable in this respect. Their subject, indeed, is composition (and they might accordingly have been listed under B), but they approach it through grammatical analyses of style. Item 1 is a collection of six essays discussing methods of teaching composition and presenting conclusions drawn from the stylistic analysis of literary texts. Perhaps the most interesting papers in the collection are those entitled 'A generative rhetoric of the sentence' and 'A generative rhetoric of the paragraph'. Item 4 is an admirable expansion of the theme of 'creative' grammar. It is profusely illustrated with examples from modern prose writers, American and British, and it effectively teaches composition by showing how the grammatical structures learned and labelled in the classroom actually spring into creative life in the work of novelists and essayists. Of particular value are the chapters on Branching, Cohesion, and Syntactic Symbolism.

Items 2 and 3 do not have so direct a bearing on the study of composition, but embody topics in stylistics and discourse analysis that have been touched upon or at least implied in the present text, and that the reader might wish to pursue further. Item 2 is recommended for its rigorous analyses of various types of discourse in English (including samples of the spoken language). Item 3 is an exhaustive technical study of a subject central alike to the theory of stylistics and the practice of composition.

D: A note on dictionaries etc

1 DUTCH, R. A. (ed) (1962) *Roget's Thesaurus of English Words and Phrases*, new edn, completely revised, modernized and abridged, Longman: London.

2 QUIRK, R. (1974) 'The Image of the Dictionary', in *The Linguist and the English Language*, pp 148–63, Edward Arnold: London.

3 SYKES, J. B. (ed) (1976) *The Concise Oxford Dictionary*, Oxford U.P.: London.

4 WATSON, O. (ed) (1976) *Longman Modern English Dictionary*, Longman: London.

Comment: The purposes for which a dictionary might be required are interestingly reviewed in item 2, a scholarly essay in consumer research. Writers might be said to make up a special category of consumers, with special requirements; they regard the dictionary as a catalogue of resources, and consult it to discover what items lie in stock, how they are used, and how they might be extended or modified. A primary function of the dictionary is to offer the assurance of a *precedent*; it is always comforting to know that a proposed form or meaning has the sanction of a previous use. (Robert Graves has reported Thomas Hardy's discomfiture on looking up a word in the *OED*, to see if he might use it in a poem, only to find that the one recorded instance was from his own *Under the Greenwood Tree.*) At the same time, the data of the lexicon provide an *impetus* to the formation of new words and the extension of existing meanings. Among such data we might expect to find: (a) definitions that are clear and comprehensive and do not send the reader on further dictionary errands; (b) a listing, preferably with illustrative citations, of the several meanings of a word; (c) indications of grammatical function – as noun, verb, etc; (d) some note on the stylistic status of the word, *eg* as 'literary', 'technical', 'colloquial', etc; (e) a listing of variant forms and associated variations in meaning; and (f) enough information on etymology and word-structure to satisfy the 'dictionary sense', the creative response to patterns of root and affix.

No dictionary could be expected to meet all these requirements exhaustively and still remain easy to handle and read. The *Shorter Oxford* is as large as may be convenient for personal use, and even that is a library work, or at least a 'shelf' dictionary. Listed above are two 'desk' dictionaries, generally suitable as companion works in compositional studies; item 4 is elegantly modelled on the French

Larousse series. There are of course many other good compact dictionaries on the market; the *Longman Dictionary of Contemporary English* might be mentioned, as a work primarily designed for the foreign student but nonetheless a useful reference text for the native user. Finally, there is item 1, a work so well known, surely, as to require no explanatory comment. The latest edition introduces great improvements, particularly in the cross-referencing of items. While there is probably no work of reference that can accurately match the psychological process of scanning the vocabulary to set words in interactive motion, the thesaurus comes nearer to this than the dictionary. A dictionary fixes points, a thesaurus stakes out fields. In the end, however, the writer must make his own thesaurus entry as the occasion arises, using elements from his syntactic repertoire to help in discovering and discriminating between lexical items. Thus the reference grammar and the dictionary enter into creative partnership.

Index

References are to pages, unless otherwise stated.

coordination, 71, 72, 73, 74, 78, 85, 138
  asyndetic, 73, 77
  syndetic, 73, 77
  cf subordination
compounds, 80
composition, 160 *f*
  inner and outer phases, 160
  linearity of, 162–3
  manuals of, 239
  teaching of, 240–1
connection, compositional problems of, 162, 173
context, as scanning device, 165: *see also* text
continuity, 6, 13: *see also* text; textual design
counterpoise (in phrasing), 72, 82
critical routines, 175 *f*: *see also* cohesion;
  lexicon; syntax; sectioning
dash (as 'scoring' device), 148–9: *see also* 'scoring'
demonstrative, 11, 15
determiner, 11
devices, compounding of, *see* rhetorical design
dictionaries, 223
dimensional block, *see* block
direction (place definers), 40
discarding, problem of, 166
discourse, 6 and *passim*
  role of endophoric terms in, 32
  role of extensional terms in, 29
disjunction (extensional terms), 28
disputant, *see* role
distance (place definers), 40
dominant (attitude of writer), 124
duration (time definers), 37

end-focus, *see* focus
endophoric terms, 30
  repertoire of, 32 *f*
  role of in discourse, 32
end-weight, 107, 108
enlargement (extensional terms), 28
entertainer, *see* role
enumerative terms, 23
  function of, 25
epanalepsis, 82
epistrophe, 82
equation, *see* syndetic patterns
equivalence (as lexicological principle), 49–53
equivalents, lexical, 49, 50, 51
Euphues, 83
etymological parallels, 165

evaluation (of sentence structure in composition), 93
exclamations (as indices of tone), 137, 138
exemplification (extensional terms), 28
existential sentences, 143–4
exploratory procedure, 14
expository structure, 23–40: *see also*
  enumerative terms; extensional terms;
  endophoric terms; interruptive terms;
  time definers; place definers
expounding, 6
extensional terms, 26
  repertoire of, 38
  role of in discourse, 29
extraposition, 142–3

figures of speech, 64, 82–3
focus, 107
  dual, multiple focus, 144, 149
  end-focus, 107, 108
French, *see* vocabulary, provenance of
frequency (time definers), 37

generalizing (property of vocabulary), 153
Germanic, *see* vocabulary, provenance of
gradatio, 82
grammar and imagination, 58
grammatical categories, stylistic role of, 51:
  see also equivalence; noun-aggregating;
  verb-aggregating
graphology, 2: *see also* cohesion
Greek, *see* vocabulary, provenance of

head (phrase head), 65, 111: *see also* phrase type
hendiadys, 75
heuristic potential
  of phonetic features, 87
  of phrase patterns, 86
hyponym, 53

image, *see* metaphor
'imagistic' ('consistently metaphoric') style, 156–7
imperative, 10, 127
  as index of tone, 137
indices, stylistic, 124
  compatible indices, 135 *f*
  see also role; tone
inference (extensional terms), 28
informant, *see* role
information, 5, 6, and *passim*
  'storage' of, 113, 114, 115